The Suppressed Memoirs
of Mabel Dodge Luhan

THE SUPPRESSED MEMOIRS OF MABEL DODGE LUHAN

Sex, Syphilis, and Psychoanalysis in the Making of Modern American Culture

Edited by

Lois Palken Rudnick

UNIVERSITY OF NEW MEXICO PRESS | ALBUQUERQUE

© 2012 by the University of New Mexico Press

All rights reserved. Published 2012

Printed in the United States of America

17 16 15 14 13 12   1 2 3 4 5 6

Luhan, Mabel Dodge, 1879–1962

The suppressed memoirs of Mabel Dodge Luhan : sex, syphilis, and psychoanalysis
    in the making of modern American culture / edited by Lois Palken Rudnick.
    p. cm.

Includes bibliographical references and index.

ISBN 978-0-8263-5119-7 (cloth : alk. paper) — ISBN 978-0-8263-5121-0 (electronic)

1. Luhan, Mabel Dodge, 1879–1962—Diaries. 2. Luhan, Mabel Dodge, 1879–1962—
    Sexual behavior. 3. Luhan, Mabel Dodge, 1879–1962—Health. 4. Luhan, Mabel
    Dodge, 1879–1962—Mental health. 5. Women intellectuals—United States—
    Biography. 6. Syphilis—Patients—United States—Biography. 7. Subculture—
    United States—History—20th century—Sources. 8. United States—Intellectual
    life—20th century.—Sources. I. Rudnick, Lois Palken, 1944– II. Title.

CT275.L838A3 2012

973.91092—dc23

[B]

                            2012008605

Design and Layout: Melissa Tandysh

Composed in 11/14 Garamond Premier Pro

Display type is Caecillia LT Std

To all women writers,

past and present, who know this truth:

All sorrows can be born if you put them into a story or tell a story about them.

—ATTRIBUTED TO ISAK DINESEN

I the Lord thy God *am* a jealous God, visiting the iniquity of the fathers upon the children unto the third and fourth *generation* of them that hate me.

—EXODUS 20:5,
the Second Commandment, *King James Bible*

In the beginning God created heaven and earth, man and woman, and venereal disease.

—F. BURET,
nineteenth-century French venereologist

The verse in the Bible . . . about the sins of the fathers being visited upon the children unto the third and fourth generation has worried me all my life. At the beginning I wondered if my father's sins were visited upon me and if I must die from his wages of sin, the wages of sin being Death!

—MABEL DODGE LUHAN,
"The Statue of Liberty: A Story of Taboos"

Contents

Illustrations

Preface

IN 1952, MABEL Dodge Luhan wrote to her doctor, Eric Hausner: "This last week I sorted & lifted and sweated over one thousand pounds of paper—supervised the packing in eleven steel-taped wooden boxes & shipped it to the Library in New Haven this morning but did not lose a pound myself!" The papers she donated to the Beinecke Library at Yale University contained Mabel's unexpurgated self, numerous volumes and thousands of pages of manuscripts, typescripts, letters, and scrapbooks that would allow scholars to continue her life's project. Mabel had a therapeutic purpose in writing her memoirs, which entailed lifting the veil on "the whole ghastly social structure under which we were *buried*, & that must be torn down, exposed, so those who follow us will have peace & freedom to make a different one . . ."[1]

At the time that Mabel donated her papers to Yale, she had all but passed from public attention, although during her heyday in the first three decades of the twentieth century, the media hailed her as one of the country's "national institutions." Writers and artists seeking to define the transition from the Victorian to the Modern era appropriated her, perhaps more than any other American woman of her time. For Gertrude Stein, Carl Van Vechten, Mary Austin, Max Eastman, and D. H. Lawrence, among many others, Mabel emblematized "the New Woman," in her various incarnations as a liberating life force for aesthetic, social, and sexual experimentation and for her castrating capacity as a devourer of men.[2]

During the 1930s, Harcourt, Brace and Company published a four-volume, 1,600-page edition of Mabel's memoirs. They appeared serially over the course of the decade under the title *Intimate Memories*, tracing Mabel's development from 1879 to 1918: from her birth in Buffalo, New York, to upper-class Victorian parents whose mutual loathing and emotional abandonment of their daughter instigated her endless quest for love and power (*Background*, 1879–1897); through her first marriage and her expatriation in Florence, Italy, where she sought to re-create the Italian Renaissance (*European Experiences*, 1898–1912); to her triumphant hostessing of a radical salon in Greenwich Village that aired the grievances and hopes of socialists, anarchists, free lovers, feminists, and modern artists (*Movers and Shakers*, 1912–1916); ending in her post–World War I flight—from the East Coast and Western Civilization—into the arms of Taos Pueblo Indian Antonio Lujan (*Edge of Taos Desert: An Escape to Reality*, 1917–1918).[3]

Figure 1 Mabel Dodge Sterne, c. 1918, Taos, New Mexico. Photo courtesy of Yale Collection of American Literature, Beinecke Rare Book and Manuscript Library, Yale University.

Figure 2 Antonio Lujan, c. 1918, Taos, New Mexico. Photo courtesy of Yale Collection of American Literature, Beinecke Rare Book and Manuscript Library, Yale University.

Figure 3 The Mabel Dodge Luhan House, 1930s, Taos, New Mexico. Photo by Ernest Knee, courtesy of Dana Knee.

For Mabel, the Pueblo Indians embodied the antithesis of all she had found wanting in her previous lives: the rigidly repressed Victorian world of her Buffalo childhood; the *fin-de-siècle* European expatriate life that stultified her; and the chaotic world of new freedoms she had reveled in during her New York years. The Pueblos offered her—and potentially her fellow Americans— what no so-called advanced twentieth-century society was able to: a model of a fully integrated society achieved through an intimate connection between individual and community, work and living space, religion and art. From the 1920s through the 1940s, Mabel published numerous articles for the popular press and literary journals to convince her fellow Americans that they could be healed through the Indian way. She presented her marriage to Tony as a "bridge between cultures" that would transform the United States from an imperialist and materialist nation of striving and unhappy individuals, into a communitarian paradise.[4]

Through Tony Lujan, Mabel achieved her mature voice as a writer and found an emotional and spiritual anchor unlike any other she had known. Through Mabel, Tony entered a life of material and social privilege and gained entrée into corridors of political power that allowed him to take on a leadership role for the Pueblo Indians in their battles for the protection of their land and culture during the 1920s and 1930s. Although he often spoke of the conversations of Mabel's friends as "flies buzzing," Tony enjoyed the role he played as a guide and mentor for their creative visitors. By 1929, the Luhans had built a three-story, seventeen-room "Big House" on the border of Taos Pueblo land, along with five guesthouses, and a large home at the edge of town, which Mabel donated, in 1936, to the town of Taos for their first hospital.

Over the next two decades, Mabel brought to Taos the artists, writers, and reformers whose cultural productions and social activism she believed would convince her fellow Americans that Taos was—as both Tony and a New York City occultist had told her—"the beating heart of the world." Among those who came were painters Andrew Dasburg, Marsden Hartley, John Marin, and Georgia O'Keeffe, and photographers Ansel Adams, Paul Strand, and Edward Weston, to immortalize the beauty of the Taos landscape; theatre designers, composers, and dance choreographers Robert Edmond Jones, Carlos Chavez, Leopold Stokowski, and Martha Graham, to capture the rhythms of Native American music and dance; Mary Austin, D. H. Lawrence, Jean Toomer, and Robinson Jeffers, to help write the gospel of her new-found Eden; social theorists and reformers who wrote about and fought for Pueblo culture and land rights, Elsie Clews Parsons, Jaime de Angulo, and John Collier.[5]

SOMETIME IN THE winter or spring of 1973, Emily Hahn and Ellen Bradbury were sitting in the reading room of the Beinecke Library, examining the Mabel Dodge Luhan papers. Hahn was under contract to Houghton Mifflin for a biography of Mabel, and Bradbury was beginning a doctoral dissertation on her. Bradbury came across something she thought Hahn had to see. A few minutes later, Hahn shouted the word "Syphilis!," turning all heads in the room. Donald Gallup, the then curator of American literature, was shown the manuscript they were reading, "The Statue of Liberty: A Story of Taboos," which Mabel had written in 1947. Within a short time this manuscript—along with most of Mabel's unpublished memoirs—"disappeared." In April 1973, John Evans, Mabel's son, gave Gallup the authority to put under restriction whatever papers he thought necessary until January 2000.[6]

When I began my research on Mabel Dodge Luhan in 1974, these papers were unavailable. At the time I published my biography of Mabel in 1984, *Mabel Dodge Luhan: New Woman, New Worlds*, I knew from Emily Hahn's biography that Mabel had contracted syphilis from Tony Lujan. But like Hahn, I mentioned it only in passing. In the late 1980s and early 1990s, a few of the restricted Luhan papers were opened, without explanation. At the time, I was doing research at the Beinecke for an essay I was writing on Mabel, when I came across a newly available manuscript titled "Doctors: Fifty Years of Experience," written in 1954, Mabel's seventy-fifth year.[7]

I was astonished as I followed Mabel's narrative of her multiple encounters with venereal disease, beginning in 1900, when she was twenty-one, married, and having an affair with her also married family doctor, John Parmenter. At one point, Mabel quotes Parmenter saying to her: "'That damn bitch of Dr. Sherman's has given me the clap.'" She responds: "'Give it to me and I will take it for you.' And throwing himself passionately upon me, he did so." In the same document, Mabel claims that her second husband, Edwin Dodge, revealed his syphilis before her marriage to him, promising her that he was no longer infectious; and that her third husband, the postimpressionist artist Maurice Sterne, had his syphilis revealed through dream analysis with her psychiatrist, A. A. Brill, who confirmed it with a Wasserman test. Tony Lujan contracted syphilis from the wife of his clan brother at Taos Pueblo and then infected Mabel, both of them manifesting symptoms that had to be treated. "Is it possible," Mabel asked, after revealing these stories, that "there is so much venereal disease in the world?"[8]

MABEL WAS HAUNTED from childhood by the Victorian euphemism for syphilis: that "the sins of the fathers" would be visited upon their children, a mantra that continued to have enormous resonance through the first decades of the twentieth century. She believed she was somehow fated to embody that prophecy, and that she might have inherited "the wages of sin" from her own father. Mabel did not *write* about her experiences with syphilis until 1947, a year after the first widespread use of penicillin as a cure. But her multiple encounters with VD—from the "family secret" whispered about when she was a child, to her first love affair, through her last marriage—were a palimpsest for her life and memoirs. That Mabel "took" gonorrhea from John Parmenter, seemingly as her due—and that she may have married all three of her syphilitic husbands *after* she learned they were infected—speaks powerfully of the hold that Victorian notions of sin and punishment had on even the most seemingly modern woman.

In her published memoirs, Mabel wrote about her schoolgirl lesbian encounters. In fact, her most convincing portrait of a loving relationship up until the time she met Tony Lujan is her account of an affair she had with Violet Shillito, a young American woman who died in France shortly after Mabel married her first husband, Karl Evans, in 1900. The lesbianism Mabel experimented with from age sixteen through her early thirties was a mark of the sexual fluidity possible before the institutionalization of Freudian psychology. But it was also clearly enmeshed with a profound fear and distrust of men, even though she ultimately chose men as her best route to power and self-realization.

Mabel adopted Freud, Sexology, and New Thought in order to overcome the Victorian fatalism of her heredity and environment. The talking cure and the sex cure seemed marvels of liberation that would allow her to free herself of both sin and suffering. The Freudian revolution was a defining element of modernity that granted women their sexual natures. But as many scholars have demonstrated, it also tied men and women to ideas of selfhood that reinforced traditional gender binaries: that women's essential selves were sexual and intended to serve men and maternity. The various forms of mental healing and spiritualist practices that Mabel engaged in throughout her life never gave her more short-term relief. Writing her memoirs over forty years was, I believe, the therapy that saved her life.

The Suppressed Memoirs is an edition of Mabel's most culturally significant unpublished memoirs and papers. I have situated them within biographical and historical contexts that are informed by my reading of all of her once-restricted papers, including the case notes from her first psychoanalysis. The papers have led me to new understandings of the linkages among sexuality, syphilis, and modernity, which I discuss in the introduction. Venereal disease was an important factor in turn-of-the-twentieth-century debates over women's rights and sexual orientation; in the representations of women and sexuality that marked modern poetry, literature, and painting; and in the development of Sigmund Freud's theories of psychoanalysis and Havelock Ellis's theories of sexology. The "fathers" who sinned are individual and collective, traditional and modern. They are moralizers who condemned women's sexuality and blamed them for the spread of sexually transmitted diseases (Martin Luther) and fathers who instilled the fear of sexuality in their daughters and sons (Charles Ganson and Henry Ware Eliot). They are pioneers in the fields of sexual hygiene (Prince Albert Morrow), psychiatry (Sigmund Freud), sexology (Havelock Ellis), and in modern art (Pablo Picasso) and literature (D. H. Lawrence), whose cultural constructions of sexuality, syphilis, and women reveal deep continuities between the Victorian and Modern eras.

The Suppressed Memoirs begins with "Family Secrets," a discussion of Mabel's first experiences with psychoanalysis, which lays the groundwork for her earliest suppressed memoir, "Green Horses." Chapter 2, "Green Horses," written in 1924–1925, is a riveting drama of adultery and incest that focuses on

Mabel's affair with Dr. John Parmenter. One of Buffalo's eminent Victorians, he assumed he could live the traditional patriarchal life of the double sexual standard, but learned otherwise in an affair that destroyed his career. Inflected by her years of undergoing, reading, and writing about psychoanalysis, "Green Horses" establishes the template of gender and sexual politics that marked Mabel's life, and, in less extreme forms, the life of her times. Chapter 3, "Family Affairs," addresses Mabel's earliest and continuing doubts about her marriage to Tony Lujan and their mutual infidelities, preparing us for chapter 4, "The Statue of Liberty: A Story of Taboos." Written in 1947, the memoir is a compelling account of Mabel's encounters with syphilis, both its presence and erasure in her life and in her era, and of the deep personal and cultural divides that marked the Luhans' transgressive marriage. Chapter 5, "The Doomed," written in 1953, is Mabel's revenge story of Millicent Rogers, the flamboyant Standard Oil Heiress, designer, and art collector who came to Taos in 1947, took up Tony and the Taos Indians, and had an affair with Tony's nephew, Benito Suazo. Mabel wrote "Millicent" to exorcise the last of her demons: a powerful, independent woman whose life and social position in Taos paralleled—and threatened to supplant—her own.

A Note on Reading *The Suppressed Memoirs of Mabel Dodge Luhan*

When I edited Mabel's four volume *Intimate Memories* into a 250-page, one-volume book in 1999, I wrote in the introduction that Mabel had always needed a good editor. Editing her *unpublished* memoirs has been a much bigger challenge. They were not prepared, and most were not intended, for publication during her lifetime. I have no independent evidence, outside of Mabel's own assertions (including those recorded in Smith Ely Jelliffe's 1916 case notes of her therapy) that confirm her claims about her multiple exposures to VD. Thus these documents have to be read with caution, in terms of their historic veracity.

During my thirty-five years of researching and writing about Mabel, however, it has been my experience that she was true to the life experiences she wrote about, at least those that I have been able to corroborate from other evidence. More important, the autobiographical "truths" of the narratives Mabel constructed have significance far beyond the personal. They can be read as a counternarrative to Mabel's published autobiography, at the same time that they deepen and broaden our understanding of the life of her times.

I have chosen selections from Mabel's memoirs that elaborate and revise the persona she created in her published works and that reveal the cultural and historical significance of the sexual and psychological crises in which she was enmeshed. I have made significant reductions in the original typescripts while trying to maintain coherence and continuity. I have modernized and standardized the spelling and punctuation of the memoirs in order to create a uniformity that does not exist across the originals, which were written over four decades. But I have kept the spelling and punctuation of the letters I have excerpted intact.

Acknowledgments

The Suppressed Memoirs of Mabel Dodge Luhan is the culmination of more than thirty-five years of laboring in the fields of Mabel's life, writings, lovers, friends, and the social and cultural circles that were part of her milieus in Europe and the United States. The restricted Luhan papers that were opened to scholars in January 2000 sent me on an unexpected journey. I decided to read them out of curiosity—for my own intellectual satisfaction, as I was denied them while working on my biography of Mabel (1984), and while editing her published memoirs (1999). But I found them so compelling that I decided to create a new edition of Mabel's memoirs, one that would open up new pathways to broader social and cultural understandings of late Victorian and early modern American and European cultures.

I could not have accomplished these goals without the help and support of scholars and editors with whom I consulted, and without the always thoughtful and generous guidance of my long-lived writer's group in Boston, with whom I stay connected, even though I have been living in Santa Fe since 2009. Thanks to Joyce Antler, Fran Malino, Megan Marshall, Sue Quinn, Judith Tick, and Roberta Wollons, who were steadfast in helping me to the successful end! And to Allan Brandt, Susan Reverby, and Dr. Barbara McGovern for their invaluable consultations in my efforts to understand syphilis in its many different ramifications. Most of all, I want to convey my immense gratitude to two editors who worked with me in shaping the ideas and structure of this book: Sian Hunter and Beth Hadas, the latter of whom has offered me her expert guidance for thirty years.

Introduction

"The Sins of the Fathers"

A Brief History of Venereal Disease

Any important disease whose causality is murky, and for which treatment is ineffectual, tends to be awash in significance. First, the subjects of deepest dread (corruption, decay, pollution, anomie, weakness), are identified with the disease. The disease becomes a metaphor. Then, in the name of the disease . . . that horror is imposed on other things.

—SUSAN SONTAG, *Illness as Metaphor*[1]

MABEL DODGE LUHAN was not being melodramatic when she wrote that her life was held hostage by the "sins of the fathers." If the Judeo-Christian God had wanted to develop a disease that would punish men and women for sex, in the most frightful ways imaginable, he would have had to invent syphilis. It is not only a disease whose symptoms mimic many other known infectious diseases, but it has been—since Columbus purportedly brought it home as the curse of the Americas he had conquered—the single most shame- and guilt-ridden disease on the planet (until AIDS, whose etiology and cultural manifestations resemble it strikingly).[2]

There is no definitive proof that syphilis originated in the "New World." It first appeared in Europe in 1495, although it may have existed earlier in other forms. The most recent phylogenetic research makes a considerably strong case for the "Columbian theory," which has had a common currency of belief in the United States and Europe from as far back as the sixteenth century. The disease spread like a plague and was a virulent epidemic throughout Europe by 1498, often resulting in early death. Edgar Allen Poe captured its horrors powerfully in his 1845 short story "The Masque of the Red Death," which opens with what can be read as a thinly veiled allegory of the syphilis pandemic in Europe during the 1490s:

> The "Red Death" had long devastated the country. No pestilence had ever been so fatal, or so hideous. Blood was its Avatar and its seal—the redness and horror of blood. There were sharp pains, and sudden dizziness, and then profuse bleeding at the pores, with dissolution. The scarlet stains upon the body, and especially on the face of the victim, were the pest ban that shut him out from the aid and from the sympathy of his fellow men. And the whole seizure, progress and termination of the disease, were the incidents of half an hour.[3]

Since the Renaissance, syphilis has been blamed on the marginal and despised—prostitutes, immigrants, Jews, and homosexuals—as the source of society's pollution. In a similar way, when AIDS came to public awareness in the 1980s, Christian fundamentalists proclaimed it God's just punishment for homosexuals. Syphilis affected women of all classes and races, but prostitutes received the brunt of society's wrath. "'If I were a judge,' roared Martin Luther, 'I would have such venomous syphilitic whores broken on the wheel and flayed because one cannot estimate the harm such filthy whores do to young men.'" In 1826, Pope Leo XII banned rubber condoms because they protected the infected from the suffering they deserved.[4]

Syphilis is the disease that "has most terrorized Western culture," not only because of its virulence but also because of its vicious irony: "Eros and Thanatos fiendishly reunited" as "One is punished by the very means in which one has transgressed." Alfred Crosby has noted its most significant ramifications in terms of its impact on heterosexual intimacy. "The fear of infection tended to erode the bonds of respect and trust that bound men and women together. . . . Add to the normal emotional difficulties of the sex relationship not just the possibility of the pains of gonorrhea, but the danger of a horrible and often fatal disease, syphilis. Where there must be trust, there must also be suspicion. Where there must be a surrender of the self, there must now also be a shrewd consideration of future health."[5]

Syphilis (*treponema pallidum*) is a "systemic contagious disease" that can be congenitally transmitted to children. Depending on the variety of syphilitic infection in the mother, it can manifest in speech and memory problems, blindness, and mental and emotional instability, a fate from which Mabel may have spared her second child by aborting Edwin Dodge's baby. Congenital syphilis can also lead to stillborn babies, saddle nose (an ulcerated bridge of the nose), incisor teeth that curve inward, deafness, and cardiovascular lesions. Gonorrhea, in women, shows up in seven to twenty-one days, and can infect the uterus, ovaries, and fallopian tubes, resulting in frequent and painful urination, vaginal discharge, and reduced fertility. It was considered a minor disease like the cold until the end of the nineteenth century, when doctors discovered that it could cause arthritis, meningitis, pericarditis, and peritonitis.[6]

Syphilis typically has a three-week gestation, at which time a sore, or chancre, develops on the genitals and then heals. Because these sores are internal for women, they can easily be missed. Within two to four weeks of the primary phase, a secondary phase manifests with very mild to severe problems: from slight fever and headaches to swollen lymph glands and lesions, severe headache, fever, aches in the joints and muscles, mouth sores, atrophy of the optic nerve, and a rash that can cover the whole body. Untreated patients can remain infectious for up to four years. After a latency period that can last from four years to a lifetime, a tertiary phase erupts in 30 to 40 percent of those infected that manifests in a number of possible symptoms that can affect eyesight, hearing, skin, the mucous membranes, and the aorta. The worst of these (5 percent) include cardiovascular disorders and paresis, or general paralysis of the insane, which typically shows up in the forties or fifties, and includes convulsions, memory loss, severe headaches, mood swings, and depression.[7]

Until the advent of penicillin, which did not become generally available to the public until 1946, there was no certain cure for either disease, although epidemiological evidence suggests that "perhaps 50% of contacts sexually exposed to early infectious syphilis actually escape infection."[8] Mercury vapor baths, or the ingestion of mercury and iodides of potassium, which could lead to loss of teeth and bowel hemorrhaging, were the most common treatments for syphilis through the early twentieth century until the discovery, in 1909, of Salvarsan, an arsenical compound created by Dr. Paul Ehrlich. European and American doctors disagreed on how long a man should refrain from sexual intercourse after contracting syphilis, and they used different dosages, regimens, and prognostications about the efficacy of Salvarsan and its somewhat less toxic successor, NeoSalvarsan. Some doctors believed a few intravenous injections would help keep the patient noncontagious, while others recommended injections for months or years. Some doctors believed Salvarsan "cured" syphilis; others did not. Although it did not eliminate the disease, the treatment made most patients noninfectious and help them avoid the tertiary stage.[9]

In the late nineteenth and early twentieth centuries, there were a series of scientific breakthroughs in the understanding of syphilis. Scientists located the spirochete as the bacterium that caused syphilis, identified its three stages, developed the Wasserman test, and diagnosed syphilitic paresis. The most influential venereologist in both Europe and the United States at the time was Alfred Fournier, who made the study of venereal diseases "a respectable branch of medicine." Founder of the French Society for Sanitary and Moral Prophylaxis in 1901, he enlisted public authorities in a crusade against syphilis, which he viewed as one of the plagues of modern society, along with alcoholism and tuberculosis. Doctors, nurses, and those in the general public who were aware of the disease believed that syphilis was inheritable through the third generation. Thus the mantra that "the sins of the fathers are visited upon their children," a thesis that was powerfully and controversially brought to the stage in Henrik Ibsen's 1881 play *Ghosts*.[10]

In his excellent study of the social construction of VD in the United States, *No Magic Bullet*, Allan Brandt has explored the moral panic over venereal disease that was foundational to a number of Progressive era social control reforms, such as social hygiene, eugenics, and suffrage. It occurred within the context of increasing divorce rates, a militant women's rights movement, and fears of race suicide stirred up by nativists opposed to the "degenerate races" who made up mass immigration. (Some twenty million immigrants arrived in the United States, mostly from Central, Southern, and Eastern Europe, between 1880 and 1924.) Venereal disease "provided a palpable sign of degeneration, as well as a symbol of a more general cultural crisis." Brandt estimates that the infection rate for VD in the United States in the late nineteenth and early twentieth centuries could have ranged between 10 and 50 percent.[11]

Among moral reformers in Europe and the United States, a "just say no" policy to conjugal infidelity became the favored protocol. Doctors' advice to patients to abstain from sex after infection ranged from six months to three years; they typically told men not to tell their wives in order not to threaten the stability of white middle- and upper-class marriages. Women of "good breeding" were not expected to have any knowledge of the disease, while working-class women and women of color, who were "destined by virtue of their origins to be of 'low sexual morality,'" were expected to avoid "contaminating the bourgeoisie." In Anglo-Saxon countries, the disease was usually referred to as "a rare blood disease." One of the many reasons it has been so difficult until recent times to document the number of cases is that doctors and medical examiners often disguised the diagnosis.[12]

As part of the widespread professional credentialing that began in the late-nineteenth-century practices of law, medicine, and teaching, American doctors wanted more control of the "moral order," which they achieved by gaining credibility from political leaders and the public for their "technical expertise." The discovery of "venereal *insontium*"—infections of the innocent—in the last decade of the nineteenth century generated the social purity crusade. There followed a virtual redefinition of VD from the classic "'carnal scourge'" to a "'family poison.'" In 1901, Prince Albert Morrow, Fournier's counterpart in the United States, chaired a VD study committee of the New York County Medical Society. His statistics helped create a venereal panic when he claimed that 80 percent of men in New York City had been infected with gonorrhea and that 5 to 18 percent had contracted syphilis. In his 1904 book *Social Diseases and Marriage*, Morrow "coined the euphemism 'social disease'" for VD because of its spread through prostitution. He asserted that gonorrhea made 50 percent of women sterile, while another doctor attributed 60 to 80 percent of pelvic inflammations that required hysterectomies or removal of ovaries to gonorrhea. Morrow wrote of syphilis as "treasonous" in its threat to destroy the foundations "of the Victorian, child-centered family."[13]

Until the second decade of the twentieth century, public debate on these issues in the United States was rare and controversial. When Edward Bok, the editor of the *Ladies Home Journal*, published a series of articles about VD in 1906, he lost seventy-five-thousand subscribers. When Margaret Sanger's infamous pamphlet "What Every Girl Should Know" was published in 1913, it was confiscated and labeled obscene by the U.S. post office because she referred to syphilis and gonorrhea by name. Sanger claimed that the majority of women in New York who married were in danger of venereal infection, warning that for women who contracted syphilis, there was a 60 to 80 percent chance that their offspring would die. Although some doctors wanted sex education to be available to parents, and particularly to men, their chief strategy was to argue for chastity and moral purity as a means of protecting the social order. The attempt to keep women ignorant of VD's potential and very real damage to their bodies drove some feminist activists and writers in England and the United States to make the claim that women needed political and civic rights in order to end "the conspiracy of silence." Christabel Pankhurst's polemic *The Great Scourge and How to End It* (1913) and Charlotte Perkins Gilman's novel *The Crux* (1911) are just two of many works by women's rights activists of the era that boldly took on the topic.[14]

Figure 4 Louis Raemaekers, *L'Hecatombe, La Syphilis,* c. 1916. Photo courtesy of Ebling Library for the Health Sciences, Rare Books & Special Collections, University of Wisconsin-Madison.

During and after World War I, there was a brief flurry of public discussion and government intervention in the United States because American soldiers seemed in mortal danger of being infected by prostitutes. But the conspiracy of silence, or almost silence, returned until the late 1930s, with social hygienists blaming the "new morality" of the 1920s on the persistence of VD and continuing to show greater concern with "preserving sexual ethics than preventing disease." In 1934, CBS scheduled a broadcast of New York State Health

Commissioner Thomas Parran Jr. on the future goals of public health. It was not delivered because moments before the broadcast he was told he could not say the words "syphilis" and "gonorrhea" on the radio.[15]

During the 1930s, statistics suggested that one out of every ten Americans suffered from syphilis, with five hundred thousand new infections a year, and close to seven hundred thousand new gonorrheal infections a year; that 20 percent of those incarcerated in asylums suffered from syphilitic paresis; and that sixty thousand babies died annually from congenital syphilis. Parran was one of the first to attack the traditional argument that "victims got what they deserved and therefore should not receive assistance." When public health officials during the New Deal began to publish the costs of VD to taxpayers, they finally got action. Parran's 1938 campaign against VD resulted in the National Venereal Disease Control Act, which gave federal grants to state boards of health to develop anti-venereal disease measures. By the end of that year, twenty-six states prohibited marriage of infected individuals.[16]

Figure 5 "Something to be whispered about *out loud*!" Handbill for the Chicago, Illinois, production of the play *Spirochete*, 1938. Image courtesy of National Archives, Records of the Works Progress Administration, Washington, D.C.

In *Microbes and Morals*, Theodor Rosebury speculates about the influence that the spirochete and the gonococcus have had throughout the ages on "philosophy, art, and literature." It is hardly surprising to find that syphilis served as a powerful trope in European and American literature and art. Often thinly disguised in Romantic and Victorian literature and the arts, VD also served as a constitutive factor in the creation of modern literature and art. Mabel was not alone in imagining and experiencing the pervasiveness of VD. In her seemingly contradictory embrace and loathing of sexuality, she also encompassed the range of attitudes that marked the lives and works of several of her fellow writers and artists who shaped the gender of modernity.[17]

The Influence of VD on Modern Literature and Art

In European and American short stories, novels and fiction, plays, illustrations, and paintings from the mid-nineteenth century through the mid-twentieth century, syphilis was deployed to describe the disintegration of borders—of gender, race, ethnicity, and class. The disease—often allegorized, masqued, or portrayed as a hideous double—infiltrated and infected the individual bodies of the privileged and poisoned the body politic. Among the European artistic avant-garde, venereal disease appeared in and influenced works by the Symbolists, Expressionists, Cubists, and Surrealists, and perhaps most powerfully in the ur-text of modern art, Picasso's *Les Demoiselles d'Avignon* (1907), with its bold distortions of form and color and confrontational women prostitutes.[18]

French Symbolist writers like Baudelaire had venom for women because they "engineered the fall of man," while French antifeminist writers, such as Émile Zola, "linked what was seen as the insidious power of New Women with social degeneracy."[19] In late British Victorian literature, the syphilitic double went underground and became the "dual personality" of Robert Louis Stevenson's *Dr. Jekyll and Mr. Hyde* (1886) and the doppelgänger of Oscar Wilde's "The Picture of Dorian Gray" (1890), which Wilde's biographer, Richard Ellmann, has interpreted as a "parable for [Wilde's] secret syphilis." Gaston Leroux describes Erik, the ghost who haunts the opera house in his play *The Phantom of the Opera* (1910), as having a skeletal frame, big black holes for eyes, and the collapsed nose that marked syphilitics, thus his famous white mask. Bram Stoker's *Dracula* (1897) has been discussed in terms of coded references to syphilis, made explicit in its most recent adaptation by the BBC in 2006, where the vampire is brought to England in order to give a blood

Figure 6 Edvard Munch, *The Inheritance*, 1897–1899, New York. Oil on canvas, 141 × 120 cm. The Munch Museum, Oslo, Norway. Photo credit: Erich Lessing/ Art Resource, New York. Copyright 2012 The Munch Museum/The Munch-Ellingsen Group/Artists Rights Society (ARS), New York.

transfusion to Lord Arthur Holmwood, the syphilitic aristocrat who is about to wed the innocent Lucy Westenra.[20]

Some modern writers, like James Joyce, coded their dis-ease with the subject through experimenting with narrative form and discourse. Joyce may have suffered from neurosyphilis, infected his wife Nora with it, and contributed to his daughter Lucia's insanity. According to Kathleen Ferris, Joyce's guilt "persistently found its way into the web of textual disguises" he created in *Ulysses* and *Finnegan's Wake*.[21] Other writers were more concerned with the impact of public hysteria on the free expression of sexuality than they were with the disease itself. As Elaine Showalter has explained: "For the male literary avant-garde, . . . syphilis was the excrescence of a sexually diseased society, one that systematically

Figure 7 Pablo Picasso (1881–1973), *Les Demoiselles d'Avignon*, Paris, June–July 1907. Oil on canvas, 8' × 7'8". Acquired through the Lillie P. Bliss Bequest, The Museum of Modern Art, New York. Digital image copyright: The Museum of Modern Art/Licensed by SACLA/Art Resource, New York. Copyright 2012 Estate of Pablo Picasso/Artists Rights Society (ARS), New York.

suppressed desire and so produced anxious fathers and divided and disfigured sons." This was certainly true for D. H. Lawrence, who published a screed about the ways in which the fear of syphilis had poisoned European and American art and literature. The pox "entered the blood of the nation, particularly of the upper classes," he wrote, and "after it had entered the blood, it entered the consciousness and hit the vital imagination," striking a "fearful blow to our sexual life." Lawrence attributed the terror of syphilis to the upper class's "dread anything but ideas, which *can't* contain bacteria." When he wrote this essay, he may well have been thinking of Mabel Dodge Luhan, his avatar of spiritual vampirism in much of the writing he did about the United States.[22]

T. S. Eliot may have found one of the sources of the misogyny and sexual loathing that inhabits his poetry in his Calvinist father's stern warning that

Figure 8 Salvador Dalí, *Visage du Grand Masturbateur*, 1929. Oil
on canvas, 110 × 150 cm. Archivo fotográfico Museo Nacional
Centro de Arte Reína Sofia, Madrid, Spain. Copyright 2012
Salvador Dalí, Fundació Gala-Salvador Dalí, Artists Rights Society
(ARS), New York.

because syphilis was "'God's punishment,'" he hoped that a cure for it would never
be found: "'Otherwise . . . it might be necessary to emasculate our children to
keep them clean.'" In the "apocalyptic vision" of *The Waste Land* (1922), "the
poet's sexual phobias result in the disintegration of not only the modern cultural
apparatus, including social, political, and gender roles, but of the very landscape."
Eliot's masterpiece is permeated with fears of Anglo-Saxon race degeneration,
brought on and passed on through venereal diseases that have increased the steril-
ity of the upper classes, while the masses breed in frightening numbers. The form
and imagery of Eliot's poetry are, of course, modern. But his sentiments about the
working class's contribution to the decline of the Anglo-Saxon race and nations
are as invidious and old-fashioned as those of his Victorian forbears.[23]

Modernist artists, like modern writers, responded to the disease in both
coded and open ways in their experimentation with form. There is perhaps no
more iconographic painting of the advent of Modernism than Pablo Picasso's
Les Demoiselles d'Avignon (1907), a painting in which art history scholars have
uncovered the trace—and erasure—of VD. Most agree that Picasso used prostitutes (and African art) to mask his own aggressively bold confrontation with

the canons of art history. Picasso frequented bordellos in Barcelona and may have contracted VD in 1902. The winter before he painted *Demoiselles*, he visited a Parisian venereologist, "ostensibly to paint the syphilitic prostitutes in his care," but perhaps for more personal reasons as well. Picasso wanted to title his painting *Le Bordel d'Avignon*, but his dealer insisted on the euphemism. Whether interpreted "as an allegory or charade on the wages of sin" or as a rendering of his terror at the reality of women "coming to power" at the expense of the patriarchy, Picasso's calling it "'My first exorcism-painting'" is certainly suggestive.[24]

Salvador Dalí, one of the founders of the Surrealist movement in post–World War I Europe, rendered his fears of women's diseased bodies in the coded language of dreams, which erupted from the irrational depths of the unconscious to paint themselves on canvas. Dalí's father, a wealthy notary and a regular client of prostitutes, believed that he had transmitted some type of VD to his son. Like Eliot's father, he wanted "to warn the adolescent Salvador of the dangers involved, and so he gave him books containing pictures of the lesions caused by syphilis." Dalí "remembered these illustrations as being frightening and repulsive and came to associate them with sexuality as a whole," which "led him . . . to rely on onanism as his source for pleasure." One of his first contributions to Surrealism was titled *Visage du Grand Masturbateur* (1929), a sardonic commentary, perhaps, on the medical community's fears that if masturbation replaced sexual intercourse it would lead to debilitating physical and social ailments.[25]

In 1933, Nelson Rockefeller Jr. commissioned Diego Rivera's mural *Man at the Crossroads Looking with Hope and High Vision to the Choosing of a New and Better Future* for the entrance hall of Rockefeller Center. Its greatest claim to fame is that Rockefeller had it destroyed because of Lenin's portrait, which appears prominently in the center of the right panel of the painting. Much less well known is the segment of the painting that stands parallel to Lenin on the left. It portrays a group of society women and men playing cards, John D. Rockefeller just behind them, toasting a woman with champagne and holding the hand of another (unseen) woman. The wealthy Americans portrayed here are placed under a "crossroads" of floating bacteria, which include prominently displayed spirochetes and gonococci. The panel is situated directly under the spirochetes, lest anyone should doubt which class was responsible for the most virulent "diseases" of modern society: the capitalist and imperialist oppressors of the working classes and of peoples of color throughout the world.[26]

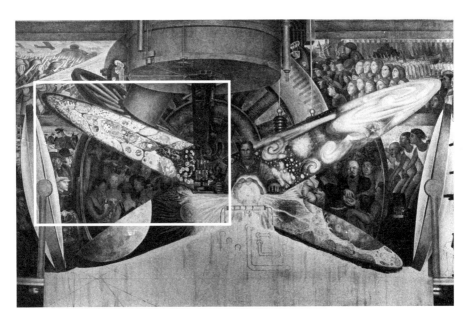

Figure 9 (*top*) Diego Rivera, *Man at the Crossroads Looking with Hope and High Vision to the Choosing of a New and Better Future*, 1933, Rockefeller Center Plaza, New York City, photo by Lucienne Bloch. (*bottom*) Detail. Photo courtesy of Old Stage Studios. Rivera restored the painting in a somewhat modified version for El Museo Del Palacio De Bellas Artes in Mexico City.

Psychoanalysis, Sexology, and Sexual Identity

Mabel Dodge Luhan's life and writings reveal the interconnections during the late Victorian and early modern eras of psychoanalysis, sexology, and spiritualism. At the same time that she was engaged with Freudian psychoanalysis and sexology, she supplemented these with various New Thought and occult doctrines and practices. Her eclecticism was very much in tune with her times. When Mabel embraced both Freud and Havelock Ellis, it was their notion of women's sexuality *as* her (modern) identity that she understood as linking them. The brilliance with which she performed the role of the "New Woman" was what attracted an astonishing array of modern writers for whom she was emblematic of modernity.

All of the mental hygiene movements have complex origins in Western society and culture. But one factor that shaped their emergence was the increasingly biologistic and hereditarian model of human nature and behavior that drove scientific and medical theorizing, investigation, and reform, and became entrenched during the last quarter of the nineteenth century. Gender differences were scientized such that women were seen as the sum of their reproductive roles. "'Her whole soul, conscious and unconscious,'" as psychologist Stuart Hall put it, "'is best conceived as a magnificent organ of heredity.'" Charles Rosenberg has noted that "Even the educated were convinced that most chronic and constitutional ills were rooted irrevocably in 'the blood,'" such that "Americans found in heredity a plausible mechanism with which to restate in appropriately secular form a lingering commitment to 'original sin.'"[27]

Damnation by blood, the condemnation to suffer the punishments of the "fathers," made the various manifestations of mind-cure movements in the early twentieth century salvifically appealing to millions of Americans and Western Europeans. Nathan Hale has documented the many ways that early psychotherapy borrowed from hypnotism, suggestion, and psychic research. This was especially true in Boston, where these sympathies were fostered by a "lingering Unitarian and Transcendentalist tradition," and where "Christian Science and New Thought Practitioners flourished, taking patients from neurologists and, what was more galling, curing them." When Mabel first decided to undergo psychotherapy in 1914, she wrote a letter about her family "inheritance" of sin and suffering to the leading Boston psychotherapist, Dr. Morton Prince, although she never worked with him.[28]

It is hardly surprising that those suffering from depression and other psychological ailments would turn to mentalist therapies that promised an escape from "hereditary degeneracy." Relying on the passive goodness of a divine god-head that offered infinite reserves of love and support was one route; the active unlearning of destructive feelings and behaviors through talk therapy, another. Mabel was "manic-depressive," as she informed A. A. Brill when she first visited him. Whatever the accuracy of the label, there is no doubt that she was subject to severe cycles of mania and depression throughout her adult life that left her despairing and suicidal. Thus *all* routes that promised a cure were attractive, as there were no effective medications for bipolar disorder until lithium became available in the 1960s.[29]

During the first decade of the twentieth century, psychotherapy increased in "national medical and popular interest" in the United States because its "environmentalism and optimism" were consonant with the Progressive Era spirit of reform (although hereditarianism continued to underlie the "science" of the eugenics movement). Since the mid-nineteenth century, women had flocked to spiritualist beliefs and practices, as founders, leaders, and adherents. In the twentieth century, they responded as well to the new talking cures, which treated their "neurasthenic" complaints with dignity rather than with ridicule and rest cures: "No longer were neurotics 'vampires' or 'silly exaggerators,' chiefly upper-class females. Most psychotherapists argued that neurosis was intensely serious and painful and could attack the happiness of individuals and families more cruelly than many organic illnesses."[30]

At the same historic moment that British sexologists were discussing free love, Sigmund Freud was discussing the ways in which the "civilized code" of sexual morality made women its chief (neurotic) victim—unable to "repress, sublimate, or fulfill their powerful sexual drives." He found Americans "very contemptible" for having what he described as the "most extreme" sexual morality. Freud was hardly advocating "free love" in his 1908 essay, "'Civilized' Sexual Morality and Modern Nervous Illness." But there were radical feminists, like Mabel's friend Emma Goldman, who took away from his lectures on sexual repression the "truth" that sexual suppression was one of the primary factors in women's lack of intellectual achievement. There were also progressive eugenicists who argued for women's right to sexual pleasure in marriage on the grounds that this would stave off the race suicide that Anglo-Saxons were bringing about because of their increasing divorce rates and decreasing birth rates. In an unpublished section of her memoir of her New York years, *Movers and Shakers*, Mabel included a eugenics lecture that Margaret Sanger had given her. It was written by a sociology professor at Columbia who provided detailed instructions for married men on female sexual arousal.[31]

Freud's theory of psychoanalysis emerged from his own dark foreboding of the ways in which a "sexual climate of gloom, frustration, fear, mutual despair, and moral uncertainty" was damaging the sexual lives and marriages of the European middle classes. Many of his first cases involved men and women who were both syphilitic and "hysterical." He was aware that the pathologies of hysteria and tertiary syphilis induced symptoms that were similar in both diseases: blindness, lameness, spasms, paralysis, and tics. Freud's commitment to a predominantly mentalist view of human nature and development may have grown partly out of his disgust with the ways in which Jews had been associated for centuries with theories of hereditary degeneracy, including the spread of syphilis. It was also connected to the marginalization of Jewish doctors to the low status specialties of dermatology (a euphemism for syphilology), neurology, and psychiatry, in which they were expected to work as clinicians, not theorists.[32]

Freud insisted that psychoanalysts should not have to be medical practitioners because of "the racism of medicine." In the United States, where psychiatric practice required a medical degree for certification by the 1920s, syphilis was "the making" of the field when the medical discovery of "syphilis of the insane" provided psychiatrists with scientific credibility. American psychiatrists cast modernity—science, frankness, pragmatism—"as the enlightened antithesis to Victorianism," a platform they used "to launch their more general attack on propriety and privacy as outmoded remnants from the pre-scientific past." Syphilis provided a "perfectly legitimate entrée into the domestic realm, and, as such, underwrote their conviction that in the future science would exempt no human activity, however intimate, from expert scrutiny."[33]

All of these interrelated concerns were embodied in Freud's first and most studied case, *Dora* (1905), which has suggestive parallels with Mabel's therapy with Smith Ely Jelliffe and with the incestuous "family plot" she embeds in "Green Horses." Most contemporary scholars read Freud's *Dora* as a narrative of the emerging field of psychoanalysis. It opens a revealing window into the Victorian patriarchal biases that made their way into modern culture, most particularly in terms of the personal and cultural dread that the "New Woman" aroused. Freud began to see Dora in October 1900, when she was eighteen; the therapy lasted for three months, terminated by Dora, apparently because of her dissatisfaction with the interpretive road Freud was taking with her.

Dora believed that she had inherited syphilis from her father, whom Freud had treated for it. She was suicidal and despairing for many good reasons, not the least of which was her father's attempt to pawn her off on his lover's husband. Dora's "mental" illness, as many scholars have noted, was rooted in her milieu and the sexual double standard that locked women into individualized explanations for neuroses that had profoundly social causes. Dora believed that her father had infected her mother with VD, and she may have been right, given the symptoms from which her mother suffered. When Dora told this to Freud, along with her fear that she had inherited syphilis from her father, he interpreted her fears as part of her pathology rather than as a precipitating cause, although he admitted "that the offsprings of luetics were very specially predisposed to severe psycho-neuroses." Dora, Freud also noted, attended lectures on women's rights, was widely read, and was ambivalent about her sexual identity, which Freud diagnosed as "repressed" homosexuality.[34]

As he moved toward his conclusion of the case, Freud speculated on its larger cultural ramifications in a way that suggests a source for his move (around 1907) from a belief in father-child incest to the Oedipal "wish" that became the hallmark of his mature theory of psychosexual development. Freud notes that Dora's governess (who was in love with Dora's father) taught her that "all men were frivolous and untrustworthy. To Dora that must mean that all men were like her father. But she thought her father suffered from venereal disease—for had he not handed it on to her and her mother? She might therefore have imagined to herself that all men suffered from venereal disease, . . ." Freud was shaken by the horrified public and medical response to his theory that incestuous sexual abuse was part of the hidden life of the bourgeoisie. Perhaps he could also not accept the links he discovered among the venereal diseases of men and some women's rejection of heterosexuality as a life-threatening disease.[35]

In making women the "privileged site" for his "sexual etiology for hysteria," Freud "gave early twentieth-century psychiatrists license further to eroticize this female malady" and "to reinforce . . . the worst of womanliness." Modern sexual identity was first inscribed on the bodies of women, marking "that symbolic (if not temporally precise) boundary—between 'Victorian' and 'modern,' 'old' and 'new.'" It became "the supreme 'secret,' the omnipotent cause, the 'hidden meaning' of our being." It advanced "the cause of sexual freedom" for women, while "paradoxically tighten[ing] the grip of the system." When the sexologists "grabbed on to Freud's theory of libidinal economy," they further imprisoned women in their sexuality. Havelock Ellis, one of the readers of Mabel's unpublished memoirs, may have argued that women were men's *sexual* equals. But that did not mean they played an equal role in sexual intercourse: women were supposed to remain passive. By reducing women to their sexuality, the sexual revolutionaries "threatened to convert them into sexual objects, creatures so preoccupied with their sexual needs as to be incapable of functioning in any other capacity." Like Freud, Ellis believed that sex for women should lead to parenthood. Thus "sexual modernism and old-fashioned romanticism join hands to reinscribe the differences between the sexes."[36]

Historians of modern women have noted that "Promiscuity and extramarital sex posed many more risks for them than for their male lovers, who believed in women's sexual freedom in theory but in practice were often alarmed by it." The risks were also, as we know, medical. A Boston gynecologist was not alone is asserting that birth control (condoms) *produced* venereal diseases, which were, in any case, "'just punishment for sin.'" Thus, radical sexologists, who condemned contraception for inhibiting women's "natural" purpose in life, made common cause with the very conservatives they were purportedly undermining. Conservative Victorian doctors shared Ellis's belief that "'in a certain sense . . . [women's] brains are in their wombs.'" Given the power of these influences over her, it is not entirely surprising that Mabel believed—even while dreading the possibly diseased consequences—that she could save herself through sex, nor that she insisted that she had intended to have a dozen or more children.[37]

There are few American women in the early modern period whose life and writings better exemplify the fraught relationship between sexual identity and female subjectivity than Mabel. When Christopher Lasch brought her back from obscurity by naming her "a pioneer in the cult of the orgasm" in his book *The New Radicals in America*, he located her problem, not her identity. Sex for Mabel *was* a means of politics, which she enacted and promoted throughout much of her life in the belief that it would affirm her existence and meaning. The Freudian and sexological regimes that Mabel adopted, however, led anywhere but to her liberation. Of undoubtedly greater efficacy was the memoir writing that she engaged in for forty years.[38]

Autobiography and the Construction of the Modern Female Self

> I started out to try & show the inward picture of a person of my own period; what heredity and environment had made of her. I did not believe, & do not believe, that she was inwardly so different from a lot of others. She was a 20th century type.
>
> —MABEL DODGE LUHAN[39]

Mabel justified the writing of her memoirs with a claim that many autobiographers have used: that one's existence is "generalizable," that it has "common ground" with the reader. If she was a "20th century type," she was a type that performed many of the self-contradictory roles embedded in the social and cultural tropes available for "the modern woman" who was attempting to create a meaningful self and world. Her "escape" from these self-contradictions into the arms of her premodern, non-Western Indian lover, Tony Lujan, was her final and most necessary fictive truth.

Contemporary theorists insist upon the constructedness of the self who is shaped through writing and therapy. Paul Eakin claims that "the writing of autobiography emerges as a second acquisition of language, a second coming into being of self, a self-conscious self-consciousness." Susan Friedman argues "There is no essential, original, coherent autobiographical self before the moment of self-narrating." In Mabel's case that self changes, sometimes dramatically, between her published and unpublished memoirs, and over time, as she revises her life stories. Donald Spence notes that talking about the past in therapy "crystallizes" memory in ways that inevitably distort it, so that there can be no authentic retrieval of a "real" past, a task rendered even more unstable by the fact that both analyst and analysand have their own agendas in the process. These observations are adumbrated in Smith Ely Jelliffe's 1916 psychoanalytic notes, which he annotated after the publication of Mabel's first three volumes of memoirs. Above his own script, he added the page numbers from Mabel's first three published volumes (1933–1936), where she referred to the same topic, sometimes with the *exact* words he had taken down during her therapy, even though she had no access to his notes until 1945. It is clear that Mabel began to "write" her life script when she began her first analysis (see chapter 1).[40]

Begun within the year after she contracted syphilis from Tony Lujan, and urged on by her analyst, A. A. Brill, Mabel appropriated Freud's theories of sublimation and catharsis for her rationale. Reliving the past through language, the painful emotions associated with the "experience" would presumably be exorcised and cease to cause disturbances. Through verbal expiation Mabel hoped she might find the psychic equilibrium denied her by her mental and physical ailments. Perhaps for the first time, at least in a sustained way, she saw writing as an active and creative use of her intelligence that could give shape to her own life, rather than depending upon others to do that for her. As Leigh Gilmore has noted: "The talking cure has been used by some critics as a metaphor for the autobiographical process of forming the chaotic elements of life into a narrative that replaces and transcends those experiences in a healing and restorative way."[41]

Mabel recognized that her life story could serve a public, as well as a private, purpose. By showing the "crude and unflattering aspects of the past," as she put it in the foreword to her second volume, she could practice therapy on a national scale. She was supported in this mission by the responses she was getting from the friends and acquaintances to whom she circulated her manuscript: Havelock Ellis, Willa Cather, and especially D. H. Lawrence. Lawrence did not believe that Mabel had the discipline to write fiction, but he encouraged her to write her memoirs because he saw her life as paradigmatic of modern American culture.

In her fourth and final published volume, *Edge of Taos Desert: An Escape to Reality*, Mabel revealed the shape and intention of her published oeuvre. After she states that her "life broke in two" with her journey to New Mexico, we begin to see the ways that she has embedded her memoirs within the genres of the conversion and captivity narratives. But she subverts the mainstream American conversion story, at the same time that she reverses the four-hundred-year-old plot of the Indian captivity narrative. Rather than white woman being returned to Christian civilization from the "savage" world of the Indian, Anglo America represents the savagery of a civilization that has exploited the earth and destroyed human community. It will be the duty of a new interracial Adam and Eve—Tony and Mabel—to bring that light to the Western world.

Isak Dinesen's biographer, Judith Thurman, called *Out of Africa* a "sublime repair job." Published the same year as Mabel's *Edge of Taos Desert*, they can both be categorized as syphilis memoirs. Like Mabel, Isak erases most of the pain, messiness, and distress of her life on her Kenyan farm—including administering Salvarsan to her African workers, many of whom were infected with syphilis. Her creation myth of Africa as a paradise, which she believed she was one of the last white Europeans to "discover," was very much a recreation in memory of what she had lost in life. Dinesen came to Africa with a mind steeped in Rousseauian views of "the noble savage." These were implanted by her father, who had apparently lived among American Indians and "never tired of reminding her as a child that the 'Indians are better than our civilized people of Europe, [that they are] closer to nature, more honest. Their eyes see more than ours, and they are wiser. We should learn more from them.'"[42]

Edge of Taos Desert was Mabel's "divine repair job," the teleological end to her autobiographical mission. Like Dinesen, she erased syphilis from her memoir,

Figure 10 Karen Blixen-Finecke (Isak Dinesen) on safari in Africa, 1918. Photo courtesy of Royal Library, Copenhagen, Denmark.

ending her story before her discovery that syphilis was rampant in Taos Pueblo, and before Tony infected her with it. Like Dinesen, she created a myth of Taos as a paradise, the key difference between them being that Mabel *ended* her four volumes of published memoirs with her having regained paradise, whereas Dinesen wrote in "an elegiac mode" from a perspective "after the fall."

Dinesen's edenic Africa was "already an anachronism in 1913." As anthropologist Sylvia Rodriguez has shown, the same was true for northern New Mexico. In the early twentieth century, the economies of northern New Mexico and Kenya were on the decline for indigenous peoples and those, like *nuevomexicanos*, who had centuries of tenure on the land. Both places were ripe for touristic exploitation, which increased dramatically in the post–World War II era. Dinesen's East Africa now has a national park and a town named for her, and she is used to sell "the safari image" to those who are hungry for an exotic colonial experience. In the 1930s, Mabel put up a sign on her front gate that read, "Tourists not welcome," due to the number of acolytes and curiosity seekers who came to her door. Her home and writings have continued to draw tourists, and amenity migrants, to northern New Mexico for an exotic experience of an Indianized landscape.[43]

D. H. Lawrence, who arrived in Taos in September 1922, at Mabel's invitation, scorned Mabel's desire to possess his spirit in service to his writing her gospel of Taos. He was equally irritated by her quest for a sublimated "higher" consciousness. But read in the light of her afflicted mind and body, her desires for spiritual transcendence are much more understandable. When Mabel took up the Taos Indians as her saviors in 1918, she was on her last flight from the many poisons of Western civilization, the war and syphilis among them. In contrast to Maurice and the others she had known, she wrote in her unpublished memoir "The Statue of Liberty" (1947), the Pueblos "seemed so clean and wholesome and free of the sin and decadence of the world." During her lifetime, Mabel could not write publicly about the negative side of her life in New Mexico because she had invested so much of her psyche, persona, and reputation in the idealized image she had promoted of herself, Tony, and Taos. Among the many things that she did not write about were the repercussions in Taos Pueblo that her relationship generated for Tony; her fear that she had betrayed her race by becoming Tony's lover and wife; and Tony's multiple sexual infidelities. She intended to keep her own darkest secret, "the secret sin" of syphilis, hidden until after her death.[44]

It is no accident that Mabel ended her published memoirs just *before* she and Tony were going to have sexual intercourse (presumably) for the first time. When she saw the bloody semen that stained Tony's beautiful white sheet, the sartorial signature of Taos Pueblo men, she knew beyond a shadow of a doubt that there was no Eden, and that the serpents of jealousy, depression, and disease would continue to pursue her, as they did, for most of her life. After she was infected, Mabel wrote in "The Statue of Liberty," she and Tony ceased to have sexual relations with each other for the rest of their lives.

Post-colonial critics who dislike Mabel Dodge Luhan's orientalizing and commodification of the Indian Southwest will perhaps read the memoirs I am editing in terms of the originating Columbian curse. Columbus brought syphilis back from the New World to the Old; now the Indians were getting revenge, so to speak, by infecting the white woman whose literary proclamations and famous guests brought touristic exploitation and real estate development in their wake. While I'll grant these critics a point, I also hope that they and others will read *The Suppressed Memoirs* as a contribution to the ongoing postmodernist project of destabilizing binary oppositions, including those that reify colonizer and the colonized into mutually exclusive categories. Mabel and Tony Luhan were locked in a forty-four-year embrace of love and anger, communion and betrayal. Theirs was a very complicated partnership that has something to teach us about the potential and pitfalls of racial and cultural border crossings.[45]

In her unpublished memoirs, Mabel claims that her refusal to give Tony up was a sign of her maturity; she wouldn't discard him the way she had prior lovers and husbands, although she certainly thought about doing so more than once. It is also true that the "myth" she built up of "her" Taos and her "Indian Tony crown"—as Georgia O'Keeffe put it in her first enchanted summer there— brought them national and international acclaim, and drew to their home in Taos scores of remarkably creative men and women artists, writers, and social visionaries who contributed to the shaping of a dynamic and continuously contested modern American culture. That venereal disease, sexual, and racial transgression were part of the foundation of the utopian vistas she hoped to sell the nation makes Mabel both indelibly *more* sympathetic—and human.[46]

Mabel's unpublished writings complicate the public myth she created about Tony and Taos over the course of many decades. They help us to better understand the personal, sexual, gender, and racial boundary crossings and misapprehensions that marked the emergence of modern Western society and culture over the course of the late nineteenth and early twentieth centuries. The power of the edenic myth that Mabel helped to create has persisted in our own time, well beyond the attempts of myriad scholars to deconstruct and undermine it. Perhaps we will understand more about its construction and endurance after bringing to light the sometimes tragic, sometimes comic, and sometimes shocking undercurrents in the life and times of one of its most intriguing perpetrators, Mabel Dodge Luhan.

CHAPTER ONE

Family Secrets

But when life is gone out of me, then I am like something banished to the outer darkness, out of touch with all that is human, feeling no recognition of the interests of others, having no sense of relationship with any human being, feeling *outside*, inhuman, unloving, insentient, an exile from the earth.
—MABEL DODGE LUHAN to Dr. Morton Prince

IN A 1999 article published in the *Psychoanalytic Review*, Patricia Everett pointed out that Mabel Luhan's relationships with her psychiatrists were beneficial to her in many ways. It is true that Smith Ely Jelliffe, and much more so A. A. Brill, helped her through some of her darkest hours. Mabel maintained lifelong friendships with them, shared her writings with them, and they with her, and she sent her friends and lovers to them for help. But Mabel's simultaneous and continuous search for alternative therapies, Christian Science and occultism among them, testifies to their limited efficacy. Throughout her adult life, Mabel pursued the question of the body's relationship to the mind, trying to talk, pray, love, and write her way out of the heredity and environment that she felt doomed her to cycles of unendurable emotional suffering, as well as to the pain and cruelty she inflicted on friends and family when she was in the midst of it.[1]

All of these therapies promised an escape from the "family secret" of which she was given only fragmentary glimpses when she was a child. In 1913, a few months after returning to New York from Florence, Mabel sought out her first psychiatrist. Bernard Sachs was a neurologist, and he did not approve of psychotherapy. Like many of his generation, he "associated 'mental methods' . . . with the 'mind cure' practitioner, the charlatan, or the vaudeville showman." Sachs told her that modern artists were insane and that she should have nothing to do with them—not exactly the kind of advice that a woman in charge of raising funds for the 1913 Armory Show would be likely to take. Mabel then turned to Dr. Morton Prince, one of the primary developers of American psychotherapy. Prince lived in Boston, where there was much greater openness among psychiatrists than in New York to "hypnotism, suggestion, and psychic research." He stressed "the learned nature of neurotic symptoms," thus weakening "the position that they resulted from hereditary degeneracy."[2]

Mabel wrote a lengthy and forthcoming letter to Prince, hoping that he would take her on as a patient. At the time she wrote it, she had already launched her radical salon, raised funds and written publicity for the Armory Show, the first large international exhibition of postimpressionist and modern art, made a name for herself as a "New Woman," and was in her second year of her love affair with John Reed. As was true for all of Mabel's other lovers and husbands, once she had sexual relations with Reed, she became entirely dependent on him as a source for her emotional well-being. She drove him away (although there were several returns) because of her "sexual possessiveness," which related to his inability to remain "faithful" in fact and spirit.

The Prince letter has Jelliffe's notation that it was written in 1914 and never sent. In the letter, excerpted here, we see Mabel struggling to express her understanding of her father's mental illness as a way of trying to explain her own. Her discourse veers between the occult and the empirical, the psychological and spiritual, as she seeks to define her manic depression and describes symptoms that suggest her father may have been suffering from tertiary syphilis, without her naming that disease. Mabel was never privy to more than fragmentary glimpses of the "family secret" she alludes to in the following letter. We cannot know what was meant when a family member told Mabel that her father was banned from having sexual intercourse with her mother because it made him "insane." Jelliffe's analytical notes provide more clues, as we shall see.

Dear Dr. Prince—
. . . . I hardly know where to begin. Perhaps about my father, who suffered mental agony all his life because he was not understood—because his case was not rightly diagnosed. The reason it was not was perhaps that in those days the intimate relation and interplay of the

physical and psychic was not so well understood as now, or perhaps because the will to live, diminished by his condition, was too feeble in him to make him reach out of his usual path of living, beyond the 'family doctor' and the 'family,' to *demand* a reason for his curious, obscure complaint and its cure. Soon after he was married (I am told in a lowered voice)—he was forbidden sexual intercourse with my mother because it made him insane. It appears he did not heed this—(I am not certain whether he did or not really) but anyway he did become temporarily insane and was for a period in a sanatorium. Then he came back and lived with my mother. I was a baby then. But I do not think that from this period until he died, when I was twenty-two or three, that he ever had any sexual life.

What I remember of my father are periods of melancholy—leading up to fearful outbursts of temper, followed by long painful attacks of gout and inflammatory rheumatism. I do not seem to remember his ever being *really* like other people, for at times when he was well he was much wittier and more amusing than they, cleverer. But these times grew fewer and fewer. His face, as I look back on it now, was mainly tormented, lined, sallow, haunted. What I remember concerning him are such words as 'uric acid,' 'monomania,' 'depression,' and finally a doctor who was merciful enough to keep him always under the influence of morphine, then death from an illness that had such symptoms as buzzings in the head, etc., a kind of poisoning, a poison distilled by himself, auto-intoxication. Had he been a biblical character he would have been said to be possessed by devils,—and *someone* could have cast them out. As it was no one understood,—it is as tho' he lived in the in-between time.—I, feeling some strange, analogous suffering, am reaching out to you.

What was true of him is true, with another adaptation, of me. Only I have more vitality. I am terrifically happy in between times.—I haven't uric acid (yet), and *queerer* things happen . . . I can't tell you all about myself in a letter. I will only try to *relate externals*, and then if you summon me I will go where you are and tell you anything else you ask me,—if you think you can help me and want to.

It is too simple to say that life alternates between two conditions, vitality and depression, yet perhaps all the rest can be confined within the definition of those two terms . . . what I want to try to make clear to you is that neither of those conditions are normal. The one is supernormal and the other is subnormal, and *both* seem to me to be states of emotion being unrelated to objects. . . . You can suspect in this matter the amount of unhappiness that I can bring to others. . . .

Sometimes there seems only one reality in the world—vitality and its fluctuations. Hegel seemed to think so too. But even so I do not think that it is necessary to suffer the entrance into one of [the] hideous torments because one is empty of vitality. One should learn how to be full of something *else*, something stable and enduring. For I seem to be only a vacuum. Sometimes the wind that is life is blowing thro' me, sometimes not, and when it is *not* something *else*,—painful, tortured—in agony—is in possession. When life is in me I am a part of life and human interests, and *of great use*, having power to influence people and keen to help and further all that is spirit and going *up*,—all that will break new roads, let in more light. . . .

But when life is gone out of me, then I am like something banished to the outer darkness, out of touch with all that is human, feeling no recognition of the interests of others, having no sense of relationship with any human being, feeling *outside*, inhuman, unloving, insentient, an exile from the earth. . . .

And all this is to say why I am writing to you. Is there a miserable spirit that must exist in me except when I have the force to precipitate it into someone else, when my vitality, drawing their vitality from them leaves a vacuum into which I push this misery? And that has a separate existence that stands *outside*, along, sometimes, so that I and one other, with whom I have the right combination, can actually sense it? Hear it? I think I must be helped to answer to this. I believe that my sanity depends upon it. So I am writing to you and putting it to you as well as I can and if you wish it I will come where you are, if you feel it will do good.

Mabel's passion for Freud had to do with the promise that "the patient's own insight cured. . . . Over and over the psychoanalysts insisted that Freud's method was radical in the literal sense; it eradicated the roots of symptoms." Presumably, the "therapist and patient were democratically engaged as equals in exploring the unconscious." This theory proved no more true in Freud's early practice than it did in the practices of the two therapists Mabel saw, although she asserted herself assiduously when she disagreed with her first therapist, Smith Ely Jelliffe, and she often ignored the advice of A. A. Brill, whom she consulted for over twenty years.[3]

Smith Ely Jelliffe

Smith Ely Jelliffe (1866–1945) was Mabel's first analyst, a man of prodigious intellect who was interested in fields as diverse as paleontology, mysticism, and drama. Jelliffe wrote some four hundred articles and books during his lifetime and was the editor of the *Psychoanalytic Review*. For all his open-mindedness in the spheres of religion, science, and philosophy, he intensely disliked the "new morality" and the "New Woman," whom he considered "mannish and decadent."[4] Jelliffe's therapy reinforced Mabel's beliefs, inculcated by her Victorian upbringing and reinforced by her gurus, Sigmund Freud, Havelock Ellis, and Edward Carpenter, that woman's biology was her destiny; that her highest fulfillment came through bearing and raising children; and that to have sex properly, a women must lie passively under the phallus and make sure she experienced orgasm in her vagina.

At the time she began her therapy with him in January 1916, Mabel had retreated from New York City to Croton-on-Hudson, where she rented a rural compound, Finney Farm. Here, she tried taking root in "Nature," gathering her resources in order to create a strong "maternal" self, rather than expend them upon a lover. This included her adoption of a young girl, Elizabeth, from an orphanage. Shortly after she moved to Finney Farm in 1915, she met Maurice Sterne (1878–1957), a Russian post-Impressionist painter who had recently returned from two years in Bali, and who A. A. Brill would diagnose as having syphilis. They soon became lovers in constant turmoil, engaged in an ongoing contest of power. On Mabel's part, she wanted to turn Maurice from painting to sculpting and to keep his roving eye on her; on his part, he wanted a muse and lover. Their impulsive marriage, on August 23, 1917, did not end their turmoil. Sterne shortly left for a short trip out West. His first night back, Mabel saw him eyeing another woman; soon after, she sent him off to Santa Fe, where she joined him in December. The battle of wills did not end until Mabel sent Sterne back to New York City in August 1918, after taking Tony as her lover, although she did not divorce Sterne until 1922.[5]

Jelliffe's fifty-eight pages of analytical notes, dated January 3, 1916, through June 7, 1916, with Mabel's accompanying letters, provide tantalizing, if incomplete, insights into early psychoanalytic therapy. They reveal several areas of Mabel's struggles with sexuality and self: her father's ailments; her sexual play with women; her emotional and physical illnesses, including syphilis; her relationship with Maurice Sterne, with whom she attempted to have a child; and her fantasies about running off with Indians.

The letters are a rare treasure, sent to Mabel by Jelliffe's wife after he died, in 1945, at Mabel's request. Historian of psychiatry Elizabeth Lunbeck has noted in her edition of the 1912 case notes of a young woman that they have to be read with caution because they "are sketchy and elliptical, intended more as *aide-memorie* than as a full account of the case." Likewise, Jelliffe's notes are nonlinear shards of memory that reflect what Mabel wanted to share, and what Jelliffe thought was significant, although there is no obvious commentary on his part. I have organized my analysis of the notes in terms of the five salient themes that are mentioned throughout.

Charles Ganson

Mabel's father was responsible for Mabel's earliest associations of sexuality with syphilis, madness, and punishment, at least in her reconstruction of her past. When she wrote to Una Jeffers in the 1930s, "my father turned me into what is euphemistically called a frigid woman at an early age," she was probably referring to an emotional trauma, or series of traumas, that she suffered during her childhood. Not only had Charles apparently been banned from having intercourse with her mother after Mabel was born, but, as she notes in her letter to Dr. Prince, he had been institutionalized at least once. Mabel's earliest memory of her childhood, at least as recorded in Jelliffe's notes, was of visiting her father in a sanitorium where, she was later told, Charles was sent for "self-abuse" shortly after he was married. As odd as that may sound to our twenty-first-century ears, it was not uncommon. According to Ronald Walters, "Nineteenth-century insane asylums contained numerous human beings whose misfortunes were credited to masturbation or sexual 'excess.'"[6]

We know from *Background* that Mabel's father had outbursts of anger against her mother, who he believed was having affairs, and who left him more than once. In Jelliffe's notes, Charles's outbursts of rage and violent behavior are more strongly articulated by Mabel, who feared he might hit her. Did her father sexually abuse her or, what is more likely, transmit to her his revulsion toward female flesh, at once menacing her burgeoning sexuality with his frightening prohibitions not to "kiss boys," easing her into the gentle and unthreatening arms of young women, and sending her on her ultimate journey toward "compulsory heterosexuality" as a means of restoring the family circle she never had? In his notes, Jelliffe quotes Mabel as saying: "Formed early hard crust. I don't feel with my heart. He [Charles] was against sex awfully." Jelliffe follows this with a note on the suicide of a Buffalo man, whom we discover in

Mabel's memoir, "The Statue of Liberty," hung himself from a light bulb, naked except for a pair of white gloves. According to Mabel's mother, this man had syphilis (see chapter 4). Jelliffe's notes indicate that Ganson was "agitated" by his death.[7]

We cannot connect the dots between these brief glimpses of her father's life, which are haunted by a statement Mabel made early in her therapy: "family secret: which I don't know." But we can ask the following questions. What did it mean that sexual intercourse with his wife "made him insane"? Was Mabel's father syphilitic or homosexual, or both? Was he suffering from paresis, syphilitic insanity, in his last years? Mabel's descriptions of his irrational and violent behavior, and his intense physical suffering, which apparently got worse as he neared his death at age fifty-four, bear striking parallels to experience and behavior of Randolph Churchill in his last years, when he was suffering from tertiary syphilis, and manifested symptoms of wild mood swings, vertigo, swollen joints, and deafness.[8]

Childhood Sexual Play and Adult Lesbian Affairs

As a Freudian, Jelliffe was very interested in Mabel's childhood and adolescent sexual experimentation. Mabel recounted playing with her friend Dorothy Scatchard when they were somewhere between ages seven and ten and Dorothy's kissing Mabel's vagina. "Her first sex experience," Jelliffe notes. She also remembers lying front to back with Nina Bull, whose mother, Mabel was told, Charles Ganson loved, but for some reason, could not marry. Mabel continued her relations with young women in boarding school. According to Jelliffe's notes, her mother took her out of her last school, Chevy Chase, because of one these relationships, with a young woman named Beatrice, which Mabel described in *Background*, although without the details about her caressing Beatrice's genitals.

"Seducing" girls, Mabel wrote, gave her no "personal satisfaction." Of course, Mabel was well aware at the time she was writing her memoirs that enjoying sexual relations with women was, in the Freudian terminology she had already adopted, an "infantile perversion," something that an adult woman needed to outgrow. She had written lovingly in *Background* about her "chaste" affair with Violet Shillito, which she claimed never went beyond gentle touching of each other's breasts. (In fact she wrote so poetically—or euphemistically—that the lawyer for Harcourt Brace said she could keep these passages in the memoir, even though lesbianism was not a subject that should be broached.[9])

After Violet's death, Mabel was very much taken with Violet's friend Marcelle, whom she met in Paris in 1904, and who tried to keep her from marrying Edwin. Mabel continued lesbian relationships throughout her time in France and Italy, before and during her marriage to Edwin. In *European Experiences*, Mabel described her relationships with women as nonsexual. But in an unpublished section of *European Experiences*, she talks about a brief affair with an English historian of the Italian Renaissance, Maud Cruttwell (1860–1939), and about what seems to have been a longer and more satisfactory affair with American sculptor Janet Scudder (1869–1940). (When Mabel told Scudder about her concern that she was being unfaithful to Edwin, Janet reassured her that the rule applied only to men.) In Jelliffe's notes, there are linked woman-woman symbols; he notes that her sexual interest in women increased during her years in Florence, and that she had at least one affair for her "own satisfaction."[10]

Madness, Disease, and Men

Jelliffe's notes record a wide variety of physiological and psychological ailments that Mabel suffered during her life, including her "mutilating" herself as a child to get the attention of doctors, whom she seems to have associated from an early age with having the power to "assuage the pain" connected to her sense of emotional abandonment by her parents. He notes several attempted suicides: she tried to shoot herself during her affair with Parmenter (an act not mentioned in "Green Horses"), and she took strychnine, which she does write about in "Green Horses."

After the birth of her son John, Mabel suffered from a prolapsed uterus, which resulted in the operation that she describes in "Green Horses" that Parmenter was unable to complete. Parmenter's name is associated in Jelliffe's notes with two other symptoms that could be connected to his giving her gonorrhea, a "bloody discharge," that seems to have followed their first intercourse, and "mucous colitis." In Florence, Mabel was finally operated on for her prolapsis, at which time the doctor removed one of her ovaries. Jelliffe's initial medical evaluation of Mabel indicates that she had suffered from "herpes of the neck of the uterus," leukorrhea (vaginal discharge), and "possible painful urination," the last two (along with her diseased ovary), possibly symptoms of gonorrhea, although it is never named in his notes, nor mentioned in her writings until her last memoir, "Doctors."[11]

In Jelliffe's notes, the medical symbol for the spirochete bacterium that causes syphilis, appears often next to Edwin Dodge's name. Mabel discusses it in one of her letters, and in one of the dream interpretations she sends Jelliffe. Although Edwin had apparently promised her that they would not have sex after telling her about his syphilis (and assuring her that he was safe), they did, at least once, and Mabel got pregnant. She went to Paris for an abortion, presumably because she feared what might happen to the child. Mabel also recorded for Jelliffe a dream she had about an old woman whose home she visited. Something was the matter with her nose—she had "saddle nose," a nose collapsed inward that was one of the most obvious signs of second-stage syphilis. Mabel commented: "Edwin's syphilis and my unconscious fear of catching it."[12]

In *European Experiences*, Mabel wrote about three suicide attempts she made while she was married to Edwin, during which time she was having passionate but presumably platonic affairs with various men, including her son John's tutor. She never explained the extremity of her behavior, or her physical revulsion toward her husband. It was not until I read Jelliffe's notes that I understood the underlying fear that drove Mabel to put ground glass in figs, and to take laudanum and veronal, as means of escaping fears with which she did not know how to cope.

In his first meeting with Mabel, Jelliffe diagnosed her main problem as "compulsory sex possession."[13] None of her therapists or spiritual advisors seem to have any idea of how to help her break her pattern of having sexual relations with and marrying men who had venereal disease, while continuing to live in morbid dread of infection. They had no theories or therapies that would enable her understand that her dependency on men for self-realization led her into the recurring losses of self and self-destructive behavior that fed and were fed by her cycles of manic depression. Brill encouraged the practice that most likely saved her life—writing, particularly writing her memoirs. But his ideas about gender and women were steeped in Freudian orthodoxy.

The Vaginal Orgasm

Like Dora, Freud's most famous patient, Mabel seems, during her therapy with Jelliffe, a bundle of physical and psychic misery, punctuated by moments of defiance. Her letters to him demonstrate her attempts to both feed into and resist his methods of curing her psychoneuroses. We see Mabel placing her most private fears and dreams at the behest of a brilliant man who tries to inscribe onto her his phallocentric theories of gender. In some of these letters, one is tempted to say that she is parodying his advice. She will carry out the letter of the Freudian law: a woman *must* have her orgasm in her vagina or she isn't a real woman; she has a vaginal orgasm because *he* directed it there; and, when she thinks that Maurice has impregnated her, she tells Jelliffe that because of his therapy, she will give birth to the first "psychoanalytic baby." Mabel intimates to Jelliffe that her earlier lesbian practices, starting in childhood with clitoral stimulation, and her desire to play "the male role" in sex, misdirected her sexual energies. But those days are apparently over.

Mabel wrote in *Movers and Shakers* that she left Jelliffe after a few months because he was too dogmatic and judgmental. "If your conscious says. . . . 'I am a man and I can procreate with my male organ,'" she quotes him as saying, "then I am dogmatic. . . . This is not forcing a philosophy on you. This is only telling you you are trying to do the impossible." When she shared her desire to cut off her long hair, he responded that it was a secret wish to shear "Phoebus Apollo" himself. In her most provocative letter, the first excerpted here, we see how Freud's psychological theories implanted "the very scripts by which we recognize ourselves as sexual subjects," that is, how Freud converted cultural codes into scientific ones. The letter also demonstrates the ways that female patients could both comply with and try to subvert that agenda: asserting their need to be collaborators in their own therapy; resisting being typologized into categories that do not do justice to the complexities of the person subsumed by them; and trying to figure out ways to fulfill gender norms without being dependent on a man.[14]

Dear Dr. Jelliffe

Here is a point where I would like your opinion. I thought of asking you about it and then dreaded a storm—or worse—a gloomy face. But please try & see it as the *first* case—see it freshly I mean—& not in the light of the conventions. See it as a case in itself—not as a type & then give me your opinion.

When I started psychoanalysis I told you I did it to get over jealousy which bothered me. Instead of that—so far it has gotten me over a lot of fantasies which I sincerely believed represented the higher & more spiritual part of me . . . my mystical notions & so on. At the beginning of it I told you I wanted to do some creative work & we believed I *would* get my energy freed so that I might. Then one day I asked you to state to me what my problem is, & you said I use my maleness femaley—&

my femaleness malely. At the beginning of the analysis you *probed* me to find my strongest desires. You will find—in turning back to your notes—that I told you I started life wanting fifteen children.

You have told me repeatedly that no relation between a man & a woman was justified save in that it was productive & I have repeatedly told you that I wanted it to be so. I *will*—and have *never* had a relation with a man that I haven't consciously desired a baby; with my whole being I have longed for it. I was *meant* to have lots of children. *But* as you said—I was *unconsciously* using my femaleness *malely*—& I never conceived for that reason. Now psychoanalysis has been teaching my unconscious something. Only twice in my life has a certain experience come to pass in me while I was merely passive. . . . When I was first married I tried to keep myself blank to my husband. I didn't strain to him & try to seize him as I had. I just tried to preserve myself & my loyalty to the other [Parmenter] by a nullified passiveness & one night to my real horror something *took* me—took place in me—in spite of my *not* straining to bring it about & in spite of my willful non-participation. The event occurred—it was some co-operative understanding between the will—conscious or unconscious of my husband & *my* unconscious. It left *me*, I remember, stunned by surprise to find *my* conscious will overpowered. That was the only time it *ever* happened to me—& it brought John. . . . Then for fifteen years it never happened again.

Whatever happened *I* worked for & tried for—I said I wanted babies & I tried to rest them out of the embrace—but my will was never strong enough. Or was it too strong—& the experience I have just written hadn't taught me anything? So of course one reason I was neurotic was this struggle between my intense *conscious* desire to have children which I tried to get in a male dominating way &—according to your theory of opposites—a possible *unconscious* desire not to receive them. Well—your analysis got under my skin at last . . . and last week—just on the eve of being unwell the same thing happened again that happened fifteen years ago. It was not only that the orgasm took place in the vagina because that has occurred more or less since the analysis directed it there, but, while my own will—on that night seemed to me torpid—slow—indifferent some other will in me seemed to act—seemed to open up the walls of the uterus to receive the flow. I was amazed at it—recalling another time long ago. I was even at the moment certain it meant a baby. My body and an unconscious will in me had operated together—while—*I*—my own strong self had lain there—hardly doing more than observe.

That was a week ago Tuesday & am not unwell yet I have had all the unwell symptoms of pain but that's all. I have even begun *to* feel that marvellous [*sic*] content & *self-sufficiency* which I have already described to you—& which I felt only once in my life—when John was moving—a sense of functioning—creating—& fulfilling. I have tried other things as you know—I have overflowed into all sorts of other channels because this one was closed to me thro' my own perversity but *no other activity* compares with this one in pure satisfaction & the sense of rightness. Now I want your opinion of it. When what I have wanted so long has come to pass—thro' psychoanalysis (which proves indubitably that therefore it is what *should* come to pass), when I have such nice children [she is referring to her biological son and adopted daughter]—when the world can use my kind of children—when I am economically *able* to do it—do you feel I ought to give up having it? In my heart it seems to me only a beginning—perhaps I will have fifteen even yet!

I want you to . . . understand that you must answer me—not as answering to a type but as to an individual. I don't see why I haven't the right to it—if I can carry it off. I am not going to marry on its account. I don't feel sure enough of Maurice nor he of himself to hurry into marriage. I am congenial with him—& after he goes to Germany to find out if he is released from that other woman & finds he is, I might marry him. But I am not thinking of rushing into it in a panic. If I have the baby I shall face having it by myself, so to speak. And I don't see why women haven't a right to babies this way if they are strong enough to do so without having to lean back on the protecting male. . . .

Please try & not answer me as you would feel obliged to answer me in a court of law—I want your private opinion. Call me up & make an appointment—& we'll talk it over.

In her follow-up letter, Mabel succumbs to the self-doubts that often racked her when she defied convention, in this case, both the Victorian and the psychoanalytic notion that all women were intended for motherhood:

Dear Dr. Jelliffe,

The enclosed note was written on Wednesday & not sent. Whenever I have tried to give it to you—as on Wed—eve—or mail it—since then—My limbs seem to turn to water & my hand seems incapable of the act, because it would mean bringing the matter into *actual conflict* and allowing a greater menace to the baby.—Of course if you read this first you don't know there is a question of a baby but that what it is & what the other letter is about. Its ten days along at present—& just in that time the right side of my body feels like something came alive & in activity—which the left side where that ovary is gone feels so different—dead like a blasted tree.

Now the conflict going on in me is awfully strong. I want that baby more than anything else one could offer me. I'd rather have it than paint the best picture or write the best book—& Maurice clings to it & yearns over it & we both feel we would hate each other if I got rid of it. Its [*sic*] so utterly against my *instinct* to get rid of it. . . . I shudder all over at the thought & my blood seems to curdle in me & *refuse* . . . and that is so different from the time I told you of when I first married Edwin & had to have my unwellness brought on because *he* was sick. Then I had a horror of keeping the baby & I rushed from Florence to Paris in a hurry to get rid of it. This time because it is right-in-nature to have it—I can hardly bring myself to even *discuss* it, my body is so unwilling to consider giving it up. Everything else but having children seems to me a makeshift & *not satisfying*. I know I might suffer more by having it than by giving it up & the baby might suffer too much & Maurice too. I want to hear from you what practical means there are by which to satisfy all the desires for good in the situation . . . & not have a conflict. If ever there was a psychoanalytic baby—this is one. It has brought about what would have happened naturally but for infantile perversion. It has brought about the submission of the female organs. What a lot of time has been wasted!

The situation would be simple but for two things. Maurice is held by a fantasy built up of hope & desire for that German woman. It's his dream. I am his reality. There is no doubt about his real honest love for me & intense desire to have a baby—& make his life here . . . now he is forty & not thirty—& he longs for a fireside & real, homely joys. . . . I think he wants to be a father. He has a strong family sense as have most Jews. He is absolutely honest & honorable about it all. He begs & begs me not to lose the baby & yet when I ask him—can he be a father to it he always replies: "I don't know what I am till I see Mira again after this year with you."

Now *in any case* he means to go in June. . . . I have told him I don't want him back unless he is free of this thing. . . . He is willing we should be married before he goes so that I could *call* the baby something—whether he is free or not *but* he doesn't know & I haven't told him yet—that my divorce comes up in June but I don't get an absolute decree until six months after.[15] As time is calculated in the conventional world this wouldn't be very satisfactory to my family—& who knows whether he'll be back here in six months anyway. . . .

I know I must decide something soon—to let it go on or stop it for there is no life the first two weeks & also I believe it is not an illegal act to bring on menstruation within that time.

Do you see a *practical* way for me to have this baby you have brought about? I want it *so*! Could I go away or something? Or just *have* it? . . .

Dreaming of Indians

In an undated interview that Mabel gave to a reporter from the *Pittsburgh Post* (probably in the 1930s), she said that she was lured to the Southwest by the paintings of Irving Couse, one of the members of the Taos Society of Artists (TSA), known for his romanticized portraits of Indians. The TSA was founded in 1915, and had its first circuit show in New York in 1917. But Mabel's interest in Indians began in childhood, as she recounts in *Background*, partly because of the rumors that members of her family had "Indian blood." During her therapy with Jelliffe, she reported several dreams about Indians that were prophetic of the turn her life would take in less than two years.[16]

On April 13, Jelliffe notes that Mabel had a dream from which she woke up feeling "marvelous, an awakening." She had seen five Indians going down Fifth Avenue. Indians, she told him, were "always—one of my favorite ideals—lots of photos about—Indian chiefs. . . . All fine animal integrity. . . . Finer creatures than we are—finer senses. Secrets of nature—more than we do. One of desires of life—to live in Indian village." On June 7, her last meeting with Jelliffe, she dreamed that she had run away with a "North American Indian" and the tribe was after them. And indeed, that would prove to be true.

Shortly after Maurice left for New Mexico, probably in October 1917, Mabel went to a medium who told her she would soon be surrounded by Indians. On November 28, Sterne wrote Mabel the letter that would change the course of her life: "Do you want an object in life? Save the Indians, their art—culture—reveal it to the world!" The night before receiving his letter, Mabel had seen

Maurice's face blotted out in her dream by an Indian face, which she later recognized as Antonio Lujan. It probably happened.[17]

Emma Curtis Hopkins and New Thought

At the same time that she was seeing Smith Ely Jelliffe, Mabel was engaged in various forms of spiritualist practices that she would continue simultaneously with psychoanalysis over the next two decades. Mabel's attraction to New Thought was based on its promise of rectifying "the sins of the fathers" that had afflicted her. The "super-self" it taught her to rely on "was the child's wish about his parents, perfect in their gratification of every need, perfect in constituting the sum of reality." That gratification had nothing, or very little to do with sexuality, which, given Mabel's experiences with VD, had to have been an attraction for her as an alternative to the Freudian imperative to find herself and her identity through her sexuality.[18]

Mabel sought help from several different practitioners, including her childhood friend Nina Bull, whom she wrote about her problems with Maurice, as well as about her desire to reconcile spiritual "science" with psychoanalysis. Nina wrote her about the limits of psychoanalysis and the dangers of sex-expression: "All this sexuality on the physical plane that M.[aurice] exhales, is like poison to you,—beyond a certain point." Some time in 1916, Mabel turned to Emma Curtis Hopkins. Hopkins became the "premier New Thought teacher" of her time, after spending years as a housewife and mother, "married to a debt-ridden and violent husband." More conservative than Mary Baker Eddy, she "imagined Divine Mind as masculine, and the carnal or mortal mind as weak, passive, and feminine," in that sense reinforcing Freudian notions of gender. But Hopkins also discounted the helplessness engendered by a belief that one "inherited the moral or physical ills of one's ancestors." For these reasons, "Luhan may have found Hopkins the more sustaining of the two sources," Beryl Satter argues. She credits Mabel with being Curtis's "most loyal and influential student in the 1910s and early 1920s."[19]

In *Movers and Shakers*, Mabel wrote that Hopkins promised to cure her "the effortless way," through a six-step program that could be repeated as long as necessary. Her patients would lie down on a bed in a darkened, comfortable hotel room, while she spoke to them in a soothing, hypnotic voice. Mabel felt stimulated and renewed after each of her thrice weekly visits (while she was in New York), but she was incapable of following the instructions she took home with her: to rely on the powers of love and health within "without the interception . . . of the stubborn will." Hopkins's responses to Mabel, filled with the kind of unconditional love she had never known as a child, offered at least a temporary balm; and Hopkins was clearly willing to adapt her advice to match Mabel's mercurial moods. In January 1918, after Mabel had first moved to Taos with Maurice, Hopkins encouraged her to "Be his woman forever—His Woman!" By November 11, 1918, after Maurice had departed and Mabel and Tony had become lovers, Hopkins wrote that it was fine if she could not live with Maurice: "Women are free . . . you are my brilliant and beautiful girl and what your free spirit chooses, I ratify."[20]

Hopkins spent two months in Taos with Mabel, in the winter of 1919. When she returned to New York, she continued to counsel Mabel on her struggles with Tony that began soon after they became lovers. Tony sent Mabel back to New York in the spring of 1919, and there Mabel met an occultist, Mrs. Lotus Dudley, who told her that her mission in life was to serve as a mediator between the Indian and the white worlds. In May, Hopkins reinforced Dudley's words, telling Mabel that she had a great role to play in bringing the truth and beauty of Taos Pueblo to the world. Hopkins encouraged her to write, and Mabel produced a short memoir titled "The Intimation," in which she confessed to her sins of wanting to know the secrets of the Indian "soul." Two years later Hopkins reminded Mabel: "*I* you know wouldn't look at the best man that ever walked the planet. I am married to God."[21]

By 1923, when Mabel contracted syphilis and was looking for a way out of her afflicted body, she hoped to find a new kind of relationship with Tony, one that didn't depend on the body for satisfaction. Some New Thought leaders claimed that if both women and men could learn to "'deny' masculine desire and matter" and "'affirm' the pure, womanly mind and spirit," marriage could be perfected and a new race created. The "desirous, greedy and competitive Anglo-Saxon man" would be replaced by the model of "the pure, moral, and cooperative Anglo-Saxon woman." By the time that Mabel came to publish her memoirs, their teleology was driven by just such a model, with Tony in the place of the Anglo-Saxon woman, ready to bring her—and the white race—to its "full evolutionary potential."[22]

A. A. Brill

A. A. Brill (1878–1944) was the most influential therapist in Mabel's life. Although she only saw him as a patient sporadically after 1916–1917, she returned to New York frequently, and underwent therapy with him periodically from the 1920s through the 1930s, during moments of crisis. Brill was one of the most influential Freudian psychoanalysts in the United States: the first to practice psychoanalysis; the first to translate Freud's major works into English; the first to write a popular book on Freudian psychology; and a teacher and trainer of other leading psychoanalysts, such as Smith Ely Jelliffe. It was through Brill that Lincoln Steffens; Max Eastman, editor of *The Masses*; and other leading progressives and radicals first heard of Freud's ideas, at Mabel's salon. And it was through Mabel that Brill met avant-garde artists and intellectuals, some of whom became his patients as well.

Brill and Mabel maintained an extensive correspondence until three years before his death in 1946. Unfortunately, his wife destroyed "an unknown number" of letters Mabel sent him that dealt with her "intimate sexual feelings." His son, Edmund, also destroyed "an unknown number of letters" from Mabel that dealt with Tony's "illnesses, symptoms, and medical diagnoses."[23]

Mabel had come to Brill in the summer of 1916, when Jelliffe was on vacation, and she needed immediate help; Brill said that he would not take her unless she became his patient exclusively, and so she broke off her therapy with Jelliffe. While his analysis of Mabel was not as simplistic as his popular book on Freudian psychology would imply, one hears echoes of his reductionism throughout her writings, particularly whenever she says that all her worldly activities were merely "substitutes" for inadequate love relationships. Like Freud, Brill saw women as having a limited capacity for sublimation, because they were "the true guardians of the sexual interests of the race."[24]

Brill was, however, a brisk, no-nonsense therapist who wanted her to get to work and *do* something as a way of dealing with her depressions. When Mabel told him that she was a manic depressive, he told her he wasn't interested in that, and that she should bring him her dreams. From the start of her analysis, Brill encouraged Mabel to write (at his urging she took on a biweekly advice column for the Hearst papers, which she wrote from August 1917 through February 1918). After hearing her read the first of two powerful stories she wrote about her relationship with Maurice (subsequently published in *The Masses*), Brill wrote to her: "I felt that you have the material and I do not doubt that once your inhibitions will be gone you will be able to put your thoughts on paper with the same freedom as you can put them in speech. Everything depends on you. I'll do my share if you'll cooperate." Brill helped her to carry on with her memoirs at times when she felt desperate and despairing. When she was hesitating over the publication of *Background*, he wrote her, "Here you are at your best. . . . So, please Mabel, hurry up and strike the iron when it is still blazing.

Your volume is interesting and fascinating, and one of the best books of mental and emotional evolution that has come to my attention."[25]

BRILL STRONGLY OPPOSED Mabel's marriages to both Maurice Sterne and Tony Lujan, although he graciously accepted them. A month before Mabel married Tony, Brill wrote to her, "Again I must withhold my approval of another marriage. . . . You know I also strenuously objected to your Sterne venture." But he added, "I am quite willing to see the other side of it." In May 1923, Brill wrote to congratulate Mabel on her marriage to Tony. But his letter also contains his concerns about her "disease" (unnamed, but possibly syphilis) and the mental "breakdown" that seems to have followed her marriage:

> My most cordial congratulations to you and Tony. May your troubles now be over for all time. My objections to the marriage were based on all probabilities on ignorance of all the facts involved but I meant well. I am sure Mabel that you understand me. Besides I felt a bit worried over your physical condition and I wanted you to come here. . . . I can't help feeling that the best work in some diseases are done in this section of the country and I wanted you here. I still feel so especially as you are somewhat susceptible to some of the medicine. Moreover I'll be frank and tell you that I wanted to do a bit of investigation about your so called "breakdown." I am not satisfied to let such things go after a superficial patching particularly when it concerns a sensitive being like you. In brief there are many more (not theological) and physical reasons for my attitude.[26]

When Mabel decided to turn to Jungian analyst Frances Wickes in 1928– 1929—with dire effect, from her retrospective point of view (see chapter 3)— Brill wrote to her, "I, as you know, do not believe in conscious introspection, and if you do not do enough of it as you complain, I take it as a good sign. However, you are not the type of person to let matters alone, you are bound to do something and try everything."[27]

Brill's belief that Mabel should just "take control" of her life came out of a mentalist view of psychological illnesses that did not take into account the complex interactions between body and mind—the conundrum that Mabel puzzled over for much of her adult life. We learn through their letters that Mabel tried at least three medical regimens in the late 1930s (including insulin) under the care of her Taos doctor, Ashley Pond, which he thought might work on depression. None of them seemed to help her for more than a short time. In 1938, when she was undergoing a severe depression, she reported to Brill that she had told Dr. Pond that she would rather "be sick with a physical symptom than healthy & sad. . . . I asked him if he couldn't induce a somatic condition for me so that I could have that instead of my dark ennui & he said he couldn't."[28]

In October of that year, Mabel wrote Brill her most moving and insightful letter about manic depression. Mabel's indefatigable desire for mental health pushed her *not* to settle for explanations like the one Brill gave her in his response:

> All I do, I do by will and without pleasure. But I do it. I am faintly considering an article in non-technical terms about these ups and downs—entitled "The Golden Mean." I will quote from Lao Tzu and also from Freud on the Pleasure Principle. I am groping for an explanation of these recurrent states, within the bounds of the psychical laws rather than in the physiological regions. . . . Riggs, Weir Mitchell, Bernard Sachs and all the old school psychoanalysts were unsuccessful in truly understanding the depressive state, and even today the most modern of them have no better remedy than the others for the duration of the latency of the emotional responses, and they, like the others, recommend a cheerful (if possible) acceptance of the condition and a rest period. The older ones put the sufferer to bed for months! Do you remember the "Rest Cure?" You yourself will not consider it worthwhile to work with the patient until he emerges from this state, will you?
>
> However being a recalcitrant person I cannot rest in resignation without research! I vaguely feel there is *a way of life* for manic-depressives to discover that could save them from these slumps and I intuitively believe it has something to do with living perpetually in loyalty to a kind of superior standpoint that ignores personal satisfaction—personal pleasure and selfish or self-seeking satisfactions and that—if found—this way of life would afford more than pleasure and could be called, moderately, happiness, balance, serenity.[29]

Brill responded on December 7, 1938: "What the average person would just consider a passing mood, your fragment of auto-erotism strives to get negative gratification by making a 'depression' out of it. Do not forget, we all have 'ups and downs,' and he goes thru life most smoothly who pays no attention to such little bumps." Brill was rarely this patronizing. He continued the correspondence, as well as his deep affection for her, through 1944. "At any rate I love you just as much as ever," he writes her in 1940–1941. In his most astute comment about her behavior, he observes: "I often think that your 'repetition compulsion' makes you blind and you just repeat the old pattern."[30]

THIS PATTERN WAS ineradicably and flamboyantly established during her first love affair, as we shall see in chapter 2, "Green Horses."

CHAPTER TWO

Green Horses

"Memoirs of a Born American" ... it's the most serious "confession" that ever came out of America, and perhaps the most heart-destroying revelation of the American life-process that ever has or ever will be produced. It's worse than Oedipus and Media, and Hamlet and Lear and Macbeth are spinach and eggs in comparison. ... It's not art, because art always gilds the pill, and this is hemlock in a cup. ... Life gave America gold and a ghoulish destiny.
—D. H. LAWRENCE to Mabel Dodge Luhan[1]

MABEL DEVOTED THE first half of the "Green Horses" manuscript to the tragic tale of Emily Scatchard. It is a dramatically different narrative than the one she told in the short "Green Horses" section of *European Experiences*. Emily married Seward Cary, Mabel's adolescent "playmate" (seventeen years her senior), the son of a prominent and wealthy Buffalo family. Mabel and Seward had spent a good deal of time together riding "green" horses before she met and married Karl Evans, secretly in July 1900, and then in a church wedding, in October of that year. Seward was a young man with whom she could have a good time, and who had no sexual expectations. In her published memoir, Mabel described the Cary's as a marriage between first families that had been destined from childhood. Emily appeared as a woman she admired, luminescent in her beauty and original in her observations. Her pregnancy aroused dreams of motherhood in the young Mabel.[2]

In the "Prelude" to the unpublished manuscript "Green Horses," Mabel writes about her first highly fraught childhood memories of sexuality and pregnancy in a much darker vein than she did in *European Experiences*. The "hysterical pregnancy" she recounts here underscores her fear of male sexuality, rape, and childbirth. It is compounded by her thought of giving birth to a "Frankenstein," a phrase that may have been inflected by the "family secret" she never learned (see chapter 1), as well as by her adult experiences with VD. The doctor's fake pill cure may have been Mabel's first encounter with medication as a means of escaping depression and anxiety.

~~~~~~~~~~

Prelude

Dorothy [Scatchard] and Madeleine and I used to go down at noontimes and watch their Aunt Emily [Cary] nurse her baby. It was the first time I became conscious of my body and the lovely feelings it held—feelings that rose and spread all through one, delicate and fiery and alive—as we stood and watched the baby suck at the white breast. When the noon hour came round, the picture would swing into our thoughts. "Let's go down to Aunt Emily's," one of the girls would say. . . .

One autumn day Emily came heavily and slowly up the path of Madeleine's house, big with another child. Madeleine's mother stood up from the garden bed she was bending over and she too was big and heavy. Emily reached out her hand to her, her small lovely face all dark and weary. "Oh, life is not worth living," she sighed. The older woman put her arms quickly around her and led her up the steps of the house, saying as they went slowly, pressed against each other—"Oh, come, Emily, don't fret. It's not long now."

We followed in a hush. We felt drawn by their significance at that time. By the important cumbersome bodies of the two women who were soon to have babies. We knew by now that babies came from people, but by what gate, nor where they had gotten them, we didn't know that yet. And we talked it over and over. For Madeleine said that they came through the little holes in our stomachs, but I said that women coughed and they came out of the mouth. And Dorothy said, "No, they come from the little place down there." So we conjectured and nobody helped us to understand.

And where they came from? I said, and I don't know how this first idea of the power of thought came to me—I said: "You think and think of a baby until you think one for yourself and it begins to grow in your stomach." And this notion took hold of me until later; one summer when I was away with my family, away from the "other girls," the thought so haunted me that I couldn't get rid of it, and I knew that I was caught by it and it would make a baby come if I was not able to overcome it. I struggled to forget it—this Frankenstein of my thirteen years—but it would not leave me. All day long I thought how babies came by thinking—and I grew more and more frightened and terribly ashamed. Pretty soon I saw that it was so, for my little belly began to swell, to grow large under my anxious hands. In bed at night I felt it growing at my touch. What an anguish I was in. I wanted to run away and hide somewhere. To have a baby seemed to me the uttermost terror, and the idea was all fused with shamefulness, already in the first chaotic material of the small, untended brain.

In an agony I went to my distant mother one hot summer day. She was always distant and unaware. When I, suffocating, managed to tell her my fear, she looked at me in cold amusement.

"What are you talking about?"

"I'm going to have a baby. I know I am!" I implored her with my eyes, almost weeping, though I had never let her see me cry, for we never showed people our feelings. Never. "My stomach is swelling up!" I went on in a low voice.

"Nonsense, don't talk so. You can't have a baby without a man." She exclaimed in an impatient voice. First intimation of a man in connection with a baby! Strange and alarming, though, it sounded in my ears, scarcely able to receive its unfamiliar suggestion. Still the fear in me began to lighten, the weight of terror slowly lifted off me. But like clouds following one another, a new fear took the place of the old one in my breast.

"A man!" I thought, groping in my imagination for a clue to this. "How a man?" and at that moment the terror of thought gave place to the terror of the male. "Oh mama! How a man? Could a man have done this to me without my knowing it? Or when I was asleep? Oh *tell* me?" I begged. For the first time in my life I begged my mother. But her own reserve was too binding upon her for her to respond to my cry. I do not know whether she felt anything then or not. She showed no feeling at all. "Well, I'm going to tell Dr. Clark about you," she seemed to threaten for an instant. "He'll tell you what nonsense you're talking."

Poor mother, in her net of silence. Baffled by the need to do something, she turned me over to the genial old doctor, who came and felt my little belly, smiling and reassuring. Now "the doctor" is omnipotent in the family life. He impresses the powerful, decisive, and ultimate character of his opinion on the whole household, from the children to the servants. What doctor says *goes*. So, though he did not make any explanations about the whole troubling question, he relieved me from my obsession, taking it away with him in his black bag.

"Don't you go on fretting yourself, young lady. You're *all right*. You're not going to have any *baby*, not for a good long time. But what you are going to have is a nice little pill that I'll leave here with Mama—and you take it tonight, and when you wake up tomorrow you'll be as bright as a penny." He took away that thought with him and I was free—but somewhere in me there lingered the new germ of another idea. The queer idea of a *man* having something to do with babies. . . . '

~~~~~~~~~~~~~

Part I of "Green Horses" contains the beginning of what I call Mabel's "Oedipal scripts" and sets the scene for her affair with John Parmenter. In this unpublished version, Emily Cary's story is a searing indictment of the lives of upper-class women in the Victorian era, in which the motifs of incest, disease, and debilitation are aligned with the power of a patriarchal elite. Emily had five children, the last two of them purportedly with her lover, Arthur Brisbane (1864–1936), the powerful editor of William Randolph Hearst's *The New York Journal*, who gave Mabel her first job, as a columnist, in 1917. A deeply conservative man, he was the son of Albert Brisbane, an ardent social reformer who promoted Charles Fourier's ideals of communal living in the United States during the 1830s. Arthur's sister, Alice Thursby, told the post-1904 part of the Cary story to Mabel while she was living in Florence.

Brisbane met the Carys at the summer place where they hunted, and there he fell in love with Emily. According to Mabel, Arthur and Emily were lovers from about the time she was thirty-five. Seward appreciated what Arthur did for Emily—bringing her books and writing to her. She told Seward she would stop seeing Arthur if he wanted her to, but Seward seemed glad that he kept Emily occupied, when he could. Seward was always out playing polo, while Arthur was mostly in New York working on the paper, so that Emily was alone much of the time. Emily drank heavily to deal with her neglect from both her husband and her lover.

Mabel writes that Emily's fourth and fifth children (John, born in 1898, and Jane, born in 1899) were Arthur's. Jane died of spinal meningitis in 1903, and Jack "grew queer and his face was vacant, his mouth always open." Mabel describes Jack as "A kind of terrible caricature of Arthur," often saying things with "double meanings" that made people wonder what he knew. He once asked his father if they had any skeletons in their closets. Although she does not mention the word, Mabel describes the kinds congenital degenerative disorders associated with syphilis. After their birth, Seward turned against Emily and called her "a whore." In despair, Emily tried to plunge out an open window, which Seward prevented.

Brisbane sent his widowed sister, Alice Thursby, to take care of Emily when she was drinking too much, and to amuse her. While Brisbane loved Emily, he was also attracted to Eleanor, Emily's eighteen-year-old daughter. But when Eleanor became a "problem," Arthur convinced her to marry the son of a friend. Eventually, Arthur married Emily's youngest daughter, Phoebe, some thirty years his junior. Emily apparently wanted to continue to have Arthur as a lover, and, according to Alice, "to take her daughter's place in my brother's bed!" Arthur and Phoebe had six children, and one was "queer," as Mabel puts it, like Emily's Jack. Mabel saw Emily once holding her first grandchild and she said to Mabel, "It's as though I held *Arthur* in my hands." The child was named Seward, after Emily's husband, and was soon taken from her because she drank too much. Alice told Mabel: "She would have dashed that baby boy . . . from the window in the same frenzy that nearly sent her that way in times past." Mabel's final image of Emily is seeing her in New York City, sitting on the floor of a hotel room, "drunk and lovely." Her last words to Mabel are "No-o-o- use at all . . ."

EMILY'S STORY FRAMES the next and longest segment of "Green Horses," Mabel's affair with Dr. John Parmenter (1862–1932). It begins shortly after Mabel's church marriage to Karl Evans, in October 1900, and continues through the summer of 1904, when her mother sends her off to Europe to end the affair. Parmenter was an attending surgeon at Buffalo General Hospital who lectured on anatomy and clinical surgery at the University of Buffalo. He was one of three surgeons called in to operate on President McKinley when he was fatally shot at the Panama Exposition in Buffalo on September 5, 1901. According to the *Buffalo Evening News*, Parmenter was "one of the most prominent surgeons of Buffalo before his retirement." He resigned from his professorship and his position as secretary of the medical department in late 1904, and he retired from his Buffalo practice in 1908, moving to Geneva where he helped to establish a TB hospital. His wife, Frances Gorham, was the daughter of a prominent Buffalo family. Parmenter died at age seventy in Geneva, New York. In a letter to me of May 4, 1985, Ross Parmenter, whose father was a first cousin of Dr. Parmenter's, said that his aunt had described Parmenter to him as "a very handsome and successful Buffalo surgeon, who frittered away his career by taking up with a rich woman." He didn't learn that the "rich woman" was Mabel until he read my biography.[3]

In the Parmenter section of "Green Horses," Mabel creates her second Oedipal script, one she has prepared us for with the Cary-Brisbane tale. Her husband Karl, who seems to spend most of his time hunting, is "relieved" when Mabel takes up with Parmenter. She and her mother become rivals over Parmenter, who ministers to both of them sexually. He medicates their father/husband into a state of morphine oblivion, while taking on the role of the father/lover Mabel never had. Mabel presents an almost classic Freudian "primal scene" when she finds her mother in postcoital bliss (presumably) after making love with Parmenter. When Mabel writes that she had to have Parmenter to "get the taste of my father out of my mouth," she is probably being metaphorical, but her choice of language is certainly revealing of her visceral feelings about Ganson's psychic invasiveness.

In "Green Horses," Mabel establishes several other tropes that appear throughout her published and unpublished memoirs. The struggle between the Victorian and Modern worlds, particularly between traditional "family values" and "free love," is embedded in the text, although there are times when the Victorian trumps the Modern as the party of moral character and psychic stability. Even the sex that Parmenter's wife Fanny presumably submits to as a duty seems more pleasure-filled than the overwrought compulsive intercourse in which Mabel and John engage. Although Mabel imagines she will triumph over her lover's wife, Fanny proves stronger than both of them. In her tenacious desire to keep her family intact, she shows a strength and shrewdness that Mabel comes to admire, even while she wishes Fanny would disappear. The equation of Love with Power is rife throughout the narrative, as Mabel constructs a struggle between the Eternal Female (Mabel) and the Eternal Male (John), each trying to possess and dominate the other. This is a battle of the sexes where neither one can let down their guard or find more than a moment's peace or equilibrium. There are only two roles for women in Mabel's script: wife or lover.

In "Green Horses," Mabel writes about the performative value of the roles she inhabits, how she tries to create a stage for every "scene," in order to give the drama she enacts wider and deeper meanings than the personal. Her narrative of her affair is clearly intended to be an object lesson in the stupidity of putting all one's emotional "eggs," as she puts it, into the basket of love. It is the beginning of what would become, in the words of her Freudian analyst A. A. Brill, her "repetition compulsion." Once she gives herself to Parmenter, she is swallowed up in a miasma of manipulation, jealousy, and dependency. She repeated this pattern with John Reed, Maurice Sterne, and Tony Lujan. In "Green Horses," she creates its first flowering, in a story that is at once riveting, horrifying, and, at times, comical.

The first fifty pages of this section of "Green Horses" was published as the opening chapters of *European Experiences*, in which Mabel recounted her meeting and marriage to Karl Evans. I have used a few brief excerpts from the published volume throughout to provide continuity. Mabel and Karl, who had eloped in July, have just been married in a church wedding (on October 3, 1900), thanks to the intercession of Dr. Parmenter, the Evans family doctor. They go off on their wedding trip to the Adirondacks for two weeks. On the second day, sitting quietly in the woods with her gun in her lap, Mabel felt nauseous and distressed. (She was pregnant.) The next morning she was "nervous and depressed. The honeymoon was over!" Mabel and Karl stayed with Grandma Ganson while their new home was being prepared. Dr. Parmenter attended her during and after her miscarriage, visiting her every day. Note the three mentions of Mary Shillito looking down on Mabel from a photograph, as Mabel makes love to Dr. Parmenter—a reminder, perhaps, of how Mabel had betrayed her sister Violet's love.[4]

~~~~~~~~~~~~~~~~

Part I

RE-MARRIAGE

. . . . Dr. Parmenter gave me a wonderful feeling of security. I knew I had him as an ally and that I could make him work for me because he liked me. And he was so handsome, so strong and so manly that he made me feel very gentle and feminine. I looked forward to his visits as the central thing of each day and I prepared for him.

One morning . . . I looked at him and was pleased to see he looked somewhat down, somewhat tired. But he looked very attractive like that. He caught my appraising glance and returned it, appraising me in a calculating, quizzical way in one of those short, significant silences during which people advance upon each other in leaps. We drew, then, near to the conscious surface of the emotion that had been preparing deep within. . . .

When he came next day I had dressed myself in a peignoir over my nightgown and I had put pink roses in my hair. . . . When he came up to me where I was sitting on the bed, I stood up and put both hands on his shoulders and said:

"Do you love your wife?" He looked at me very gravely and answered as one does a catechism of the holy life:

"As one does a child."

"Then I want your love," I told him. And, "You have it," he replied. And Mary Shillito looked down on us from the chimney place in the slightly frozen surprise of a portrait; and Grandma Ganson in her bay window below beamed at the clubmen as they passed bowing to her. God was in his heaven.

LOVE

Now there began a curious duel between this man and me. I did not want him in any obvious physical way, and yet I wanted to have him hold me in his arms and show me all his tenderness and protection. It was his *love* I had asked him for, his deep feeling and his quick, protecting, sheltering, masculine power over me. I wanted to find at last in the world a *man* who would be as much a man as I was a woman, that is, someone to summon up my subtle electrical female forces and someone who would even overmatch my own strength of will and endurance and courage. I wanted to get the taste of my father out of my mouth and his odor out of my nostrils and his contemptible, his ignoble weakness out of my memory—blotted out by another. And here was one who could do it for me. A man who was self-possessed and strong and burning like a lamp.

But I did not want to take him into myself. I did not want to give him the extreme hospitality of my body. I did not need him in any such way. I only needed his affection and his powerful reassuring embrace. I loved to feel him hold me against him and to feel so small and weak in his arms. And, besides, I could not face the deception between Karl and me that such an act would necessitate.

From the first I have had that principal of fidelity strong in me; that one could do most anything with other people and still remain faithful, but to do "that" was unfaithfulness. The same rigid attitude that I had held about keeping myself for the husband that would come had gone over in marriage into another feeling—that of obligation to be true and to be truthful. I could not conceive of living with a man and at the same time having the same relation with another and not telling the first one to whom I owed my open allegiance. It seemed to me then and it seems to me now that such deception at the very roots of life would make one's soul split in two and grow in different directions. I was actually afraid of this, then, as I am today twenty-five years later.

I told the man this. I did not call him *Dr.* any more, nor would I call him Jack like everyone else did. I called him *Parmenter*, just like that, and I liked the way my voice sounded saying it, clear-cut, authoritative, and possessive. It made him mine to call him so when no one else did. He had his arms around me and he was looking deep into me. We had gone very fast in a couple of days.

"I love you very much, my dear," he said. "It seems to me I've been waiting a long time to find just you. And now I've found you, I want you *all*."

"But Parmenter," I said, hugging him very hard, "I know. And I've been waiting for you. I've never known a real man except you. They've all seemed like boys and children or else like old pigs, never a man. Oh, dear! Why am I married! You see I'm afraid if I go ahead with you, I'll tell Karl!"

This made him look very serious and then he laughed. "That would hardly be fair, would it? To make him unhappy unnecessarily just to make yourself feel more comfortable? That's usually what all these confessions amount to—self-indulgence at someone else's expense. I thought you were one of the strong ones."

"Yes, I'm strong," I said, slowly. "Strong enough to keep you and yet not give in to you," I was saying to myself. But I didn't let any sign of this appear in my face. There showed all the love I felt flowing out of me at his look and his touch.

At this time I was feeling stronger in myself than I had ever felt before, and to feel *strong* was always my great aim. Anything that reinforced me in my belief in myself, or anyone who made me quicker and more alive in any way, that was what I wanted and I would give up anything else to these satisfactions I needed so badly: anything for the sake of feeling life flow. . . .

Parmenter satisfied once and for all something that had been hungry since I was born. He gave me the kind of love that is at once authoritative and submissive, that makes one feel like a child and yet a woman, too. . . . But though he appeared so positively authoritative as to be really like a law-giver (and to exert this power was one of his principal pleasures), in actuality, he was without any feeling of social lawfulness at all. Like me, what he wanted he took. Both of us were unusually vital. . . .

He had lost all sensitiveness if he ever had any. Part of the piquancy of love for him was stealing it and hiding it and passing falsely among people for the most righteous of them all. He did not think he had a right to the wives of his friends and his patients. He really felt it was wrong and that people were right to punish offenders when they were caught. He was, in his opinions, what is called a *good* man. Yet, early, he had formed a love habit, and he had no scruples left. But he was careful never to be caught. And he managed to make his skill in deceit contribute to his own feeling of superiority among men. It gave him quite an air.

But at first I was scorched in my heart when he laughed at my grandmother's pleasure over his visits and at Karl's satisfaction at our friendship. In the first days he did not try and urge me too much. I think he did not need me in any ultimate way. He had other relationships as I learned afterwards—for he told me of them when he broke them off. So at first we were just happy and stimulated and gay together. He felt perfectly natural and relaxed with me. He told me. "With most women you have to remember this or that all the time or you'll make them mad and start something. But with you I feel as free as though I were with myself. You are like the other side of me I have never found before. Oh, It's good to have you, dear—*dearest!*" he said, with a sweeping, exhilarated embrace. . . .

So he was, when he found me, thirty-eight years old, the leading surgeon in the neighborhood, one of the chief operators at all the hospitals in town, handsome and strong and successful—but just ready to be a little weary of play. Not of love—for (and this is one of the strange parts of this story) he hadn't loved yet, he had only played with love.

Of course it was a dangerous age! There are several of them in one's life! But of our two lives, we were at the most dangerous age of all for each of us! I was so young, and so repressed and intense. And he was just beginning to get old and to grow tired of the easy surface satisfactions of the flesh. Obscurely, somewhere in him, he wanted to satisfy the spirit that had been waiting and lurking in the background of his light love life, he wanted to grow, to feel deeply and seriously for once in his life, to *be* the man he in reality was in embryo.

And there isn't any way except through love. "Go through it!" cries the Boy in *Peer Gynt.* "Don't go around—you must go through!" he cries. Well, we did. And this is what happened.

THE ABYSS

Soon the house my mother had taken for Karl and me was ready and we moved into it. In the dark hall downstairs Karl nailed up all his beautiful incongruous Indian things. I didn't like them there much, but they were all he had to bring to our house, so he brought them and he liked them and nothing else so well. For he didn't like things. He had no feeling for them at all.

But I loved them—they were the settings and the costumes of the life-drama. Whatever one did must be properly staged. And wherever one lived one must animate one's surroundings above all things, make it alive with live things. So I have always wanted to make a background for myself and then live in it. To make an outer atmosphere from the intense, ardent life going on inside me, and to project it about me so that it would feed me and reinforce me so I dwelt in a kind of magic circle of living and the emanations of living. . . .

I had rather a hard time bringing life into my new house, for I had to furnish it with wedding presents, the furniture that had been in my room at home, Karl's Indian things and the things I could persuade my mother to buy for me down town, which wasn't much. There wasn't much to choose from in those early days. Factory made stuff. Imitations of mahogany, white enamel, and mission. That was about all the choice! But somehow even that first rented house—half of a square of red brick, it had an atmosphere. But the atmosphere was strongest up in the front bedroom. There where Parmenter came to spend an hour with me every afternoon.

Without realizing it we began, Parmenter and I, to organize our lives around each other. He was particularly nice and attentive to my mother, and through her my father changed his old dull doctor and took him instead—a most unlucky thing, for Parmenter was unimaginative about drugs and thought nothing of giving my father a shot of morphine if he asked it. He wasn't careless or criminal about it, he simply didn't realize, imaginatively, what would happen in a case like my father's. Parmenter was only a psychologist of light love. The lesser fates, and the greater, these he didn't know.

I wanted to know Fanny, his wife, and I was both curious and calculating. In the early days of love, particularly before the final step has been taken between lovers, they are singularly free of each other. They are mind-free and not yet too possessive and obsessed by each other. So I was not jealous yet. I was coolly curious to know what Parmenter's wife was like. And she was curious about me, too, because . . . he had talked a lot about me at home, freely amused by me and what seemed to him my original ways. That had been before he had been Karl's messenger to my mother. And since then doubtless he had talked some—but maybe later he had ceased to say very much. Anyway Fanny was curious and he brought her to see me one day.

Of course I had heard of the Gorhams all my life along, with lots of other people whose faces did not emerge for me when their names were spoken. Mr. Gorham lived in the old-fashioned house opposite Mr. Evans on North Street, and they were old and intimate friends. When his daughter Fanny had wanted to marry the rather unknown young doctor, Mr. Gorham had looked sour—but he had given in because, though no one in Buffalo had ever heard of the Parmenters (who were of German descent and lived somewhere in limbo outside the real best circle), yet this young man was a brilliant hospital surgeon and would surely make his way when he picked up a practice.

Fanny and her connections had helped this, as doubtless he had expected and possibly had married her for. Certainly no other reason could have actuated him— and he told me that the night before the wedding he had stood at his bedroom window looking out and asking himself, could he do it, could he go ahead and promise to live with Fanny always. And the night of his wedding day again he had hung back before going to her, hung back in a deep physical reluctance, for he felt he could not bring himself to the point of taking her in cold blood, and his blood was turned to vinegar in him. But he had, perhaps sentimentally, shed a few tears there before he squared his shoulders and "went to her like a man," he told me.

Fanny was very thin and dry. A little old-maidish woman with her eyes for her sole beauty. She had great brown eyes full of expression and feeling. More feeling than she ever showed in her crisp, matter of fact behavior. She had no temperament at all, but she had a terribly deep devoted love of Jack—that alien she had chosen to bring into her own group. He seemed to her the finest person in the world, greatly above her own father—small, wizened, but ethical-minded Mr. Gorham—and a kind of god among commoner mortals. And Parmenter was a god among the moderated men he ministered to, but a god of pleasures she had never learned in life and only dreamed of rarely.

When we grew to know each other better and she talked with me, all my thoughts had to be expurgated, for there was so much she did not know in life. And Parmenter told me that she had never experienced the pleasure or expression of love with him and that it remained for her always a sacred duty; it was a pleasurable thing to her that she procured for him the relief he needed, that he depended upon her alone to satisfy certain peculiarly masculine insistencies. For so she believed it was, and that hers was the significant, the unique right to minister to this need of his. Naturally he had never deceived her. They had lived together for years and his life, his blood, his rhythms were never revealed to her. They were not susceptible to her vision or her expression. She *could not* know him.

But once a strange thing happened after they had been married for quite a long time. She dreamed one night of a man taking her in his arms, and the intercourse between them brought to the surface of her nerves a startling and lovely sensation, something unbelievable and indescribable. When she awoke she tried to tell him about it, but there were no words for the strange, sweet feeling she had had. And after that, at long intervals of months, the dream had recurred, and it became a curious haunting reality to her that she never quite forgot. But in her waking days she had no romance, no glamorous way of life. She was brisk, literal-minded, thrifty in her housekeeping to the point of stinginess, and very critical. A small, thin woman with dank, meager hair and a long nose, unattractive, unaware, and sure of herself. Only the large dark eyes, sensitive as a deer's, were there to check one if one dismissed her too carelessly as entirely negligible and one of the world's mean averages.

We became friends in a way, on account of Parmenter. I felt nothing for her, she didn't interest me at all; her manner of life, calculating every slice of bread and every lump of sugar, was actually repellant to me, who wanted to cut a wide swath. But I overcame my indifference and ennui at her small bourgeois ways enough to get upon a kind of intimate footing with her so I could run in and out of their house.

Parmenter, to whom now I had grown to be something like a child one is fitting for the novitiate, wanted me to learn to be a good housekeeper. I didn't know how to order anything for my kitchen. I didn't know one cut of meat from another and I don't to this day. But like the other Buffalo women, Fanny used to go down town every morning and pick out her meat and her vegetables, and she lived on a budget that she never exceeded.

Parmenter told me to go shopping with her and she would teach me how to buy things. I certainly had the greatest distaste for this plan, but I went with her for a few times. It was a satisfaction, in a way, to all three of us. There was an ancient, ancient custom being carried on—the older wife was educating the younger one for her lord, teaching the care of the house and the kitchen, the appetites of the man, the art of procuring for him as much as possible for the least amount. It gave Parmenter, I could see, a peculiar pleasure to see Fanny taking me down to the market in the morning. Some might say this was a perverse pleasure, but I do not think so. I believe it is the expression of something inherent in men since the beginning of time.

Fanny and I would go down then, together, to Boyce's store, and she would help me decide upon what to order, and she would hesitate and linger over the vegetables and fruit. From there we would walk down the unlovely street of the shops with trolleys clanging in the centre, to the other places where there was a one-minute errand to do for her house or mine, a cord to match, or dusters to select or something equally dull to my seeming. And at eleven or half past we would arrive at Huyler's and go in and have hot chocolate and crackers.

A morning like this made me either chafing with impatience or sleepy-minded and dull with depression. I simply rebelled against such a routine. But after lunch, and after his office hour was over, Parmenter would come to see me; and up in my bedroom behind the closed door, life rose up in great waves of color and beauty all around me. He would open his arms with a smile and I would fly into them and give myself up in silence to the great streams of electrical energy our proximity induced.

Still, in those early days, he did not try to compel me any further than his kisses. Once he said: "I am waiting for you. When you are ready . . ." I turned my face away from that and he didn't say any more then. But even while I kept my sense of fidelity to Karl, after Parmenter left me, I would succumb to an anxious and guilty feeling. I was sorry it was as it was, sorry for what had happened, and yet I felt fatalistic about it as though it were inevitable and as though my anxiety and guilt were inevitable, too.

While I was making the pattern of my life around Parmenter and Fanny and trying to be friends with her so I could see him oftener, he too was weaving his part of our web. He went now daily to see my father who was continuously sick with gout and inflammatory rheumatism, and he had attached my father to him both by his strong consolatory presence and by his generous, carefree use of the morphine needle. Nothing else, now, relieved my father of the terrible anxiety and anguish that had engulfed him. Only oblivion—in repeated doses.

When Parmenter had gone into my father's room and quickly given him the small portion of miraculous powder, then he stopped in at my mother's room for a moment to report to her how things were going. My mother always spent the whole afternoon out of doors and at five o'clock she would come in and lie on her couch in her bedroom in a peignoir, resting before dressing for dinner.

And she too, as well as my father, grew to look forward to the doctor's visits. He was so strong, so cheerful, so full of authority. He told her how I was trying to settle down and learn how to take care of my house—and that Fanny was helping me. It must have been rather comforting to my mother to hear that someone else had, at length taken a hand with the queer, wild, incalculable child she had had to have in her house all these years. She must have been relieved at last not to have that silent, observing, unfilial presence about. There had never been any combination between them. The child made her uncomfortable.

So Parmenter administered to us all. It was growing into December [1900] now, winter and snow, and Karl went off on several hunting trips. I didn't go because I didn't want to. Karl didn't care much, he went with Jack Piper. I don't remember just how or when it was, but I noticed one day just the slightest change in Parmenter. He was a trifle absent-minded, not quite so interested, so wrapped up in me when he was with me. In a second of time I was on the alert to this. All my invisible antennae were sent out to search the air around me and find out what was there. I grew more intensely alive and aware to life and was awakened out of the lovely, thrilling, yet restful dream I had been in since he had come into my existence.

I had continued to share with Karl the nocturnal marriage of our bodies—it was as though we met together to drink, impersonally, almost as strangers, at a public fountain. Then, daily, I went into the accelerated, gleaming, atmosphere that arose like a cloud obscuring the flatness and commonness of things about us when we met together, Parmenter and I, an atmosphere where I became intensified in my sense of identity, enhanced in my own eyes, and empowered. All my life had become centered around this experience now, and I had sacrificed everything else to it except those people and those activities that could contribute to it. I did not see any of my old friends any more. I scarcely went anywhere. Unless I went out with Fanny, I did not go out at all. For without knowing it or realizing it, I had fallen into the real harem existence.

All my eggs were in one basket, as I concentrated more and more on the compelling authoritative man. All my thoughts, my attention, my vitality went to him and were in turn nourished by him, the sole material of my spirit. So when a shade of difference showed in his tenderness, when his wide gaze looked a little past me instead of deep into me, every cell in me was immediately on the defensive. My very life was threatened if he looked away now.

The next day he telephoned me he had to operate at three o'clock—at the hour he was usually with me. It was the first time he had ever put me off. Usually he had been so eager to come and, at the very first, more eager than I. I did not know what to do, but all that afternoon alone in my room in the silent house I burned in every kind of intensity. I was in despair of something, I knew not what.

My deprivation, now that I had grown so used to that powerful, that delicious exhilaration from his tender and adorable presence galvanizing and empowering me for hours to come, my sense of loss was like a drowning. I lay on the bed and every nerve in my body cried out for him to come. And mingled with the loss, with the pain that came from the broken current, was my terror. I did not know what I was afraid of, but the anxiety was so acute that sweat was on my hands and forehead. . . .

The abyss opened beneath me. I had nothing to live for but him. I had lost everything else. I had lost the rest of the world and all of life by taking my attention off them and putting it all on him. *That is the only way we ever lose the world.* And I knew I could never forget him, I had so completely given myself over to him. . . .

THE DESCENT

By the time that it was six o'clock, and I had lain there in the silence on the big four-poster bed until it was dark in the room except for the light that came in the window from the street lamp below, I had imaginatively gone through the weeks and months ahead without him. All alone. Karl, undetained by me, off on his hunting trips and the other people I had known in Buffalo reduced to shades by my own loss of interest in them. Shades that I felt I could not turn to any more and reanimate by my own will after having focused all my attention on Parmenter. He was such a vivid person, so vital, so mysterious in his deep psychic processes, so wonderful looking, and above all, so life-enhancing for me. I did not realize then that almost any human being upon whom one concentrates one's attention as fixedly as I had mine upon him, will reveal, contained in one bundle, all the wonders of the world. For a while. . . .

At six the maid came to my door and knocked, frightened perhaps that no sound had come for so long. And I got up and washed my face in cold water and drank some tea. When eight o'clock came, I wrapped myself in a fur cape and ran all the way to Parmenter's house two blocks away on Franklin Street. I knew that after dinner he usually went out to his office behind the house for a short time.

I felt numb when I went in the door to the dreary noncommittal waiting room with its leather chairs, magazines and a picture, of course, of the *Night Watch* on the wall.[5] But when Parmenter opened the door of his inner office, in a flash I was alive again. I started and ran to him and flung myself into his arms. I crashed into his arms. . . .

"Don't, don't do that again," I sobbed. "Don't leave me, don't leave me alone." He held me close, moved at once by my passionate grief. "Nothing matters but you," I cried, the tears flowing fast, "Nothing and nobody. I'll die without you if you leave me."

He tried to console me; he spoke of his afternoon's work, but I scarcely listened. What did I care for Rob Lawson's peritoneum? I was breathing in again the odors of his flesh, and warming myself at the gentle, continuous flames of his body, which always seemed to burn with a comforting, unfevered heat, well stocked and regulated. . . .

"I want you. You are mine. I won't lose you," I sobbed into his shirtfront.

"Well, dear, you have me, all you'll take of me," he said rather wryly. "I thought you really didn't care so very much. You've held me off for so long."

"But I *do*. I *do* want you. I'll do anything you say."

Something inside me seemed to turn over when I said it, but I hardened up against this sensation. Without answering me, Parmenter drew me, my face still buried and blotted on his breast, into the inner room where a gas light burned low. And there on the shiny leather couch, while the tears continued to pour automatically down my cheeks, was consummated, in the over-flow of grief and abandonment, the sacrifice of the only law I knew.

Parmenter seemed satisfied to drink salty tears along with his kisses. As for me, I felt a dull relief—no passionate pleasure or delight was here, but instead, the conviction of a bargain made between us. For I felt that I had bought and paid for him, that he might be mine forever and save me from going out like a lamp whose oil is spent.

BELOW

Now began a time of living by the will. I had succumbed to Parmenter's will, but only in order to hold him more firmly. Had he hesitated long enough to contemplate for a moment my reckless acquiescence, he would perhaps have hesitated longer still. But he was not a thoughtful man, and besides, the frequent love affairs he had glided in and out of had lessened in his eyes the significance of the act of love, a significance that cannot be calculated and that never grows less as the world grows older. The dynamic and esoteric power of it affects human destiny more deeply and inscrutably than we ever know. No less when we treat it as a bagatelle than when we raise it to a religion, no less when we deny it altogether than when we indulge it as carelessly as other hungers.

The next day, when Parmenter came to me as usual in the afternoon, everything was changed between us. With few words he leaned to me again, and now I responded to him. Overnight, by the curious invisible mechanism of the human creature, I had shifted my whole moral equipment. I had not only withdrawn my allegiance from Karl, but with incredible swift ingenuity had raised a faint barrier between us, a barrier of tardy indignation because he had taken advantage of me, had taken me unaware and caught me, and I was tied to him.

The indefinable sense of guilt I had felt towards him was gone completely. Till now I had felt friendly enough towards him, if not very loving or very interested. But as soon as I deceived him, as soon as I gave myself wholly to another, it was necessary to feel justified in my deception. I could not relinquish my good opinion of myself, so I began to feel more positively about the faults in Karl. I divorced myself from him psychically, and though I did not dare refuse him the right to have me when he wanted, yet I learned to withhold my pleasure and to contain myself completely so that it was only with Parmenter that I experienced any feeling.

The infinite adaptability of the body and the soul! When we can seem to so completely control the life in us, is it not strange that it ever overcomes us? From the time I submitted to Parmenter in his office, I felt I was his wife in the inner reality and all that was left was to work out the thing into practical external life. From that first afternoon when there passed between us the complete, flooding and clarifying exchange of passionate love, I only lived for Parmenter, and he too became at last, in his late thirties, the subjugated and dominated lover.

But that was not what I wanted. I wanted, I had always wanted, a husband. And not only a husband, but children. Twelve children I had wanted all my life, sitting around the table with shining faces and full of a happy life. To take the place of my solitary childhood alone in the desolate nursery, I treasured this picture in my heart and meant to bring it to fulfillment.

And now, in the exercise of my whole self, I blossomed and grew very strong. I think I reached my own perfection, my own unique blooming, in the early months of happy love between Parmenter and me. For each of us there is a moment of the physical life towards which the years approach, and it endures for a little while in purity and intensity, and then forever afterwards we depart from it, a slow incline to other levels of another life than that. Other levels of life, not less significant, often more precious, usually more wise—but we never return again to that hour of the body's triumph. We cannot even detain it for very long. Ask any gardener if this is not as true of his peaches and plums. Our laws resemble theirs.

So to Parmenter fell that inimitable hour. We exceeded others in our extravagant outpourings. We could never get enough of each other. Not he of me, not I of him. But we differed in one thing. I was determined to have him wholly and openly for my own, for my husband. I wanted *to live* with him, to take care of his house and have his children. But he, I think, was at first content with things as they were, and he laughed at my plans for our house together. But he, too, wanted me to have his baby. That he did want. And he never took me in his arms that he did not say: "Now——."

But, let us admit it, Nature has some curious way of outwitting us, so that even while we think we control her, she it is who uses us. I learned to hold myself in check during the inevitable moments Karl seized for himself, and this was all right for a while. And then one night with him it was as though my body were not my own but belonged to itself. The gates opened to him and involuntarily received him: it was the same, inevitable, natural, unwillful fusion of our two essences that it had been the first time I had undergone this mysterious baptism into the sexual life.

"*That* is a baby," said Karl succinctly in my ear at the conclusion of the flowing moment. My heart sank as my brain acknowledged the truth. I knew it was so as clearly as though I held, already, the baby in my arms, and I felt like a traitor. It was then that I experienced deceit, and I felt like dying of shame, like sinking down, down into the earth from shame and remorse. I had betrayed my man, the man I loved, the man I schemed to own for mine in the world of all others—Parmenter!

That was a terrible loss to me, that loss of my self. That unconscious, natural expression of my body despite my own strong will. But the curious part of it was that my deepest instinct, hidden away from us all, was to be "right"—and that it was, I think, that secured the baby to me from my husband. Parmenter and Karl, Fanny and my mother and father and I—we are all woven into a pattern as clear and sharp to my vision today as the designs seen crystallized on sea-fossils. But in the making, while our sharp wills labored against each other, we could not see what we were doing.

Every day, Parmenter's motor stood before my door. Almost immediately people started to talk about us. Naturally. We were both conspicuous. He was always so—and I was too. Live people are dazzling bright in their surroundings. Whatever we did threw radiations all about us! Then Fanny heard the echoes of this talk and spoke to Jack, and he told me what she said. She remonstrated with him and told him that he oughtn't to come and see me so much, that I was so young and willful that I always had people watching me to see what I'd do next, and she told him he shouldn't lend himself to gossip.

I asked him what he had answered and he told me he wouldn't have her or anyone criticize his actions—and somehow he shut her off. Fanny was silenced for the time—and Parmenter and I continued our love. It was as though we dwelt together at the bottom of a deep place where we were in the sunshine, while somewhere else, apart, the rest of the world separated from us by our indifference to it, dwelt in the sordid shadows of everyday life. . . .

It was in October [1900] that Karl and I had been married in Trinity church. In December I had given in to Parmenter. And in March I had lost myself once more to Karl.[6] I began, almost at once, to feel confusion in my thoughts and feelings. I did not tell either of them how I felt, but in despair I tried to outwit nature. By the power of thought I sought to substitute Parmenter's seed for Karl's. I wanted so desperately to have his baby. I wanted it as women have wanted it from the beginning of time, to have more power so that he would love me more, even, than he did, and would stay with me forever. . . .

I told Karl I was pregnant and he was overjoyed. To him it was like expecting a foal or a litter of hounds, and not less exciting. I told Parmenter the same news and I made him believe it was his baby. I told him I was sure—and he was also so overjoyed that I became almost convinced that it was true whenever I was with him.

Now for the first time he contemplated divorcing Fanny and marrying me. "We would have to go away from here, though," he said. "It would make too much trouble. Fanny wouldn't—I don't believe she would—make it impossible. She's a good sort, really. But all these damned prudes here in town; we could never make them face it. Well, I'd lose my practice but I'm tired. I don't mind stopping for a while. I feel as though I had a right to loaf for a while, I've been working for so long, ever since I was a kid, really. I'm tired."

He said we would go and live in Europe, and after a while he would work up a practice again over there. He told me he was awfully tired of the people he'd been working with so long. Then he used to say, too, that little Dick [his son] could come and stay over there with us. "He's a good little kid—too delicate, though, like the Gorhams. You know, old blood."

He often talked to me about the future in the early days of my pregnancy. He grew more and more loving, and more tender now. Once when Karl went away on a trip with Jack Piper, Parmenter and Fanny asked me to stay overnight at their house, so I wouldn't feel lonely. But this was too sad. I couldn't bear it, when he went to bed, to see them go into their room together and close the door, leaving me in my room at the end of the hall far more lonely than I would have felt at home.

It was the first time I felt jealous. And it wrenched me all night, the misery of my situation. I *hated* Fanny for being alive and for being between us. My hate flamed up in me against her. I think Parmenter, with the clairvoyance of passion, caught my feeling. In the morning he came to my door and said: "Don't get up, Mabel. Fanny will send your breakfast up to you." But I was still miserable. I could not forget the picture I had caught of them together in their room—and that the right to be there was theirs.

Soon after breakfast Fanny ran up to see me, cheerful and practical. I really had to fan my jealousy when I looked at her, for I knew no one need ever fear her in that respect, so lean, so unattractive, so positively unaware. She left me to get dressed at my leisure and, putting on her stiff dark blue sailor, she went off down town to order her food. I lay there depressed. Parmenter has gone out in his motor soon after breakfast. I was all alone and whenever I was alone nowadays I grew worried and sad over my mistake.

But I did not lie like that there for long. I heard the front door downstairs open and shut and he came up the stairs still in his overcoat. He came in, closing the door, and without speaking he took me there in a deep, positive silence; in a kind of promising, irrevocable way. And then at that moment I felt for the first time most clearly that I *had* him, that he was committed to me, that now our two wills were fused together at the inward forge, and that neither he nor I was henceforth free.

FOOLED

. . . The days of the pregnant woman gradually change in their outward aspects. Very gradually all the values of things change about her and while some drop in favor, others become enhanced. The pregnant woman ceases to be an individual and becomes a part of the undifferentiated cosmic order about her. Only a short time and it was as though I ceased to be I. Instead of living on love and longing, I was supported, now, by nature, and cradled in comfort with no need of a man's arms.

By degrees my feeling for Parmenter oozed out of me, leaked away and was no more. Was that not amazing, incredible? Even while I watched my diminishing love and languidly tried to hold it firm in my self, it departed out of me and left me cold. I simply didn't need Parmenter any more. With my brain I wanted to continue to love him and hold him, but it was no use trying to want this. I was helplessly a slave to my deeper instincts.

Did I have no further use for him on the day I knew he was irrevocably mine? Or is it always so—that women cannot divide themselves between the man and the child? Was I given over now, completely, to the baby? I did not know, nor, truth to tell, did I care very much. I soon gave up thinking and trying to make things different by a cerebral activity, and as soon as I gave up, the powers of life inside me took complete control.

Then a very curious metamorphosis occurred! My instinctive loyalty to Karl returned to its unseated place in me and I began to feel the most dreadful sensation of guilt towards him and his baby. I could scarcely bear it. It filled every moment of the day and I dreamed of it at night. My love for Parmenter was as though it had never been at all, and he seemed a stranger to me. I could not summon up one flicker of feeling for him when he came to see me.

And I wanted Karl to stay with me, even to being with me when Parmenter made his visits. They were both lovely to me. Seeing a cloud on my face and a silence wrapping me away from them, they drew closer together and spoke of my pregnancy, of their patience and their need to make it as easy for me as they could. Two men, shut out from the mystery of a woman.

But soon I drew to feel I could not carry the baby to the end if I had to carry too the guilt I had in my heart. I could not look Karl in the face with that secret between us, and yet I wanted him about me in the house. In a desperate mood one day I opened my dry lips to Parmenter about it. "I can't bear to think I've deceived Karl," I said.

He answered me very gently: "Don't fret yourself, darling. Just be patient for a while. All these feelings and thoughts will leave you once the baby is born. Our baby, dear," he added, tentatively, to try and comfort me a little.

Nothing could have been worse chosen. My whole insides save a great heave as though they would spew out of me forever every vestige, every memory of this man. I turned faint and put my hand out to the chimney place nearby. Parmenter saw I was ill and said no more about it. He became the physician and drew me over to my bed and helped me lie down. Then he went to the kitchen and himself prepared for me some lemon juice and ice that he bade me sip. Drawing down my curtain quietly, he left me there to retain my inner balance. . . . Soon a compulsion to speak caught me by the throat as soon as I awoke each morning.

One day I called out hoarsely from my bed to Karl in the next room: "Karl, Karl, come here! I must tell you something." He came running in, fresh and gay and free of all care, and the words were caught in my mouth and I couldn't speak to him through that day and the next until evening. When the light grew dim in the house and, in the street, the lamps began to show, then was the worst time. Then the burden of guilt weighed most heavily of all on me and finally, at that hour of the day, overcame me.

Karl had come in from out of doors, cool cheeked and cheerful, undaunted and undismayed, he was the epitome of a simple, healthy living. He came to me where I was sitting on a low bench by the window and sat down on it beside me and put his arm around me.

"Parmenter has been my lover," I said to him, and began to cry. "He's been my lover ever since you had the jaundice. And I tried to have a baby with him. But I didn't. This is your, baby and I don't like him any more," I sobbed. Blessed relief! Like clouds lifting off one mountain top and settling upon another, the terrible weight left me and came down upon Karl. He looked at me as though I were crazy. Or as though he were.

"Gosh, Peg!" was all he said in answer. I continued to cry and cry. In a deluge of tears I washed out of me the last traces of Parmenter.

Karl got up and left me. He didn't say another word. He went downstairs and out of the house and got into his motor that was standing out there. Turning it swiftly around, he made off downtown at top speed. A few days later he told me he had dashed down to Brownley's and bought a magnificent pigskin saddle he had wanted for a long time and hadn't been able to afford. That was the way it took *him*!

He was back in the house by dinnertime and now his behavior was incomprehensible. He came up to me and kissed me and begged me to come down and eat something with him, and he said the same old words I'd been hearing: "Don't worry, Peg, everything's all right."

I was amazed. But I gave a kind of mental shrug. Men were queer. Also women. I didn't understand any of us. But I didn't care. My burden was gone. I didn't suffer any more. I wanted, now, to give myself up to the baby, to luxuriate at peace in that community of living that I felt had become possible to me. I went down with Karl in content—and we ate our evening meal.

The next day, punctually at three, Parmenter—that dogged and determined man—arrived smiling. Playfully he took my hands, the hands that didn't thrill to him any more. And he looked deep into my eyes and he said, kindly, sweetly, and yet with more than a suspicion of infallibility:

"Foolish girl, to upset the apple cart!" he said. And then he told me what has happened. Karl had telephoned him the afternoon before and without making any fuss had said that I had told him that Parmenter and I were lovers—and he had acted as though he were asking Parmenter to fix it up somehow. I was not surprised. I asked him what he had said and he told me.

"Karl," he said, "try and put this out of your mind if you can and let her have her baby. And then after the baby's been born a month, you go to her and ask her if this is really true, what she's said now in the condition she's in. That's all I ask of you, and I ask it for her sake. She's really not responsible just now."

"You bet, Dr. John," Karl had almost shouted to him—and then he rang off!

"Now, my dearest," Parmenter added, to me, "you do as I say too. Put all these thoughts out of your head. Give yourself up to your job. That's what you're to do now." And he gave my cold hands a little squeeze. No kisses, no possessiveness. Just a strong, helpful, reassuring care. After all, he *was* a real man.

[After her son John was born, Mabel wanted nothing to do with him. In *European Experiences*, she wrote: "I saw the pathos and the pity of life and I thought, 'I don't like it,' and my heart shut right up then and there." In "Green Horses," she writes: "I saw the pathos and the pity of our life and what I had done to injure us all; and my heart shut up right then and there."]

Part II

THE CONFLICT

Parmenter came to see me every day while I was in bed, for the first two or three days I had a temperature after the baby came. The nurse was rather worried, but he wasn't, and he wouldn't do anything about it. I lay listless and sad there in the dark room and couldn't take any interest in anything about me. No milk came for the baby and they had to put it on a bottle. I didn't care and I didn't want them to keep bringing him into my room. I didn't like to look at him. He was a good baby from the beginning and slept all the time and never cried. And he took the first preparation of the food they made up for him and thrived on it right away.

Nothing seemed to matter to him. He had had a good start and he pushed right along, gaining all the time. He has been pushing along ever since. When he goes on hunting trips for game or for blankets—"Well, let's push along," they tell me he keeps saying.

But in me there didn't seem to be any push at all. The heat in my body flickered up and down following my tormented thoughts. I wished I needn't get well. I hated to have to get up and live in that conflict I had brought into my life. My mother came to see me, too, every day. She was bluff and had a suspicion of tearfulness about her. She was worried, too, I saw that. Things didn't feel right to her, but she never analyzed anything or thought about things.

I noticed after a day or two, that she always came when Parmenter was there—and he had a joking, familiar way of talking to her. Then as I lay silently watching them from my dark corner, one afternoon, I saw a swift, vital look come to her face as she looked at him. And when she left, she gave him a questioning look and he replied with a slight, almost imperceptible nod. Then the life rushed all of a sudden through me again and my heart beat faster and I raised my head up and said: "Parmenter, is my mother after you?"

"My dear girl, what a question! What do you mean by that?"

"I saw her look at you in a way—as though she—as though—"

"Nonsense, child. Don't get ideas like that in your head. You know I have been waiting for you. You know it's been very long since you even looked at me—all these months. I've been patient, don't you think I have?"

"I never wanted to have you wait for me," I said slowly. "But if you think I'm going to have my mother take you, like she wants to, I won't *have* it. Do you hear me? You've got to be *mine*," I went on, more and more heatedly.

He sat on my bed and took my two hands. His touch was reborn to me again. As though I were new to life and to love. His touch was made new and desirable to the blood and nerves of my body. I pressed his hand to my face and all the trouble I had been harboring vanished and made a place for my leaping interest in him, and I felt as though I had returned again to an abandoned house that awaited me. . . .

Day by day, then, I grew rapidly better. My curious reluctance to see the baby dwindled away and though I did not feel any sadness, neither did I feel any love for him. He, I saw, was a beautiful baby, but I could feel nothing for him. . . .

The days, happy again, flew by, and the nurse left me and the baby's nurse was there to take care of him. I was up and dressed now, and going out every day to drive. The life streamed through me—I was stronger than ever and hell-bent, now, on securing Parmenter to myself forever. When Fanny came to see me and when she praised the baby and fussed over it, I was scarcely able to control my impatience at her. She was in my way—the obstacle to life.

One day she said to me, laughingly, but still rather prim:

"Well, it's a good thing you got over the notion you had about poor Jack when you were pregnant! He told me about Karl telephoning him! A nice mess you might have made if Jack hadn't been so levelheaded. He didn't know what you'd be saying next and he told me about it to get ahead of you in case you took it into your head to want to spring some story on *me*! These doctors! The things they have to put up with! I could tell you some things—"

Well, even in my barren delight in his shrewdness and, yes, his level-headedness, I was aghast at his real coldness in being able to handle the situation like that. It took such perfect balance, such certainty of himself. But he had it. He was not the kind to weaken and falter. He would carry anything through to get what he wanted. And he *liked* the danger of it. I liked danger, too. But I hated the messy part of this—I hated the deceit and it made me feel dirty. To forget this feeling

I shut my eyes, my outer and my inner ones, and flung myself deeper and deeper into loving him. If that was what it was.

And every day he came to me now, after his office hours were over at the old hour of three o'clock. And soon I was stronger in passion and will than I had been before. And he, too, was deeper in the fusion of our two fires, welded more firmly into the passionate link we had formed.

One day when the baby was about two months old, I was coming home later than usual from my drive, . . . As I passed my mother's house in the dusk, I saw Parmenter's car just driving away, and on an impulse I stopped and went in. I went up stairs with a terrible wind blowing in my veins—like a stupendous tornado sweeping over a sea. Straight to her room I went and walked in. She was lying on the couch at the foot of her bed, and as soon as I looked at her I knew everything as plainly as though I had assisted at their amorous activities.

She lay there on her white pillow, flushed and warmed, her hair, burning brightly in the light, a little loosened. Her eyes were not cold now, as they always were,—no, they were dark and sapphire blue, heated and accentuated by her quickened, strong blood. The air in the room seemed throbbing to me as I looked at that woman who was my mother but who had never been a mother to me; who had been a stranger, but who was no stranger to me now: a sister, rather, she seemed, another version of myself, my real, secret, passionate self filled with life—with the life that was my life, with the fires that I considered I alone held the key to loosen, that I only could control . . .

The terrible intimacy that I encountered there in the room was enough to madden one! I reeled in my spirit between the visions that filled my eyes. To see her so was to see myself after Parmenter had left me, after his hour. To see her so was to see another woman as she appeared after his fire had lighted her veins. To see her was to see my mother, after her lover had left her, burning like the embers after the flame has escaped. I looked at her and she looked back at me. And then we spoke and I said: "I was passing and I thought I would stop. How is my father?"

"Oh, just the same. The doctor has been here. He keeps him quiet. You ought not to be out too late, had you?"

"I'm just going. I stopped at Mary's. Her house isn't bad. Too much white enamel."

"Oh, I like it like that. So clean."

"Well, I'll go along."

"How's the baby?"

"Oh, he's all right. He sleeps all day and all night. Well, good-bye."

"Good-bye."

I went out and down to my house two blocks away. And Karl was there when I went in. I could hardly drag one foot after another now. I asked Karl to call up Parmenter and ask him to come that evening. I felt sick. I went up into my room. The room that had held so many different emanations from my changing life flow. . . . I felt terribly exposed. And I was frightened. But as I moved about the room, after a while the strength to fight came into me and my fear left me as the dark, inflammable current filled my blood. I gathered myself together and pacing up and down the quiet room, my fists tight shut, I waited for Parmenter. He came just after eight o'clock. . . .

Parmenter had sat himself down in a chair and drawn me, unresisting, to him where I stood between his knees, looking down at him. "Why, my dear, what's happened to you? Why do you look at me like that?"

"Because I *know* now," I answered, bearing down on him with a look.

"Know what my girl," he said bravely. But catching my eye he looked away.

"I know about you and my mother," I said, dully. My eyes, vigilant, hovered just above him, charged with their cargo of magnetism. But he avoided the danger. He leaned forward and bent his face against my thigh.

"My darling, why will you torment yourself? Why can't you be happy after all these months? You never want to leave well enough alone. You always seem to want to stir things up and have something doing between us. Really, dear, you know when I'm tired you rest me, when I'm bored you stimulate me; now why can't we be happy together?"

This man's perfidy stirred me so at that moment that it left me speechless with hate. It seemed to me I couldn't grasp his deception—it was too much to bear. And yet at the instant I knew that what he said was all true. He loved me, I was everything to him, he wanted to be happy with me—and I always stirred up our sweet brew and disturbed its clarity, its dubious transparency. . . .

"How dare you talk to me like that! You're just playing with me! Do you think I'm a fool like Fanny—that old prig that saves the orange peel at your house?" I sneered.

"Here, here, that's enough of that. We'll leave Fanny out of this!" He stiffened possessively into angry authority and dropped my hands.

"Yes, I've been wanting her out of it for a year now," I returned, deadly. By this time there was no more love left between us. We were become enemies, the fire of passionate conflict died down in us both and left us cold and almost indifferent. We looked at each other in dislike and criticism. The feeling I had had since leaving my mother's room was gone—and I only wondered now how I could have depended on this man for my flow of life—this obtuse, this stupid, lumpish man.

A deep, sluggish disgust rose in me when I thought of him driving his awkward body against my mother's cold sensuality. This is a mental picture that never can appear graceful to an onlooker. It is well that love remains blind to its own antics. When it is one's own lover whom one visualizes with one's mother in the fumbling, frantic adjustment, the reaction is too bitter; and the stark truth of the fatal grotesque takes on the character of desperate and unhappy canines driven by their mutual heat, helpless, into ridiculous attitudes.

I laughed outright. I felt as cold as ice through and through. Parmenter looked at me again to see if he believed his ears. And again, at what he saw in my eyes, his own dropped.

"My God, Mabel! Don't look like that. I wouldn't know you. Come, don't let's fight. Don't let's spoil everything . . ."

"Will you admit the truth, then?" I probed him. "Will you at least be honest with me?" Suddenly I longed for an opportunity to forgive him.

As I looked at him again, he appeared to me as I knew him. I noted his strong, masculine hardiness, his bold, certain movements, and I recalled in gazing at him, the release that his proximity brought to my heart, tired from containing itself. I longed to have him, but I wanted him on his knees. I had to have him—my medicine he was—but I wanted him *down*. . . .

"Won't you tell me the truth? Won't you just say, 'Yes, I am her lover, but I don't love her.' I know you love me and I know men do these things. Maybe they do them even if they don't really want to. Parmenter, won't you tell me about it? Will you *admit it*?" I begged him, my mouth close to his ear, my arms around his neck.

"Hell, no!" he replied, and I started back and saw a laughing devil flashing in his blue eyes; a special male deviltry, audacious, unburdened and ruthless, glinted like steel in his self-possession. He was more on the defense than ever, at my demand for truth. . . .

What a pity, when we were all ready for love, that we took the wrong turning! I looked down at him, at his vain, habitual self-assured masculine certainty that he was master, that no girl was going to trip him up and make *a fool* of him—and I was glad he was so sure. It gave me more chance to catch him in some careless moment, off his guard. I gave myself up to conquest now. I relaxed deeply, deeply. My resolution was taken. I could trust it to sink down into me and guide me along the difficult surface to the end.

I looked at him and let my love mount in me now: this flood called love. It had been there, damned back and waiting for the waves of all those other conflicting feelings to recede before it could rise and rise and fill me and flow on across to the man who wanted me filled like that till I was like a Leyden jar brimming with the dangerous, passionate fluid. . . .

"My God, Mabel! What are you? What is there about you that you can make me feel like this? There's no one like you. There's not a woman in the world can move me as you do. When you look at me in that way, I don't know what it is, I grow dizzy . . ."

He kissed me as though he would never let me go. He kissed me as though he wanted to dissolve me and assimilate me into himself. He, too, wanted to dominate and overcome and absorb me. Each was become to the other one the goose that laid the golden eggs!

LOSS

That spring [1902] we never could get enough of being together. Karl was away more and more, hunting off with other people, and though I had arranged my life now so that I often ate over at the Parmenters, or had them at my house and went to the theatre with them or something, yet we could not see each other enough without interruptions. There was for certain only our hour alone in the afternoon. We had that right along—though indeed people were commenting more and more now at Parmenter's daily call with his small black bag. So he began to leave his car at home and walk around to me—only two or three blocks away.

So Parmenter and I used now to meet down at the Iroquois Hotel a couple of days a week and stay all the afternoon. The ease and carelessness with which he carried this out and taught me to should have shown me how habituated he was to such ways. But I did not think of this. I thought only of my role in it and of how well I must act it to succeed and pass through the dangers I had to meet before we would be safe together locked in a room. I went into the hotel dressed quietly, wearing a thick veil and carrying a bag and I sat, demure, in the ladies' sitting room off the Lobby.

Outside, many men walked up and down or sat chatting. Many of them I would have known at least by sight had I examined them, but I kept my face from them. The hotel was owned by Mr. Gerrans, Monty Gerrans, who lived only two doors from me. I saw him every day up in my own neighborhood and his wife was very friendly and nice. He must often have seen me there in the hotel if he did but look in my direction. But I was a mouse. I drew all my feelers in and curled up inside myself.

In a few moments, Parmenter would come to the door of the sitting room and, taking of his hat, he would say: "How do you do!" in a business-like way, and then: "Will you come this way?" I would follow him meekly to the lift, trying to impersonate the retiring manner of a lady from the country, and we would shoot up a few flights together, he with the door key in his hand and a grave, powerful look in his face. I remember the first time I saw his face under the light in the elevator. It looked so mask-like, so dominant, so imperturbable. Like a beautiful Roman coin.

But safe inside the room he would drop his bag and open his arms, and his face would become brilliant with life and the sly, male laughter of antique abductions. Together we burned up the hours: one, two, three, until little was left of us save flesh and bones.

We would drink the beer I had fetched, ice cold, in my modest traveling bag, and for a bit we would lie waiting for the hardy glands of us to refurnish our veins with fresh power. Then he would go—leaving me to follow after. And I would walk down and out of the place light as air, feeling completely transparent and purified. A couple of times a week we met like this, and Parmenter always engaged the same room from the office for the lady who came up from Elmira for treatments. . . .

As the months went on, my father was ailing more and more. My mother and I were feeling like eagles in the sky, but my father sank lower and lower. One day after Parmenter had left me at four o'clock, I wandered into my mother's house. My brain was busy, while my heart ached. I had some vague idea of hiding in the house somewhere and waiting for Parmenter's visit: to see what I could see, to have *proof*, to *know* once and for all and confute him, to end the tiring strain of our two wills, neither one of which could give way before the other.

The house was quiet downstairs. Upstairs—(my mother was still out and the nurse late in coming back to her patient)—upstairs I heard a sound of regular moans coming out of my father's room, and I went in. He was lying in the darkened room, his head low on the pillow, his chin covered with a dark stubble thrust up, his fleshy nose hung pendulous over the querulous mouth. He turned as I came in. His yellow hands lay over the sheet, drawn nigh. He whimpered louder when he saw me.

"I'm awfully sick," he moaned, as his breath came faster. "I wish I had a cross. Do you think you could find me a cross in this house?"

Cold as ice, without a single throb of response in me anywhere, I said: "I'll look." I didn't feel anything. It's queer how one gives the whole of oneself in some direction, and there is none, nothing left over for anything or anyone else. I went out and thought over coldly where on earth I was to look for a cross. I couldn't remember one anywhere. As I went into my mother's room, I saw the hour: quarter of five. I must hurry if I was to hide before anyone came. I glanced around me. There *was* a cross! Of course. It had hung there for years. A large inlaid cross of olive wood and mother-of-pearl made for the tourist trade at Jerusalem. Someone had given it to my mother. It hung by a yellow ribbon to the side gas light at the left of her dressing table. I untied the faded ribbon and carried the cross, the large, impersonal cross with no consolation in it, to my father and, offering it to him in some embarrassment, I said: "This is the only thing I can find. I'm sorry." If only that nurse would come back, my thoughts kept saying.

"Put it down on the pillow," whispered my father. "There are devils here. All around the ceiling, all night and day—" His yellow eyes glanced up sideways in a stealthy way at the sky-blue signs of the zodiac pursuing each other around the pale walls, as though he would catch and impale them on his look. "Your mother doesn't care. She doesn't care what happens to me," he muttered; and his breath shuddered a little and weak tears were shaken from him.

"Oh, my goodness!" I thought. I had seen so many of these attacks, these journeys of his into the depths and out again. But though I didn't know it, he was caught this time at the bottom of the pit. . . . I left my father then, and I never saw him again. The nurse returned as I went and I heard my mother come in the front door. . . . Like a shot I withdrew into the dark closet of the spare room across the hall from hers. I was in there for more than an hour. I heard nothing save steps coming and going, doors opening and closing, and I had no particular feelings except discomfort from the closeness and impatience to be out again and busy on my task.

I calculated exactly enough when it was that he finally opened my mother's door and closed it softly behind him and walked firmly downstairs, and I opened my closet door and very quietly I followed him and caught up with him in the hall as he was taking up his overcoat. I felt absolutely nothing but resolution and my own heartbeats as I walked towards him. No jealousy, no anger, no anguish as so often before. I walked up to him and was in front of him before he saw me. And when his eyes met mine—I do not know what he found there. Something that conquered his will.

"My God, Mabel, my darling. Forgive me, I couldn't help it. I will tell you all about it—" He fumbled brokenly with these words. I didn't answer him. I was watching myself act a part that was directed from deep, deep somewhere. I just continued to look at him and to feel the streams of living energy pour out upon him. And then, after a moment, I slipped past him and out of the house and ran all the way home. But my break came then. I got into my house and fell on the floor in the sitting room in the kind of weeping that I had only experienced once before: when I had to tell Karl about Parmenter. Karl was there this time, too. He raised me up and tried to get me to talk, but of course I could not. There was no one in the world I could talk to—no one.

"Great Scott, Peg, *don't*. You'll make yourself sick. Come on, eat some dinner. Have you seen the kid in his new jacket? Here, wait till I get him . . ." And he was off in a clumsy attempt to find something to distract me. But the baby was the last thing I wanted. I motioned him away when Karl came back with him. I wept until I was faint and then, because I was too weak to sob any more, I lay quiescent on the couch while Karl sat, puzzled, by me, patting my hand. And then, as with lovers when their blood receives new strength, they fall to expending it again—so I broke into fresh convulsions of sobbing as soon as my force returned to me.

Finally, Karl got frightened and naturally he thought of the doctor. I heard him call Parmenter on the telephone and ask him to come over. And even while my body shook involuntarily from the storm in my heart and the tears poured down from the wound I had received, yet my cool mind found itself speculating upon him and upon now he was feeling, how he would act, what he would, could say *now*?

He came immediately and, hastily throwing off his things, he raised me up and tried to help me walk up the stairs to my room. He treated Karl like a negligible child—just threw me over his shoulder: "Bring me a pitcher of ice-water," and went on, half carrying me up the stairs. I gave myself gladly to his physical strength. I was worn out from him: from having conquered him. . . .

"Well, tell me about it," I breathed, finally, into the silence, not looking at him. He felt me reversed from him. He saw I was removed from him. His future depended on getting me back, my youth, my strength, my attention, like a bright beam of light reinforcing him. He bent his head down by me on the edge of the bed where he was sitting by me in a stiff chair (like a doctor for once in his life!)—he bent his head down by me, on his hands, and all of a sudden he began to shake without any sound or any fuss. He just shook hard and he shook the bed and me on it. I opened my eyes at this. This was something new. This man cried horribly here. There was something terrible about the dry regularity of his rapid sobs. As though some other force than his had caught him and was shaking him fast like a rattle.

I was through, myself, and empty of everything. A weary, sarcastic reflection about the lack of correspondence in our feelings came into my depleted mind. He continued to shake silently and I, feeling like an actress now, put one hand weakly on his head and murmured kindly: "Stop, don't do that!" For myself I had reached the point we all must pass and re-pass where nothing matters. And he? Ah! He was meeting, at last, his destiny, his destiny of loving and loving, until he could love no more. The barrier had broken between us—and his will was overcome.

"Oh, Mabel, how could I hurt you like that? I only feel it now, what you have suffered. What if I lost you on account of these women—these *women*! Don't you know why I lied to you? To *save* you. I didn't want to hurt you. I couldn't make you understand how little it meant to me; I never *thought* of her once the door was closed on her: but *you*, you are in my thoughts all the time. I *can't* lose you now. Not for *that*. I was sorry for her. Her life has been hell. And it was nothing; to me—nothing."

"Are you going there again?" I asked him, coldly.

"I leave that to you. You know your father's condition. God knows I don't want to go back into that house! If you only knew how sick I get of all this—"

"Will you promise me never to go into her room again?" I continued.

"Yes, yes, of course, I'll promise that. But *you*, will *you* come back to me—will you feel the same to me? *Will* you?"

"I don't know," I answered, and I meant it.

And then the telephone rang and Karl came knocking at the door and summoned Parmenter. He rose and shook himself and ran his hand through his hair. His face looked older and crushed and somehow defiled. He came back to me, almost a petition in his eyes. "Your mother says your father is very bad," he said. "I shall have to go." He stood like a soldier, numbly, attentively, asking the order from me.

"All right, go," I said. And at three o'clock that morning, after a night of delirium, my father died [November 25, 1902]. . . .

Two days later we drove, an uninspiring procession, to the crematory in the cemetery. The whole dreary lifeless performance seemed infinitely boring and rather disgusting to me. I had no other feelings. It has taken a lifetime to be able to have the right feelings at the right time!

I remember with what surprise I saw my mother hidden under yards of dark veils, step forward in the chapel, out of the group before the coffin that stood on three raised steps, and kneel suddenly with outstretched arms flung out protectively or imploringly over the dumb wooden box. It seemed to me the freest gesture I had ever seen her make, and the most tragic. I wondered what thoughts and feelings were in her now, and my heart hardened against her more than before.

After the funeral my mother summoned Parmenter. She wanted to be comforted and she wanted him to be her comforter. I do not know what he said to her, but not enough to discourage her. He would not know how to do that very well. Anyhow she sent for him again the following day and he told me that she expected him—at five o'clock. My stomach heaved in me at the thought of this. "You're not going. That's finished. When a thing is finished, it's finished."

"What shall I say to her?" he pondered.

"You'll tell her you love me, that I know about you both and that I won't have you go there!" I ground the words at him passionately. He looked at me as though fascinated.

"If *you* don't tell now, *I* will," I went on. Hastily he agreed to go for the last time and make it all clear to her. He told me the next day of the scene he had had. He was rueful and sad over it all, but he realized it couldn't be helped. He told me he had felt sorry for her.

"'I've never had anything in my life,' she kept saying to me, over and over. She never said a word about you and me. She seemed to think if she could see me sometimes that would be enough. I told her it was impossible, that I couldn't hurt you any more. 'How about me,' she said. 'I love Mabel,' I answered her. It was damned hard. But I knew she would take it like a man. She's a strange woman. Very strong. The night your father was dying—there in that sitting room next to him, where that pink couch is, she tried to take—"

"Stop that, Parmenter! I won't listen to any more of that. If she's strong, then let her be strong. This is her chance. Never tell me any more about her."

Now never a look or a word passed between my mother and me of all that. We talked of the external aspects of life as mothers and children do, when I went to see her or when she came to see the baby—whom, by the way, I called John after Parmenter. I had him christened John Ganson. I had asked Parmenter to be his godfather, but he dissuaded me from this and I had left it, then, to Karl, who asked his cousin Evan Hollister to do it.

When John was nearly a year old, I had Neely Sage paint two miniatures of him and one was on my dressing table and the other I gave to Parmenter. He, nothing loath, took it home and showed it to Fanny. To her, from that time, it figured on her bureau as one among the several other babies he had brought into the world and whose pictures, given him by young mothers, she always framed and put there.

I had him christened John Ganson because of our eminent great uncle [who fought in the American Revolution], but John Parmenter was how he figured in my heart. He grew beautifully, never crying or complaining, but seeming to unfold from day to day. Once in a while when Parmenter was with me, I would fetch him from his green and white room and sit him up on a chair beside the big man and in small ways try and draw fatherhood to him from this willing but doubting lover. His own past divagations prevented him from finding certainty anywhere. He could believe no one but himself and himself he doubted, as well he might. The baby eyed him calmly with a kind of noble patience.

"You don't handle him as though you *loved* him," said Parmenter, split between feelings of identity with the large, blooming child and fear that after all he had nothing to do with him.

"I don't love anything, but you," I answered, and carried the baby away to his nurse.

Parmenter had capitulated wearily to love, and every time he gave up to me after that fatal surrender of himself, it was in fatigue. He could not fight any more to keep his independence. He gave in to everything that came up in issue between us. I often begged him to come back again and see me in the evenings now and he came willingly, indifferent to the increasing gossip, dumb and indifferent to Fanny's discreet remonstrances. We talked more and more together of leaving her and Karl and going off to Europe. He cared for nothing but me now, and he wanted to find me everywhere. . . .

Karl was away more and more. Where? I scarcely knew. . . . I saw Fanny less and less now for I had dropped that attempt to have a combination with her. She bored me and I did not need her any more. The autumn came [still the autumn of 1902] and people came back to town and the activities of a cooler season were resumed. Professional people knuckled down harder to their jobs after the summer heat—but Parmenter didn't. He had grown careless. He neglected his work.

Since the baby had come, I had had backaches and pain when I walked, and Parmenter had been trying to make up his mind to do a necessary operation. So now he brought himself to do it. It was, of course, a major operation needing as it did an incision through the abdomen; and he, always so cool, so bold, the adventurous surgeon as he had been called, he was shaky over this. I didn't mind. I would have let him do anything to me, except be stronger than I was.

The nurse came, and operating, tables and things, and at three o'clock they gave me the anesthetic—some other young doctor and he. When I came out of it, I was lying in my bed and the room was quite dark. Maybe it was five o'clock. Parmenter was there bending over me—and the same nurse that I had had when John was born, Miss Ganue. "Go to sleep, now, everything will be all right," he said. So I closed my eyes again. I enjoyed convalescing: the week after the pain of the healing wound stopped hurting me was lovely and restful.

Parmenter was with me a good deal, people came and brought flowers, always there was some reason for my room to be full of flowers and I loved them so much. I had had only one present from Parmenter—only one thing I had wanted him to give me—a little watch to tell me the hours of his coming, of his approach. It lay, now, by my pillow, and I lived by it.

Karl had stayed around for a few days when I was first sick, but I saw he was impatient to be off and at the end of that week he left, going to the Barretts for duck shooting. And I was glad. There was less between me and my thoughts when he was gone. I remember lying, almost in a magic spell of rest and attainment the afternoon and evening; it left—but it didn't last.

When the nurse, Miss Ganue, was putting things away for the night, she let out a secret. I was chatting with her in a desultory way, sleepy, and I said: "What did he do, anyway, when he operated? I never asked Dr. Parmenter about it."

"Well, you'd better," she answered dryly.

"Why, what do you mean?" I had been struck by the tone of her voice.

"Oh, you ask him when he comes in the morning," she demurred.

"No. Now you've worried me. *Tell* me! You'll make me wonder about it all night if you don't. What happened?"

"Well, nothing happened," she said.

"What *do* you mean?" I urged, impatiently.

"Well, my dear, Doctor made his incision, and just when he was going to start the work that was before him, he shook his head and sewed you up again. He didn't say a word till it was all finished. Then he remembered us and he said: 'The light wasn't good enough.' Of course it wasn't for me to have an opinion. Us nurses aren't supposed to, you know. But it seemed a pity you had to have that great opening made in you for nothing. Oh, well, these doctors! They have their own ways. . . ."

[The rest of this chapter was published in *European Experiences*, describing Karl's death and funeral. He died on February 25, 1903, the day before Mabel's twenty-fourth birthday. He had been accidently shot while hunting with a friend.]

"LA FEMME A TOUJOURS LE BEAU ROLE"

I

Immediately after the funeral they took me away for a change of scene and air. "They" were Parmenter and Fanny. He had arranged it all with my mother who continued, as from the first time he had approached her, to do anything and everything he said; and with Fanny, who no matter what happened would always stand by him. He had authority. He could always make things go his way— nearly always.

But at Atlantic City, where we three went for the sea change, we found we had all undergone another change than that of air and water. The imperious instinct that does not wait upon taste and time lifted itself in my depths and made me realize I was nearer my goal now since Karl's death. I did not shrink back in any way. I wanted Parmenter for myself more than ever when I found I was nearer to him through the removal of a husband. Only Fanny stood between him and me now. Only! That little, uncomprehending, dried up thing!

Parmenter was wonderful to me in those days. He felt, more than I did, all I had gone through. In some way, he felt it *for* me, with the vicarious suffering of a lover. Every chance we had to be alone we took, and some we made. After I was in bed at night, he would leave Fanny, and, crossing the sitting room between our rooms, he would come in to me. And because he had her so entirely under his suggestion, we were as safe from interruption as if we had been there without her. She reverenced his character; she regarded him as a kind of omnipotent king among men. Whatever he did was sure to be right, wise and kind; and she was happy if she could cooperate with his benignities.

I was happy. Human life is so precariously balanced: the ups and downs depending on such trivialities. Nothing mattered now but the lovely fresh air from the ocean blowing in our windows, and the exquisite renewal of convalescence. I don't know how I looked then. Very young and quite frail in black, I suppose, or maybe I showed, somehow, the glow I felt burning, strong in me. Anyway, the second day at the hotel, Daisy Davidson, who was at the table near ours, came up to me and put her arms around me right there in the dining room and whispered with tears in her eyes:

"I *have* to tell you! I think you're *wonderful*." I was a widow! I could not remember it unless people said things like that. It was, to me, as though I had never known Karl—and indeed, perhaps I never had. Now in the weeks and months that followed, I spoke often to Parmenter of our future. He wanted to have me as much to himself as I wanted him. But he had his hesitations. He did not think there would be the slightest trouble about Fanny.

"I can handle her all right," he said. "It isn't that there were the same feelings between us as there is with you and me. She will be unhappy for a while, but more on account of losing 'the doctor' than the husband! She's always been rather proud of my success, you know. Proud to be married to the best surgeon in the country and that sort of thing! Poor girl! That's about all the satisfaction *she's* had from me! But you'll not have *any* of that, darling. You won't mind going off with your old man somewhere where nobody knows him?"

"*I* want a husband," I answered him, throwing my head back, proud of my need and disdainful of Fanny's neutrality.

"God! You do! And you'll have one!" he exclaimed in great male delight, feeling his prowess. . . .

So we talked and still he hesitated from day to day. Imperceptibly now, a little change came over people in regard to us. As long as Karl lived and there was a husband in the house, people had only smiled and looked and whispered. . . . Now they began to alter towards me somewhat in their manner, growing cooler and less sympathetic. . . .

Someone really approached Fanny about it all. It was, of course, her best friend Violet Townsend. . . . She had told Fanny to speak to Parmenter because everyone was talking so—and even saying I was making a fool of him. "She's only a child," Fanny had replied, on the defensive. She couldn't bear it said that Jack could be made foolish by anyone, much less by anyone as young as I was.

"She's only a child and she's had a very hard time and Jack is trying to *help* her. She's had no upbringing *at all*—awfully handicapped by that mother and father of hers! Jack is trying to develop some seriousness in her. He thinks she has *very* good stuff in her. And as for people criticizing Jack, well Violet, you know I really think it's ridiculous that they should presume to criticize him! Look at him and compare him with *them*! Does *he* drink? Does *he* play cards all the time? Does he have affairs with type-writers [secretaries]? Look at what he's done in this town! What was the Children's Hospital before he reorganized it? And the Buffalo General! Did it have any operating facilities until *he* shook up those old directors? No, Violet, people are jealous of him and they're not worth considering."

So she had silenced her friend, but that night she had spoken differently to Parmenter. She told him how worried she was, that it did me no good, that I wasn't worth it. She told him I was idle, restless and frivolous, and that he shouldn't let people talk about us. Then she said:

"Why don't you persuade Mrs. Ganson to send her away for a trip some-where? *You* can't go on looking after her *forever*!"

"That's just want I want to do," Parmenter had answered. The moment had come to face the issue.

"You want to *what*?" demanded Fanny, not believing her ears.

"I want to *marry* her," replied Parmenter. He was surprised at the effect of these words on his wife. She turned deathly pale, then paler still. She had shrunk back in her chair and the lamp-light streamed on her stricken face and showed Parmenter the ravages of the truth as it wormed its way into her, deeper, deeper, until she was eaten through with it, as though by a terrible poisonous acid.

He said he was touched into response to her by her helpless agony. The doctor was alive to her at once. He had begged her not to take it like that. I knew, when he told me, how the tenderhearted side of him had come uppermost. She had asked him then if it was really true—if he wanted to leave her and Dick and his position and all,—for me. And he had answered that it had grown little by little and that he did love me and he was even afraid of what would happen to me if it were broken off now.

"And what am *I* to do in all this?" Fanny had asked. I could imagine how she had gathered herself together—practical. And then he told her he wanted a divorce.

"When?" she had asked.

"Soon," he had replied.

Then she told him she would not have believed it of him, that he couldn't be in his right mind, that he was as though bewitched. And she said she couldn't imagine anything worse for him than to marry me. I asked him quickly: "And what did you say?"

"I told her that was for me to say," said Parmenter. But she had exclaimed: "No, it's for *me*," and she had seemed suddenly to become full of strength and determination. "Don't forget that *I* have a voice in this matter," she told him. Already she was hardened back into a kind of stiff, self-support.

He asked her if she wouldn't do her part, and she said, yes, she'd do her part and save him if she could. She said she wasn't going to divorce him when she felt it was the worst thing that could happen to him. And he told me he had felt perfectly helpless for a moment, helpless to make her see the truth. He begged her not to be so hard and he said we depended on her, that she was the only one that could help us. I think that "we" must have decided it. Maybe if he hadn't used that word she would have acted differently. But, the stupid, he *loved* to say it at last—to no matter whom!

She told him she wasn't going to be hard, but she wasn't going to be soft either, but that she wasn't going to get a divorce until she was convinced it was the best thing for him. She said she'd wait and see if we really loved each other. And she finished this argument of theirs by saying that if we really cared enough, we wouldn't mind waiting.

He looked baffled as he told me about it, for he knew what this would mean. He knew the impatience, the passionate, urgent impatience in me. Of course he could look ahead and see the angers and the chafing, the wounded pride at being dependent upon Fanny's opinion of our love for our release. He saw all that it would mean for him in the months to come. Jealousy, argument, and that terrible will bearing down on him!

And at home the cat was out of the bag, now! He could never fool Fanny again. He had thrown away his freedom to gain a larger one—and in the end he had neither. Poor Parmenter, things had gone entirely differently from what he had expected! He looked terribly harassed.

II

After Parmenter finished telling me this conversation, I was in a rage of impatience and anger. What have these prudencies to do with me? Fanny's ultimatum insulted me, infuriated me.

"Why should we wait upon her opinions? What has she to do with *me*?" I cried, the angry tears flowing. "It's ridiculous that a person like *Fanny* should be an arbiter for either you or me. Why should we stand it? Let's go anyway. We needn't wait for her old divorce. Let's go and live somewhere where it won't matter. Come on! Do let's!" But Parmenter shook his head sadly.

"It would never do," he said. He was wiser than I—older. He tried to convince me that Fanny would come around to our help in the end. "She says she's doing it for my good," he repeated. "She is fair."

"Nonsense," I broke in, "She wants to hold you for herself and it's the only way she can. Legally! I'd be *ashamed* to prevent a man from going if he *wanted* to! If I couldn't keep a man because he wanted to stay with me more than anyone else, then I wouldn't have him at all. It's indecent. Oh, these *laws*! Always they're there, to force some unwilling person to do something he doesn't want to. If he doesn't *want* to, doesn't that mean he *shouldn't*? Of course it does. Why do we *have* these feelings unless they are to *tell* us things we should do or not? Well, how long does she expect to watch us? How long do we have to wait to show her whether we're suited or not?"

"I don't know, dear," Parmenter said, wearily. "We'll just have to see. Be patient. I'm sure it's going, to be all right."

"All right. We'll see if it is," I answered grimly.

The prevailing note of things was grim from that time. I resented my position too much to show any grace in it. It offended and outraged my vanity. I couldn't bear any feeling of coercion. Neither did I care about being on my good behavior so that Fanny should decide in my favor—should find me good enough for Parmenter! For, secretly, I felt I was too good for him.

I decided to act as though it were a fait accompli—and as though Parmenter and I were engaged to be married at the end of a few months. I went down town and bought a bolt of fine linen and a lot of lace and I cut out dozens of towels. I was making my trousseau! This was something I had never thought of before, but now it gave me a decided sense of certainty. I bought a carved wooden chest and had it in my room, and whenever Parmenter or my mother came, they found me (grimly) sewing. And, often I showed Parmenter the piles of linen things increasing in the chest. The day after he told me about Fanny's stance was my birthday and he wanted to give me something. He asked me what I wanted him to bring me.

"I want a gold cross to wear," I told him, "a plain gold cross to wear on a ribbon. That's what you mean to me," I told him, grim, "a cross." This was rather melodramatic and he laughed at me but humored me and brought me the cross. I wore it on a black ribbon. That and the little watch he had given me were the only things I ever had on me.[7]

It was inevitable, I suppose, but now that Fanny *knew* Parmenter and I loved each other, she couldn't be as complaisant as she had been before. She couldn't, of course, realize how we cared, or visualize our ardent hours together because she herself lacked ardor altogether. But she was afraid all the time. And, of course, jealous. So almost at once she found ways to prevent his being with me so much. I don't now how she did it, but she began to telephone me that this or that prevented him from coming over to see me, but always he found time to stop and send me a little bunch of freesias because he knew I loved it so much. There were always freesias in my room now, and I sitting there, grim, sewing on my trousseau! I who had always hated sewing! I learned to like it during those weeks. I made dresses and underclothes and folded them into the chest. They were, to be sure, rather elementary in design and workmanship, but they were my symbol of the future life and they satisfied me, or I pretended to myself that they did.

When Parmenter began to let things interfere with our time together, I didn't notice it at first, not for the first two or three times—but then I did. It came to me that it was Fanny that was preventing him from coming. I had a clairvoyant realization that she was determined and that he was not so strong and free as he had been when I first knew him: he was weak because he was tired, too tired to struggle very much. That he was losing his vital interest in me enough to let anything come between us, even for an hour, was bitter to me who would have gone to any lengths for him. . . .

I sat and sewed day, determined and decidedly grim! When he came, now, I went on sewing just to show him! I was becoming obsessed with my task—it began to mean everything to me now and the symbol overshadowed the reality! So I sewed when he came in, sewed when he was gay and wanted to make love, sewed when he was fagged and discouraged and wanted to be consoled. Like the old woman at the foot of the guillotine who "knitted and knitted with a look upon her face. . . ."[8]

III

My mother used to come and see John quite often. He, in his room with Nelly the nurse, was always glad of company. Then she would come and knock at my door and come in awkwardly with her feelings frozen in her, as mine were in our contacts. She saw me unaccountably sewing soon after I began it and asked me what I was doing.

"My trousseau," I replied, briefly, though my heart did skip a beat at admitting this to her.

"What do you mean?" she asked in a blank voice.

"Parmenter is going to make Fanny get a divorce and we're going to be married," I said, wetting my thread and trying to appear far more cool and matter of fact than I really felt! To speak of divorces as casually as that wasn't done in those days. Nobody we knew had divorced anybody except two or three women who had suffered the greatest cruelties and hardships.

"She'll never do it," said my mother, suddenly.

"Why won't she?" I asked.

"She's not that kind," she went on. I didn't want to talk about it. I felt a quick nausea in me. But I continued to sew and the chest was getting full.

But I was getting ill over this. I couldn't eat any more, scarcely took anything at my meals, and I hardly ever went out. I felt weak. Once I dragged myself up the street to my mother's, suffering all the way up the slight hill to North Street and when I got into the house my mother was having some women to lunch.

As I entered the room, they ceased talking, a constraint fell upon them from my presence; they were aloof and unfriendly and I left at once and went home in a great depression of spirit. I didn't want those women for my companions, but I didn't want them to feel towards me as they did. It made me feel very badly. And very lonely. Really all alone in the world, except for Parmenter: and I must continue to fight to achieve a perfect aloneness with him—to be the only one in his life.

Soon after this I stayed in bed, too weak to get up any more. Parmenter came with trouble in his eyes and sat by me on my bed. He didn't know what to say to help me. I searched his face and asked: "Does she say when, yet?" But he shook his head. He himself was in an impasse. He could not move Fanny a particle. When he went home and told her I was ill from the uncertainty and the worry, she said I hadn't the right stuff in me, and she asked him what kind of doctor's wife I would make!

"It's not sensible to act as she does. I have given her a chance to prove what she is—and how is she making use of it? To go to bed and sulk like a spoiled child, Jack, *that* isn't going to make me feel very certain about its success!" And she told him he would thank her some day.

Parmenter was really in despair sometimes. He lost interest more and more in his work and his patients began to drop away from him. It had leaked out *somehow* that he had tried to get rid of his wife—that excellent, that able Fanny, who had always managed everything for him so wonderfully, economizing for him, and helping him set a practice. There was a lot of sympathy going to Fanny in these days and quite a lot of criticism to Parmenter—"playing fast and loose with that girl! These doctors! They take advantage of their positions every time."

I sank a little lower every day and, because I couldn't sleep, Parmenter gave me some veronal powders. He gave me ten grains and when they were gone, I had the prescription made up again and doubled the amount at night so as to be certain of sleeping, certain that I would not lie there open-eyed listening to the wind in the leaves outside and whipping myself up into a frenzy of nervous fear and exasperation. Then, when Parmenter would telephone me he couldn't come, I would hastily swallow another couple of powders so as to get through the day without him, with *anything*, since I had not him! . . .

So I was constantly under the influence of this drug—and it made everything easier. The pain was not so sharp. But I was really growing very weak and emaciated from lack of nourishment and when Parmenter came I could only lie and look listlessly at him. He knew well enough what was the matter. Hadn't he told Fanny I would die if this fell through? He tried to persuade me to eat and brought me soup from the kitchen, where the two dismayed maids continued to run the machinery as best they could with no one at the head of the house and everything apparently going to pieces.

But I couldn't swallow the soup. I was willing myself back to the place where I had come from. If I could not go forward the direction of my wish, then I would retire. I knew this. I could have put it into words had I wanted to.

Parmenter looked wild now. Driven into a corner by that incredible Fanny, who never relented, never showed a sign of giving him up. He knew well enough I was dying, and really he didn't know what to do. He wanted to ask De Witt to come in and see me, but he had quarreled with him over me once when he had come in to see me in his absence, had insulted him. Things were uncomfortable there now. So he stopped Dr. Cary on the street and asked him to come in and see me, telling him that I wouldn't eat, and that he was worried. Dr. Charles had looked at him and told him he looked as though he needed sleep himself. And he said:

"Aren't you taking this rather hard—for you?" I can fancy how he grinned like an old faun. But he promised to drop in and see me. He stopped in that afternoon and came up into my room with that bursting good cheer that healthy doctors sometimes affect. He came up to the bed and took one of my hands that were always dripping wet now with the sweat of lowered vitality combined with nervous agitation.

"Well, well," he said, as though nonplussed. "Here's a pretty howdy-do! I never thought I'd see you lying down on your job! What's the trouble?" I didn't answer him. It didn't seem necessary and besides I was too tired and dulled.

"Well, what's Jack been doing to you to put you in this state?" he asked me, thinking maybe to provoke some response. But I answered, "Nothing," sulkily, and said no more.

"What have you eaten today?" he asked, looking around the room.

"Nothing," I repeated.

Then he got mad.

"Well, look here. I'm going to get you up out of this, see? You're a damned little fool. I thought you were a girl with a lot of spirit. You were, only a year or two ago when you and Seward [Cary] were running things to suit yourselves. And here I find you lying down on your back and looking like a dying duck in a thunderstorm! I'd hate to have Seward see you like this! Where's your telephone?"

"What are you going to do?" I asked.

"I'm going to call up your mother and tell her I'm bringing you up there where you'll get some attention, and then I'm going to call up a nurse and tell her to meet me there. See? That's what I'm going to do. So prepare your mind for it."

I didn't make any resistance. I couldn't. It crossed my mind that it was an anti-climax for me to return to my mother's house after all that had happened. He bundled me up in my big fur coat and took me there, and when they helped me on to the bed up in the spare room, I fainted. But I was more comfortable after that. My mother had a talk with Dr. Charles. The case was his, now. He made his ultimatum:

"Now I don't want Jack to come and see her for a few days. I'm going to feed her up and get her back—and when she's herself, something can be decided. It's no use leaving things in the air any longer."

I heard them talking together in the hall. I thought my destiny seemed more propitious than it had for some time. It was a relief to me to hear the problem that consumed me taken out of the silence of our circle and discussed by *others*: it took off some of the unbearable tension to have others, besides ourselves who were involved in it, talk it over coolly and seem to weigh the pros and cons. "Something can be decided!" These were blessed words to my ears, I who believed that the decision must be in my favor.

So now I had something to live for. The next morning the nurse brought warm water to the bedside to give me a bath. When she saw my body, she exclaimed, for my legs and back were covered with black and blue spots that I had acquired on the short journey from my bed to my bathroom at home—for I could not walk without falling from weakness, nor steer myself straight without bumping into things. When Dr. Charles came, I saw the nurse had said something to him, for he came and turned down the sheet and looked at these dark bruises.

"How did you get these, Mabel?" he asked me, very short.

"Fell down," I answered him economically, for I was still too weak to talk.

"I want you to tell me *the truth!*" he said, sternly. "How did you get these welts on here?"

I looked at him in amazement and then turned my face away from him. He didn't believe me! I couldn't credit it to him, but it was true. He turned away from me and muttered,

"She'll talk later," and went on his way. . . .

I grew better day by day now. But I was still very weak. Only my wish kept me going at all. My mother didn't say much or even come near me very much. She had John and his nurse there too, and she loved that. John she had always unreservedly loved from the beginning. But though she didn't say much, she knew what she meant to do and nothing ever held her when she wanted to go her way.

She waited till I was really out of the woods and then she went to see Mr. Gorham, Fanny's father. Now Mr. Gorham was a very lean, narrow-minded man of the old school, whatever that is. He was the kind that passed the plate in church and always carried an umbrella whether it rained or not. He and Mr. Evans had been old friends for years and had maintained a dignified and respectable relationship without any intimacy in it. Their mutual respect for *privacy* was so great, that had either one of them by accident lapsed into a confidence that touched on anything *real* in life, the other would have been struck dumb on the spot: his ears would have refused to receive it! Karl had told me that he used to hear Gorham reprimand his pretty, grey-haired wife for running across the street between the Evans' house and his in her little velvet slippers.

"It's not dignified," he used to tell her, "to go on the street in slippers."

My mother went to call on him down in his office. When I think of what that interview must have been, my flesh crawls even now! I never heard the conversation in toto. My mother is too inarticulate a woman to have been able to repeat it had she wanted to. But evidently what she said to him was, in effect:

"My daughter is dying because she wants your son-in-law; and he's gotten her into this so now he's got to get her out. Besides, they *both* want each other. Only your daughter won't give him up. Now you've got to go and tell her that she must give him up. Because my daughter wants him." Something like that, it must have been!

Mr. Gorham must have writhed internally. It was probably the most naked interview he ever had had in life, bar none. But there was some robust human quality in those older people upon which they seemed able to fall back in a tight place. They could always face the music and did, when they had to. The habits of the Victorian age did not annul the manhood and the womanhood that they masked; there generally were real men and women underneath those protective colorations. Far more then today, I think, where the expressive gestures and the freedom of speech conceal, quite often, a human void!

After he rose from his ducking into the elements whither my mother had plunged him, one fancies him giving himself a slight shake and, with a firmer grasp on his furled umbrella, replying: "Indeed. Jack and—ahem—Mabel. Quite so. Well, Mrs. Ganson, I will go and see Fanny. Doubtless we will, ahem, arrange matters." Something like that.

He went. And the next day mother came and asked me when I thought I would be able to get up—that Fanny wanted us to come to her house and talk things over. When? Immediately! If it was a question of that, strength returned in waves. It really did. It wasn't there—and, then it was there, as changeable as that, those fickle life forces! I told her to say we would go that very afternoon. My nurse helped me dress and I was so happy, though I trembled with weakness. It was the first time I had ever been physically weak like that, so very shaky. We drove over in our carriage at three. . . .

When we went into Fanny's room she rose from her chair. She had been crying and she couldn't speak to us. She just motioned to us to sit down. So we all sat down and for an instant there was silence and then, as though he couldn't bear it, Parmenter leaned his head over and buried his face in his hands. The talk began tentatively. My mother began by saying something; about things couldn't go on like this, that she couldn't see me go to pieces, that she was sorry if she had upset Mr. Gorham but she didn't see what else to do.

"Mrs. Ganson, there was no need to say that to my father. Why didn't you come to me first?" said Fanny.

"What have you done up to now? Nothing," said my mother.

"I've been waiting," said Fanny.

"For what?" asked my mother.

"For Jack," said Fanny.

"For Jack?" asked my mother. "For Jack to what?"

"Decide," answered Fanny implacably.

My heart leaped. If it was to be left to him, it was all right. But he got up and moved to the window across the room, away from us all. Then my mother turned to him. Her face was a mixture of all the emotions a woman can have about a man: love, pity, commiseration, and fear, distrust and contempt.

"And what do you *decide*?" she asked.

Again an instant of silence in the room, and then the man buried his head out of sight again and shook it slightly in loathing and despair.

"Parmenter!" I called him. "Parmenter, why don't you speak? Parmenter!"

But he never looked up or answered me, and the room turned round and I gave myself up to darkness. I don't know how we got home. But soon I was in bed again in the spare room, staring in front of me. My mother, that strange woman, came to me and stood by me and uttered the only wise thing I have ever heard her say: "Never mind. When a thing is taken from you, something better always comes to take its place," she said, "Always. . . ."

INTERLUDE

In a few days my mother sent me to New York with my nurse. We went to a small hotel in the forties somewhere, and I passed through the dreadful distress that one suffers when the object of one's heart is withdrawn. There is no pain to equal this. No pain to match the sense of a void within where once there was fullness and flow. Like raw nerves cut and left in trembling unattachment, my antennae were loose on the air and groping blindly in their empty surroundings. The whole of my self, body and spirit, had the habit of this man, of looking towards him, directed to him and received by him. Now he was not there and I was like one lost in space. My nerves screeched after him and my heart wept blood.

My sense of loss was ultimate. To tell the truth, I felt like a shell without its oyster. The depression of this time was bottomless. I did not write to him or hear from him except that every day or two a box of freesia and violets came to me—and I knew they must be from him. Afterwards I learned that he had asked my mother to arrange this!

My sitting room was full of all the lovely spring [1904]: flowers daffodils and hyacinths, and the windows were open, bringing in that wistful New York April atmosphere compounded of dust and asphalt and the sea—with the music of organ-grinders rising on the moist, spongy air. When shall I ever forget that first spring in New York? Never—never—. . . .

Very slowly I was beginning to raise my head out of the dust. By the force of my prayer that Parmenter would come back to me, I was beginning to emancipate myself from the need of his return. And then he came back one afternoon when the nurse was out and I was lying on my couch reading a new book of Henry James.[9]

Not a trace of pain was left, not a *memory* of it. It was as though a great piece of our lives had fallen away into oblivion and the two parts (the past when we had been happy together, and now that we were together again and happy) met and closed without a sign or a scar. We lay on the couch together and told each other happily all we had suffered in absence. It was *fun* to tell of the *degree* we had found ourselves capable of enduring. . . .

"I never thought anyone could mean so much to me darling. When you were gone it was just as though the bottom had fallen out of everything. I'd just as soon be dead as to try and go through that again. I don't know how we're going to manage but we will, somehow."

I asked him about it all, but he evaded me when it came to details. Maybe it had been impossible for him to abandon Fanny when he learned how she cared; maybe she had made him see it all as she did. But we were in a harder position than ever before. More and more people were in it now and watching and judging us all. Fanny had finally given way and told Violet Townsend all about it. And Mr. Gorham of course knew. Then Dr. Charles had come close, and as for my nurse, she had helped me through the worst days.

She came in later, while we were talking, and stood speechless to find Parmenter there. She gave her head a little shake of hopelessness and smiled ruefully. It was the expression of one who is used to building slowly, bit by bit, and to seeing her work knocked over as it nears completion. She didn't say anything, though. Parmenter shook her hand and exclaimed: "I just ran down for a night to see how you are getting along with my patient."

"I was getting along very well," she told him. She went out again and left us to dine together. The most remarkable change had come over the room. There was a tender and poetic atmosphere there about us that was exhaled by the poignant spring night and shining, singing flowers. The few things in the room that had any charm, silks and bright shawls, books and flowers, they all came to quick life and contributed to our delight. What a strange miracle takes place when the lethal chamber turns, of a sudden, to the bridal chamber. . . .

But it was so short! Only that evening—and then the nurse came back and he left me again, and was to take the early train back to Buffalo in the morning. But he had told me a lot about things. He had heard rumors that he might get dropped from the General Hospital. Dr. Charles had come to him after I had gone and begged him to be sensible again.

"You've been perfectly extravagant in this matter, Jack. People really won't stand it any more." Besides that, he was worried about Fanny. She had just escaped nervous prostration and was upset now at the slightest little thing. He'd hardly been able to leave her for a night, she was so jumpy. He had had to tell her he was going somewhere else: she couldn't have stood it if she'd known he was coming back to me again.

My mother wouldn't speak to him now when she met him on the street—but he supposed that was natural. Mr. Gorham, too, would hardly speak to him and many people were extremely cool when he saw them. But none of that bothered him as much as his loneliness. He just couldn't stand that. Besides, it seemed to him, he said, that night after night he heard me calling him to come back and it nearly drove him crazy because he felt drawn by everything in him to go; and yet he was held there by conventions and promises and unrealities. Finally it was too much for him; he had to come to me.

"I believe I would follow you to the end of the world," he told me.

"You know they want to send me to Europe," I said.

"I'll never let you cross the ocean without me," he cried. "If you ever do that, you'll find me with you. Life is too short to suffer the way we have. We will try and be patient and see if there is any chance to get our way right, and then if there isn't, we'll just take it into our own hands."

He had a plan, for the meantime. In three weeks, he had already told Fanny, he was going away for a month alone, to rest and forget all this trouble and find some fishing—up the St. Lawrence River—up in Canada somewhere. This was all true. He didn't mean to go alone, however, but with me. She had agreed to it. I think she, too, wanted a rest from the sight of him, if she could feel he was safe somewhere out of her sight. I think she was awfully tired of keeping tabs on him.

He told me just how it would be done. He had planned it all out. He was going to get Grandma Ganson to help us. He would go to her and tell her that he wanted to take my nurse and me on a trip and help nurse me into a stronger condition; and then get her to take care of John and his nurse, Nelly, while we were away and not tell anyone where we were. My mother would be away then—we all knew she had planned to go to Lenox for July. I forget all the details, but he had worked it out, the tale for Grandma Ganson, and part of it was the truth and part of it was lies. He did not intend to have any nurse along. That was certain!

BEGINNING OF THE END

When I joined Parmenter in Quebec, he said I startled him by my increased attractiveness. He had never found me so wonderful, so glowing, as I was now. Well, I felt wonderful. I was brimming full of spiritual vitality and gleaming with the lambency of the burning vision I had held before me. . . .

We went on a boat to an island somewhere up the river and there on that island he had a house engaged for us. I don't know how he had worked it all out, but there it was, a summerhouse with flowers growing down the path that led to the swinging gate and beyond the gate another path to the beach and a boat landing.

Canada and the St. Lawrence! That river has left no picture in my memory, though I lived on its brink for several weeks and in that house. But there is nothing of it left in me to tell about. I was happy and alive again for a little while, a very little while, and then a curious nervousness and weakness came on me. I was quite shaky and upset. Parmenter and I had to get our own meals and neither he nor I knew much about cooking and very little about cleaning up. The food was brought in a boat from somewhere; I suppose he ordered it. But we certainly had no picnic there on that island.

The old ennui came back to me when I was with him alone for every day and night, and the color went out of everything. When I was very weak and troubled, he gave me a little morphine and that helped me for a few hours; and he also gave me strychnine tablets. He was moody, too, puzzled.

One day when we were eating, to our surprise a knock came on the door. And when Parmenter went to see who it was, he found his brother standing there. I had never seen this brother. Richard, his name was. He was much younger than Parmenter and was just finishing at the medical school. He lived with his parents and Fanny and Parmenter saw him only occasionally. He was a big, rather common looking fellow, I saw, as Parmenter brought him in.

They both looked very self-conscious and disturbed. I felt an enemy in him immediately. I recognized by the look in his eyes that he was an enemy. So I was frozen as long as he was in the room. We gave him something to eat and conversation was naturally rather forced. Then Parmenter lighted his pipe and said: "Well, Richard, what is it? Out with it!"

"Fanny is here," said he.

"*Where?*" exclaimed Parmenter, looking awfully annoyed.

"Well, I'll tell you. She got wind that you had gone away with—Mrs. Evans, and she had no one to go to. She thought of me. She came and asked me to bring her up here. She's staying down the river at the Traymore in Quebec. She came so that people wouldn't think you were here alone with Mrs. Evans. She came to protect you, really." He said this last with a touch of contempt in his voice. One could see plainly he was disgusted.

Well, Parmenter was certainly disgusted too. He couldn't bear to be spied on and followed up like this. It offended everything in him. As for me, I had a new rush of life in me on the instant. My waning vitality burned up again in pride and resentment. Parmenter flicked his eyes towards me and noted my rage; and, getting up, he took Richard out into the garden. I started after them and vowed to myself that that *lout* and that meddlesome Fanny should never get the better of me.

After what seemed a long time to me, Parmenter came back into the house alone, leaving his brother waiting outside. He looked old and tired and all in. He knew, I suppose, he'd have two women battling over him again. "Well, I suppose we'll have to face the music again," he sighed as he sank into a chair. We were both furious at this interference. It didn't matter at all that we hadn't been enjoying ourselves very much. We wanted to go our own way whether we liked it or not.

"What are you going to do?" I asked him in a hard voice. I had taken up the fight once more.

"Well, she has summoned me," he said, "And I suppose I'll have to go. Richard says she's about worn out with worry and so on. I told him I'd go down tomorrow and talk it over with her."

Instantly, the dreadful menace of isolation without any hope in it, struck me again in the heart and I flung myself on him.

"Oh, Parmenter! *Don't* go! *Don't* leave me here alone. I can't stand it, I *can't* stand it here alone—and seeing you go off with her. I can't stay. You won't!"

Poor man! He was terribly torn. He knew he had to go and he knew I was really not in any condition to be left alone on an island either by day or night, and he couldn't make the trip and return in less than twenty-four hours.

Well, Richard stayed that night with us. He had to. The boat that would take him away only came by in the morning. He disliked very much having to stay there. One could see that.

We had a terrible time, Parmenter and I. I was fighting like a tiger to keep him from Fanny, but women could draw him to them. I knew that. Fanny was calling him and he had to go. I was so exhausted by morning that I couldn't get up. Parmenter made some coffee and toast and brought it up to me and he was alarmed at my unearthly color and my jumpy pulse. When the boat came in sight of us, when he saw it from our window, he came to me and gathered me in his arms and held me tight and begged me to help him!

"Don't make it so hard for me," he implored me. "I am so worried about you. Now look, I am going to give you a little injection of morphine to tide you over the day and I'm going to leave two half-grains here on the table. You take one tonight and one in the morning and then tomorrow at dinnertime I'll be back. Please, dear, try and be a woman. I'll fix everything the very best I can, you know I will. I'll arrange *something* with Fanny. We'll have our little vacation through just the same."

While he talked he fixed his needle and, pinching up my arm, he plunged it in and hastily kissing me he moved away. The boat was docking. As his steps fell on the wooden stairs descending away from me, I dragged myself out of bed and snatched up the gold cross he had given me that lay, overnight, on the bureau, and flung it after him, hitting his cheek as he turned to look back.

"Get out of my life," I screamed. "Never come back, I hate the sight of you. You kill me!"

He rushed back and seized me with a sort of groan and put me down on the bed and kissed me again and again. Then he hung the cross around my neck and ran once more down the stairs and down the flowery path to the boat and away. . . .

When Parmenter came back, I was weak and cool and, feeling the lack of exhausted morphine, I asked him almost at once to give me a little more. So he did.

He told me then about Fanny. How worn and pale she was. She seemed to him to have lost pounds that she could ill afford to part with, just in the short time since he had left her. She had broken down and begged him to be sensible, not to ruin his life and mine and hers—and all of us, in fact. He told her that I was ill, too, that he was going to get me well and then he would come home. But she said she would have to stay there at the hotel, that it was the only way to keep people from breaking out against him, that everybody was ready to throw him over if he didn't behave himself now. She had cried and carried on and he had been dreadfully bored but had finally calmed her down. And then that evening, when he was sitting reading in their room, she had broken forth again, very strangely for her.

"I had brought up some newspapers," he explained to me. "You know I haven't laid eyes on a paper since we left Quebec! Well, I was sitting there reading and I had forgotten all about her." (And me, too, I added to myself.) "When all of a sudden she jumped up and pulled the sheet out of my hands and began to harangue me!"

"'You stupid, unfeeling *man*,' she shouted, 'Why do I waste my life on you! You're not worth it! You're not worth either Mabel or me. You're not worth any *woman's* suffering the way you made us suffer! You—you,' she screamed, glaring, at me. And then she called me, 'You toad!'" laughed Parmenter. "Gad, I never saw Fanny excited like that! I don't know what got into her. But pretty soon she gave up and was crying again."

"Well, what on earth have you decided to *do* now?" I asked, numb enough but still interested.

"I told her I'd have to stay with you for a few days and then I'd go down and stay with her there to close people's mouths if that's what she wants. And I've arranged to have a nice little nurse come up and stay with you while I'm away. You won't mind, will you, dear? It's the only thing I can see to do. . . ."

The days passed by, dull and unrelieved. I thought I saw a look of relief on Parmenter's face when the boat came that would bring the nurse and take him back to Fanny. But I didn't feel much about it. I only *saw* it. The nurse was pretty, with red hair and white skin and a Canadian accent. Parmenter instructed her what to do and how to give me injections of morphine at certain times, but no more than he said. He left quietly. We were both quiet and unemotional. So for three days and nights that stranger with the red hair and I lived together on an island. . . .

At night the nurse tried to question me about it all. She couldn't understand, but she suspected. Her own experience had evidently taught her something of mine.

"These men, they have it easy," she said. "They know how to slip through." She took her needle out from its shiny box to prepare my dose, and when she finished with mine and squeezed up the flesh of her arm between finger and thumb and gave herself a jab.

"Yes, I use it," she said. "It helps one along."

The rest of this visit is more dream-like than the first part to my memory. But the time came when this thing called Parmenter's vacation was over. He had taken the house for a month and the tenants who were to follow us were coming in two days. We had to leave. And the plan was that Fanny and Parmenter would go for a few days to another place on the river, and I should go back to Buffalo to Grandma Ganson's.

In a kind of dazed despair I passed dream-like on my way. I went from boat to train and to another train, and finally I was in the noisy, dirty Buffalo station with my bag in my hand and too much, too much suffering in my heart. There seemed nothing ahead but an endless repetition of these terrible separations. I could never bear the way Parmenter took me up and then dashed me down again on to the rocks. It was not good enough. Life like this was just not good enough.

I drove up to Grandma Ganson's and went in. She sat there in her vestibule in her usual interested way, taking everything that happened for granted. She had the most innocent perceptions. I kissed her and went in and she chattered. "Go right up to the spare room, your father's room, my dear. The baby is out, but he'll soon be in. Are you better? Did you pick up some? You look fine!" she exclaimed obtusely. People always looked well when they came back from trips!

I went up to the spare room, there where Parmenter and I had accepted each other, where I had first demanded his love and he had told me it was already mine. I saw everything was as before: the big walnut bed, the stiff bureau containing the vanilla bean in the top drawer, and the portrait of Mary Shillito staring down at me more pinkly than in real life.

I went into the bathroom (that bath that Grandma had had placed there for my father to fly to when he got mad at my mother) and I turned on the hot water and took a long, comforting bath. The pain in my heart continued to weigh me down; it was too heavy to endure. After I was dry, I put on a clean nightgown and brushed out my hair and braided it as for the night. Then taking a glass of water to my bedside, I put it there, ready. I drew the bottle of strychnine tablets from my bag, the tablets I had promised Parmenter to continue to take three times a day. And pouring them all out into the palm of my hand, I swallowed them-one-two-three big swallows of water—till they were down. And then lay back and waited with my eyes on Mary Shillito.

But, oh! I hadn't known it would be like that! A cataclysm, a hurricane of unseen forces seized me and nearly broke me—and then subsided. I sprang to my feet with desperate energy and flung open my door: "Grandma! Grandma!" I yelled, but my voice that began in terror, ended in a muffled roar as the convulsion came on me and bent me backwards in an arc, and I was flung unconscious on the floor.

The first miracle of my life occurred then. DeWitt told me over and over he would never understand it, how he had saved me. That much strychnine had been enough to kill several men. Anyway they got him there in time and he did things and I was alive. Terribly weak and about smashed in every way, but alive. Something stronger than love or death wanted to go on in me. . . .

De Witt drew from me some more facts than he had known about Parmenter and me. He didn't, like Dr. Charles, leave it to us to talk over and decide! He tried to take a hand in our sad game. "You've got to go away now, Mabel," he said. "You've come to the end right here and now. Go to Europe and stay a year. Take John and be somewhere where its lovely and you'll get better little by little. This is enough, isn't it?"

Tenacious, I had the habit of Parmenter in my blood and nerves. Obstinate, I wanted him even now. "I can't go abroad without him De Witt," I said. "I promised him I wouldn't cross the ocean without him." De Witt looked at me kindly with his beautiful, expressionless eyes. He had no fire, no smoke, nothing but brain.

"Will you go if Jack tells you to go?" he asked me.

"Yes," I answered, stoutly. "I know he won't, so I'll say yes." Then De Witt told me he was going to find Jack and ask him if I should go or not. This threw me into a curious trouble, though I was certain it would make no difference. He left a nurse with me and some medicine and he left that night.

At midnight the nurse stood by me with the bottle of chloral, a spoonful ready for me.

"What is love?" I asked her. "Do you know anything about it?"

"Bitter-sweet," she answered, sentimentally, a blindness swept over me and I seized her bottle and put it to my lips.

All that night the signs of the zodiac turned to blue flames and pursued me round the room. I was always just ahead of them, but in mortal fear, for they were devils. Then I lost consciousness even of these—and remained out for three days.

There were two doctors with me when I came to myself: De Witt and a stranger. I turned to look for Parmenter, but he was not there. The doctors talked among themselves. "You said she'd never come out of it, but you see?" De Witt was saying. He brought me water to drink.

"I never thought she could," said the stranger.

That evening De Witt came to me again. He was very sweet. He told me about it like a story. "I went up there and found Fanny and Jack were staying at a little hotel on the beach. Jack looked stubborn when he saw me. He knew I meant business. I didn't say anything at first, but I made him take me out on the water in his sailboat.

"When we were way out and he had loosened up a bit, I told him what I wanted. I said, 'Jack, there's only one thing you can do for Mabel now and that's send her away. Send her for a year and give her a chance to see things differently. You've nearly killed her. Do this for her now, will you?' He looked hard and sad and uncertain. 'She can't stand one bit more,' I went on. He stood by the mast looking out over the water thinking. He certainly was up against it.

"I saw him considering and I took out the paper and pencil I had taken with me, just for that. 'Here, Jack,' I said, 'write her a note and tell her you want her to go. She will do as you tell her.' He looked at the paper and then at me, then he shook himself and sat down and wrote this and gave it to me. He had tears on his cheeks but his voice was like steel to me when he said: 'Take it and get out. I never want to see you again.' Here is his note. Read it. You see he says, 'Go.'"

I took the crushed paper, but the words danced around at first: "My dearest— Do as they say and go. Try and get well so that everything will come out for us as we want it. Forgive me. Parmenter."

I looked up at De Witt and I felt my eyes shine. "All right, I'll go," I said. Why not? I *knew* he would meet me on that boat. I knew he couldn't let me cross the ocean without him. I tried to sit up but I was weak.

"I want to go soon," I said. "When?"

"As soon as ever we can manage it," replied DeWitt, gaily. "This story is going to end all right yet."

They bustled about and made preparations! Two nurses, one for me and one for John—lots of packing and fussing. Sheets brought to me to sign, arrangements made, hurry, false cheer and departure, soon, quite soon, and orders and anxiety.

I remember nothing but my steadfast faith bearing me towards Parmenter. We were off at last for Germany, I thought, in secret. To those breakfasts on balconies and to an end of pain. I struggled somehow, in my weakness, onto the steamer. And I wasn't surprised that his face was not among those of the other passengers as we moved amongst them to our cabins. "He will wait till we start, and then come to me," I said to myself.

But the great ship moved out from shore on the July blue water and he never came to find me. Then I didn't stop to wonder very long. I knew, quickly, as soon as I saw there was no hope. He had really sent me away from him over the ocean that he had made me promise never to cross without him. And in a flash, as though a swift knife cut him away, something in me divided that man from the fatal admixture of our two beings and thrust him out and away from me then and there forever.

That night I took the gold watch he had given me and the gold cross, and gave them to my nurse. "I don't want them any more. Do you?" I asked her. "If you don't want them, I'll throw them overboard," I told her. So she took them, though she didn't like to. And I had, for an instant, a strange, an ugly wish that someday Parmenter would see them on her and know what a careless thing I had done with them. And that was the end for me. . . .

Parmenter lost everything then. Quite soon he was asked to resign from all the hospital boards he had been on for so long. His practice fell away from him . . . people avoided him. . . .

He and Fanny left Buffalo and went to live in Geneva [New York]. I was told he and she used to drive about the country there in a buggy—visiting an occasional sick person, like a young doctor just beginning. . . .

~~~~~~~~~~~~~~~~~~~

The end of Mabel's memoir bears an uncanny resemblance to the last lines of F. Scott Fitzgerald's 1933 novel, *Tender Is the Night*, when the once-brilliant and accomplished psychoanalyst, Dick Diver, moves from one small town in upstate New York to ever smaller ones (including Geneva, where Dr. Parmenter ended up). He has spiraled downward into tawdry sexual escapades and unethical medical practices, until his ex-wife, Nicole, the victim of an incestuous relationship with her wealthy father, loses track of him. "In any case," Fitzgerald concludes, "he is almost certainly in that section of the country, in one town or another."[10]

Mabel reviewed the novel for the *New York Herald Tribune*, writing about the story as a reversal of the Orpheus myth: "In these days it is Orpheus who must be saved," because Eurydice is a "kind of 'Typhoid Mary'" who carries "potential battle, murder and sudden death in her wake. He sacrifices himself for her—." One has to wonder if Mabel was thinking of herself and the havoc she had helped to wreak during her affair with Parmenter. Fitzgerald saw his wife Zelda as a major cause of his own ruination. He was very moved by Mabel's review and wrote to thank her: ". . . your appreciation has given me more pleasure than any other." When Mabel edited *European Experiences* for publication in 1935, she left out the story of her love affair with Parmenter.[11]

CHAPTER THREE

Family Affairs

The best I have had in life has been finding Tony in this world: the one who
stirred my heart where all before him had exercised my sense of power, so that
sexual tension was more important to me than fulfillment, and the threshold
more significant than entry. I do not doubt that if I had missed Tony, I could
not have written the review of my life that has helped me to understand it.
—MABEL DODGE LUHAN, "Family Affairs"

O N T H E C O V E R page of "Family Affairs," Mabel noted that it was "unde-
leted, unshown, unpublished."¹ The least coherent of all her unpublished
memoirs, it covers the years 1923 to 1933, including Mabel's relationships with
her mother and her son, and her son's first marriage; Mabel's analysis with
Jungian psychologist Frances Wickes, which focused on Tony Lujan's infidelities; Georgia O'Keeffe's arrival in New Mexico in the summer of 1929; and
Mabel's decision to publish her memoirs. I begin with excerpts from Mabel's
"journal intime," about the days surrounding her marriage to Tony, on April 18,
1923, which Mabel wrote to and for her friend, and her son John's mother-in-
law, Alice Corbin Henderson.

Written in the white heat of the moment, Mabel's letter is a fascinating indi-
cator of the doubts and confusions she was having about marrying Tony; it also
provides a first glimpse of a less romantic Tony Lujan than the one who appears
in her published works. The threats talked about here are related to advice that
many of her friends in the New Mexico Association of Indian Affairs were
giving her. Both Mary Austin and Alice Corbin Henderson, among others,

told her that her relationship with Tony was causing problems with the Indian Bureau that could harm the work that they were doing against federal legislation that threatened to undermine Pueblo land rights. They had urged the marriage and seem to have frightened both Mabel and Tony into it.

~~~~~~~~~

"Journal Intime"[2]

Tony is coming back today and a new direction must be chosen. His & Candelaria's divorce was probably granted yesterday at Raton. Now Tony & I must marry or separate or the Indian Bureau will be after me to use as a scapegoat to break up the Indian work.

It doesn't feel *right* to give up Tony. For real *reasons* & for feeling ones. The real ones are a certain hidden responsibility about him and then the one of my having taken him out of the Pueblo life and made him live with us all & see a different way of living—a way that seems better to him in some manner & worse in others. Our *talking*—like flies buzzing—seems of no good use to him. But our responsible ways to each other seem good. He has lost his place in the tribal ceremonial life through me. Jealousy—on the part of the Indians—he says it is. He says he has not failed in his Indian duties—that he has done nothing to cause this indignity. Just that they are jealous because he has this life here.

Tony Romero has promised me he can be put back in his place if he will accept it. Neither he nor I know if Tony will. Maybe he has lost his sense of the significance of those endlessly recurring ceremonies. I don't know what they consist in. Seems that they have each to take their turn & go long climbs up the mountain to get certain herbs that will be used in the ceremonies. . . . When he was still a part of it all it used to be very hard for me. I used to lie awake & wonder & wonder. He seemed so lost to me. I wondered what he was doing. If there were Indian women in it too. If maybe he wasn't at a ceremonial at all but with some woman—out in the forest or fields or sagebrush—spending himself—living. So I think my presence took him away from the Indian rituals as much as the Indians put him out. And now does he want to go back? Will he feel the significance of it as he did before? I don't know.

But in our life together here there is not enough incentive to activity for either of us. We don't *have* to earn our bread & meat. And I am not rightly energized so that I move without having to. Most of the world is like this. Most of the finest things wouldn't get *done* unless people were impelled by the pressure of personal *need*. . . . All our projections—our beauty & science—are propelled by this. Nearly everyone sits down & *talks* if he has an income.

The Indian life that we feel is so glowing & alive has this at the bottom of it. I asked Tony if he would be happier if he were back in the pueblo living the Pueblo life—*doing* more. He laughed & said: "What is the Pueblo life? Do you know? It means getting up in the morning & . . . spending all day looking for an *egg* to take home. Working for it—or begging for it or stealing it. All day long looking for that egg—there's nothing in *that*." Of course that's putting it baldly but that's the structure of it, I guess. Tony thinks very straight & clearly. He never fools himself. He can only do things if the real motive for doing them is present. He doesn't want to go off hunting unless it's *really to get meat*. It seems amateurist & faked to him to go hunting for hunting's sake. . . .

But I can't just pretend I haven't any money & do it any way. I have to have the economic pressure just like all the great artists & great scientists & builders of the world! Tony & I were put together, in my feeling, for some ultimate purpose. I believe in a Plan. One sees it as one looks *back* on life; no matter how weird or mixed or untidy & idiotic life seems while one is in the midst, as one looks back one sees Purpose and Plan—where one has been used deliberately—pushed here & there—& put up against things—out of which order & strength & beauty have been forged. All the horror & pain & worry that we've gone through since I just saw Tony in his house—& then deliberately chose to take him for mine, & he to leave it all & come with me—have taught lots of things as we went but only now, it seems to me, are we approaching anything like the *beginning* of intention in it—this matter of marriage that will be a real change of life. For Tony tried hard at first to keep his life & have me too. He tried to keep his wife until he was forced to choose & let her go—& his house, & his tribe and his Indian ceremonials.

And I tried to keep my life—to give white people the chance to disbelieve I was living with & loving *an Indian*; to keep my habits of life, my white ways, my idle purposeless life of talk & pleasure wishing. But Tony let all his go & I kept mine until I was pushed up against sacrifice *hard* and *forced* to capitulate & let it all go if it *wants* to. There is where we are today. Everything can fall away from me if it *wants* to when I openly take Tony & marry him. I leave the world no choice not to know.

So we have to make a new form of life now. The old form we have lived in for five or six years is outworn or we wouldn't be driven to break the crystal & build another. Our life has to be re-symbolized. A new symbol must be chosen—to have more *living*. We were almost become that lifeless things—an institution, Tony and I! That's been a weariness lately. Not that Tony & I were through with each other, that we ceased to make each other feel & grow & expand!—because that's the one thing we do do to each other. The only thing that seems to make each of us stretch a spiritual muscle—or emotional tendon is each other. Therefore we each need the other. But we were bored with the form of our life. That was what made Lawrence say that I'd be a different woman doing my work & Tony out hunting. Lawrence was intelligent enough to see that Tony & I were both bored doing nothing—*having to do* nothing except take trips for our pleasure or to amuse our guests. A round of unimpeded pleasure ceases to be amusing. Going *to see* things for the sake of seeing them only, not to utilize them somehow afterwards, is absolutely palling & appalling. I envy Mary Austin her personal ambition & her economic pressure! . . .

Tony comes back today. It's been a terribly depressing 3 weeks. Turning things over & over. Facing giving up Tony because of family, people—you all—the world. Because of deteriorating Tony, by an easy life—because of lack of outlet with Tony—because of everything one could think of. But always coming back to one central truth. Tony can make me live, given the right conditions, & grow! I can make him live & grow. We are not wrong but our situation is. Somehow I must get it changed. We will get married soon I guess, & maybe 'things' will begin to move then. I suppose the noble thing to do would be to write my mother & say I was doing a thing she would disapprove & render up her $1000 a month income to me. But it wouldn't be a real motive—it would only be that one of trying to improve one's own situation. This must work out *true* & *real* & *square*—like geometry, to be any good. We will see if it does!

~~~~~~~~~~

In "Family Affairs," Mabel refers to a theme that she will develop further in "The Statue of Liberty," the sense of racial self-betrayal that she sometimes felt because of the of discomfort that her marriage to Tony caused her mother and son, although they liked him and got along well with him:

> I suffered, in secret, and sometimes burned with a white heat, with a flush that flooded my whole body, when I had a momentary realization of what I had done. When I identified myself in my imagination with my race, and knew I had broken a barrier and left it and crossed to the other side to stand with these dark men, their river of blood dividing me forever from my own kind, I had a sense of drowning horror at having done the impossible act. But when I was just myself and disentangled from my family, I knew I had done what I was meant to do, and I had a deeper feeling of rightness than I had ever had before. . . . So that when I lived with Tony, it was more like being on a visit in a strange country, but when I married him, I became naturalized, one with him and his,

accepting the good and bad of it, and above all, the different, and making it mine. No one who has not actually married into another race can realize in imagination what a plunge it can be.

MABEL BEGINS THE memoir with the arrival in Taos of her son John and his new wife Alice "junior," the daughter of William and Alice Corbin Henderson. They were married on December 20, 1922, and were returning from an extended honeymoon in Europe in the summer of 1923, not long after Tony had infected Mabel with syphilis. Mabel's only hint of this is her reference to her "distraction" when she talks about why she could not attend to the young newlyweds: "my nerves were ragged that summer. . . . I was quivering and raw and disgusted with life."

John and Alice first settled in Santa Fe where, from the fall of 1923 through 1926, John ran the Flying Heart Development Corporation. After it was bankrupted, he returned to Buffalo and joined the firm of Brody, Herod, and Co., becoming a successful broker, the pride of his grandmother Sara, and the bane of his mother, because he had chosen to follow in the path of the family she had repudiated.

In 1929, in Buffalo, John built a magnificent Spanish hacienda that made his mother's eccentric home in Taos look jerrybuilt by comparison. After the stock market crash, both Evans's income and his marriage were bankrupt. Mabel interfered, on the grounds that she wanted to make her son happy. She encouraged him to go to Mexico in January 1932, where he bought a home in Taxco; she also encouraged him to have an affair with a young woman who was visiting her home in the summer of 1932, and who was devastated, according to Mabel, when she learned that John didn't intend to marry her. At the time Mabel was writing "Family Affairs," John and Alice had divorced (December 1933), and John was having an affair with the woman who would become his second wife that same year, the writer Claire Spencer, whom Mabel would come to dislike even more intensely than she did her first daughter-in-law.

John had five children between his two marriages. A handsome, charming, and intelligent man, he was also at times, at least in the experience of his youngest daughter, Bonnie Evans, "melancholy, violent, and perverse." In a letter to me, and in an unpublished memoir, Bonnie asserted that John had been sexually inappropriate with her as a child.[3] Throughout the 1930s, Mabel wrote Una Jeffers about his shortcomings. She accused John of being weak, effeminate, and unable to get over his "Mother complex." Her letters leave the uncomfortable impression that she encouraged in John an unhealthy attachment to her, even while deploring it, an impression that is reinforced by some of the poems that he wrote to her during the 1920s, which have an erotic tinge.[4] The "Oedipal scripts" that occur throughout Mabel's memoirs were part of her son's writing as well, and if his daughter Bonnie was remembering correctly, of his life.

Evans had many careers, including trying his hand at fiction writing during the 1930s. The second of the two novels that he published, *Shadows Flying* (1936), is an overwrought story about brother-sister incest and homosexuality. John wrote it as an homage to Robinson Jeffers, whose poetry he loved. Jeffers used the trope of incest as a way of talking about western civilization's narcissism; John turned it into unconvincing melodrama. After he married Claire Spencer, they lived for a while in Carmel, in order to be near the Jeffers. *Shadows Flying* infuriated Mabel. The loving inscription John wrote to Una and Robin might well have fed her underground discontent with them, although that was based primarily on Robinson Jeffers's disinterest in writing poetry about the Taos Indians. Mabel's rage burst forth in the summer of 1938 when she encouraged an affair between Jeffers and a woman guest at her home, which led to Una's attempted suicide in Mabel's bathroom.[5]

From 1943 to 1945 John served as Superintendant of the Pueblos for New Mexico, at which time he worked with reformers who were promoting a bill that would guarantee New Mexico's Indians the right to vote, a bill that was passed in 1948. During the early 1950s, John spent time in both Tehran, Iran, and in Israel, working for the U.S. State Department under the "Point Four Program," which was a part of Truman's Cold War containment policy in the Middle East. In the 1960s, when he came back to Taos for a while after Mabel's death, he worked on the restoration of Blue Lake to the Taos Indians. This was a project started by John Collier, in the 1920s, when he first became active in Indian Rights issues. Evans died in 1977, in West Brookfield, Maine, where he and Claire Spencer had bought a home in 1945.[6]

Frances Wickes

Frances Wickes (1875–1967) was a Jungian analyst in New York City for forty years. She studied with Jung in Zurich in the 1920s and had several clients who were artists and writers, including Martha Graham. She wrote plays, stories, and poetry for children. Her best-known work is *The Inner World of Childhood* (1927). Mabel sought her out for therapeutic guidance during one of the critical periods in her relationships with Tony, from the fall of 1928 through the summer of 1929. She saw Wickes in New York City for six months, in the winter of 1928–1929, when the analyst insisted she live there alone in order to learn to be independent of Tony.

Mabel might have turned to a Jungian analyst because of her interest in Jung's theories of the racial unconsciousness, his decentering of the ego in favor of a larger "Self," and his early views that "the psyche has knowledge of what is good for it, a capacity to regulate itself, and even to heal itself." Mabel was attracted to Jung's mysticism, to his interest in finding a "synthetic under-standing of matter and psyche," and to the role that he gave to the feminine in his belief that male and female forces—the animus and anima—needed to be balanced within each individual.[7] Jung's ideas about gender were, how-ever, no less traditional than Freud's. When Wickes told Mabel she needed to control her overactive "animus," as Mabel writes in the Wickes section of "Family Affairs," it was no more helpful to her than when Jelliffe told her to learn to be passive rather than dominant in her sexual relations. Several of Mabel's letters to Wickes reveal the ongoing difficulties that she suffered and instigated throughout her marriage with Tony. But they are also revealing, in both bitter and humorous ways, of her sense that she never belonged, in some fundamental way, to the community of Taos and, in particular, to Taos Pueblo, in spite of her making them one of the foundations of her life's work and reputation.

In her first undated letter to Wickes, Mabel notes that both she and Tony had turned to other people to love over the past few years: "Tony has been lov-ing someone (or several) others & really had no love left in him for me," leading her to feel as though she had "no power & little energy or wish to live," which she says is exacerbated by her going through her "change of life." He claimed he turned to others because she had.[8]

Mabel had intensely emotional, if not sexual, "love affairs" with other men during the 1920s, including writers D. H. Lawrence (1922–1925) and Jean Toomer (1925–1926). Her passion for Toomer came close to destroying her marriage and drove Tony to suicidal behavior. Mabel gave Toomer fourteen thousand dollars in the hopes he would start a Gurdjieff center in Taos. She gave D. H. Lawrence's manuscript of *Sons and Lovers* to A. A. Brill to pay for the analysis of a man named "Everett" with whom she had been "in love" for a while. In one long segment "Family Affairs," she writes about her flirtation with Eliseo Concha, her son John's "blood brother" from Taos Pueblo, which she claims ended in nothing more than a kiss. Tony had sexual relations with many different women, perhaps including his former wife; and he had at least one, and perhaps two, long-term mistresses over the course of their marriage.[9]

By March 20, 1929, Tony and Mabel had cleared things up, to the point that Mabel expresses her wonder and pride in Tony's attraction to women, as well as a sense of humor about her "sexual possessiveness." She writes Wickes about "a wonderful conversation" she had with Tony in which she confessed her mistakes. He told her that it was not necessary to name them, and then said: "It makes no difference what you do. I always love you & you love me." He explained their interest in new people as "fresh fruit." On April 9, Mabel writes to Wickes, with startling (and short-lived) equanimity, that Tony is repentant about his love affairs of the past winter. Mabel believed, and Tony apparently admitted to her, that he had an affair with Marion Shevky during the winter of 1928. Marion was a medical doctor who was married to Eshref Shevky, the man who uncovered syphilis at Taos Pueblo (see chapter 4). Mabel then writes of Tony: "He is so attractive to women & women to him there is always something in the air! I know we can hardly regulate these matters!" By April 20, Mabel and Tony are "the dearest of friends—depending on each other—trusting each other—& putting each other first." But, of course, he still wants others. To reassure her, he wryly tells her, "Never mind—pretty soon I be old." Mabel reports that she doesn't have "any of *that* life left in me—but I have so much *life*!"[10]

In May, Mabel is suffering from a weak heart, low blood pressure, and hyperthyroid, and from rumors in the "Mexican" community that she had "dropped dead," which led to many offering condolences to Tony. Mabel had friends in the Hispano community, and a godson, Eliseo Armijo, whom she put through college. But the community's prevailing opinion of her was less than favorable, including a legend they created that she was responsible for bringing with her from New York the sunflowers that "invaded" their crop fields in Taos Valley. Mabel's multiple affairs and marriages violated their values, and her stereotypical views of "Mexicans" as fatalistic, shiftless, and driven in their religious rites by masochism, were highly insulting them.[11]

That month, Mabel landed in St. Joseph's Sanitarium in Albuquerque. Her doubts about Tony returned in full force, most likely because of the presence of Georgia O'Keeffe, whom she had been trying to attract to Taos for several years. When Mabel saw her at an Indian dance in the spring, she convinced her to come to Taos, which she did, in May. "Of course," she writes Wickes in an undated letter, "its [*sic*] just wonderful that O'Keefe [*sic*] will be here this summer & that *at last* this country will really be painted." Mabel humorously revised the meaning of what her marriage meant, while she was in the hospital. Ansel Adams was also in the hospital, recovering from appendicitis, and his wife Virginia was apparently spending "all her spare time with Tony": "I tell you in confidence but I know Georgia O'Keefe [*sic*] is terribly drawn to him & I fancy she *needs* him or someone like him (& there are few of him about!). After her cerebral, old, neurotic Stieglitz. And I *love* her & feel like being generous but Oh dear! This ego!

"Here it is the same! All the women in the place like Tony! They do little things for him. . . . Maybe that was mission when I married Tony! To provide a bridge between Indians & white people! It is made easy for them to pass over to Tony since I took the initial step & made the trail! My goodness! That's a fine mission for a selfish egotistic woman to find herself involved in!"[12]

In June 1929, Mabel was diagnosed with fibrous tumors in her uterus and advised to have a radical hysterectomy, which she decided to have done in Buffalo, in July. When she returned to Taos in the fall, she went into the netherworld of one of her cyclical depressions. During this time, Mabel wrote to Wickes two of her most revealing letters, about the mixture of fear, pain, jealousy, need, and love that marked her and Tony's relationship, and about her sense of outsiderness from Taos Pueblo: for all her devotion to the pueblo, her various philanthropic and political work on behalf of the tribe, and her deep bond with some of Tony's family members, she had never penetrated the community or been embraced by it. She first writes Wickes that she has never been honest with Brill about what she "really feels" about Tony: "I have been absolutely loyal to something wonderful in him & therefore could never utter anything critical about him or admit any lack to myself. Because you understand I care more for something in him than for anything in myself—yet this is possibly annihilating me—this strong willed allegiance to him, because I do feel *starved to death*, you see, crushed back & out of any waters that might sustain me. . . . Several people who are geniuses have told me I would lose my soul if I staid [*sic*] with Tony. . . . Either you or he will have to be sacrificed."[13]

A few days later, on October 12, she writes that she can't leave Tony because of her sense of responsibility of having taken him out of the pueblo: "He has told me repeatedly he couldn't bring himself to go back into it & live there even if I left him. That if I left him he would, then, have nothing. Besides me he loved his mother & she died two years ago & it has taken him all this time to get over feeling it *actively* & suffering from it—& that makes me need more than ever, to sustain him. . . . To love Tony & to love anyone else *splits* me. To love Tony like this starves me. To this problem I see no solution yet I suppose there is one & I hope to find it with you."[14]

In this same letter, Mabel reveals that Tony has told her that none of the Indians care for her, though she has done a lot for them. "They, in reality, *care nothing* for anyone outside the pueblo." Their lack of responsiveness and gratitude for her interventions on their behalf has left her "becoming more and more unresponsive to them & more than that—[I] find myself becoming *tired* of them . . ." Then, in a rare moment of self-recognition, she understands. Talking about the "secrets" that she believed the Indians kept alive, she writes, "First, it occurred to me that there is no special *truth*, they have no Secrets, they *have* no mysteries—as we count them. Then it dawned on me that what it all is, is *embodied* in them, incarnated in their very flesh, their truth is in themselves, in their lives—in their response to the world around them, in their actual behavior. . . . Sometimes, at special & accidental moments when I have been at ease in my body, flowing evenly, feeling happy & comfortable, suffused with life & enjoyment of it, one of the Indians would look at me encouragingly, recognizably, answering me with something like the handshake of the Freemason to another Freemason. At such rare moments I have had an exchange with Indians—a mutual & comprehending *corroboration* of shared knowledge. Then it would pass. For the most part Indians are merely polite or not even polite with me. Indifferent—apart—as though leaving me to stew in my own poison."[15]

By the end of the October 1928, she and Tony had one of their many talking it out and reconciliation moments. She had told him that their love was over, that they had made a failure of it. His response: "You going to say those things all night? Better sleep." And they both "slept *perfectly* all night & I woke up all refreshed & over my depression and quite cheerful & he & I feeling more friendly than ever. . . . But he has a wonderful *effect* on me without words." The effect, as always, did not last; and so, at Wickes's urging, she came to New York for six weeks to work with her and separate from Tony. By December 1928, Mabel was visiting her son John in his new home in Buffalo, and "everything is marvelous between us," for which she thanks her "skillful, determined, knowing analyst" with whom she looks forward to many more months of therapy.[16]

Mabel's therapy with Wickes came to a bitter end after the six weeks she stayed in Buffalo, in the summer of 1929, during which time she had her hysterectomy. Although Mabel had spent six weeks seeing Wickes in New York in the winter of 1928–1929, and thanked her for helping to repair her relationship with her son, she dramatically revised her view of Wickes after her recuperation from her operation. Their therapeutic relationship was terminated in the fall. In her last letter to Wickes, written on November 25 [1930?], Mabel states that she has heard rumors that Wickes was spreading about her and felt compelled to write her. She is "horrified in the months that are past, to watch the harm you did," although she says Wickes has also done "great good." She threatens her with terrible losses in her life "unless you find out about things in yourself." Wickes had apparently discouraged Mabel from getting medical attention. Mabel also believed that she was the cause of her deteriorating relationship with her son and daughter-in-law which, like her marriage to Tony, was in a constant state of turmoil. Wickes's visit to John and Alice, from which Mabel had hoped "so much good to come for us all, completely smashed anything budding & beginning." Wickes's responses to Mabel are gentle and supportive, relaying her "gladness" that Tony and Mabel seem to be "right again," as reported by one of Mabel's friends.[17]

Georgia O'Keeffe

Ironically, the summer of 1929 was a banner year for Mabel in terms of the extraordinary stars she had visiting her home and producing great work: photographers Paul Strand and Ansel Adams, and painters Georgia O'Keeffe and Rebecca Strand. It was a new and tremendously productive time in O'Keeffe's creative life that followed a period of personal and professional difficulties. In Taos, she would begin to create her sunlight-drenched high desert paintings, artfully abstracted from the landscape, paintings that gave a sense of its eternal presence and beauty and became the signature for most Americans of the "look" of the Southwest. O'Keeffe was thrilled during her first summer about the new world she had encountered. Her husband, as Mabel writes here, was not at all happy about her being there; and with good reason. He had betrayed her with his lover Dorothy Norman, and he feared he might lose her.

When Mabel left Taos and went to Buffalo for her operation, O'Keeffe wrote her ecstatic letters about what she had accomplished in Taos with her "Tony crown." She recounted the wonderful times she was having with Tony, who took her on road trips and taught her how to drive. She seemed to think she was writing on Tony's behalf, keeping Mabel informed, but Mabel read these letters as evidence they were having sex, which soured her on Georgia, to say the least. When O'Keeffe returned the next summer, they saw little of each other; by 1932 O'Keeffe found in Abiquiu the landscape and home that she would make her own.[18]

That same summer of 1929 a depressed young woman, Miriam DeWitt, the oldest daughter of Mabel's closest friends in New York, novelist and playwright Neith Boyce and radical journalist Hutchins Hapgood, visited Mabel with her mother. Taos transformed her as well. It was there that she became a painter; married her first husband, Edward Bright (at Mabel's insistence—she had picked him out for her); and lived in Taos for thirteen years. When I interviewed Miriam in 1984 about her years in Taos, she began to cry when she recalled that Tony had wanted to make love to her. She had been mortified at the time, she said, and declined. But she told me that her tears were mostly about how dear the place and time, and Mabel, had been to her. Miriam was the only one of Mabel's friends I spoke with who talked about Tony's casual interest in sex with women who attracted him. While Mabel may have imagined some of the extramarital affairs she attributed to him, Tony always claimed that for him having sex, and even loving other women, had nothing to do with his love for Mabel.

~~~~~~~~~~~~~~~~~

One year [May 1929] Georgia O'Keeffe and others arrived to spend the summer. She had arrived out here with Rebecca [Strand], demure as a nun, in black, with a shadowed face and quiet, resigned hands. In a week, the fountain began to play, and her frail, sensitive body was shot through and through with the influences of this place, which custom has agreed to sum up in the word "altitude."

Her eyes deepened and her voice escaped her control; it rose in flooding ecstasies; unbelieved excitements thrilled her through and through, and feelings that had slept beside her old man [Alfred Stieglitz] awakened and reminded her she was alive and disinterred. This sudden startled awareness rose to the surface and fell upon the most vital being in the environment: Tony. She could not believe her eyes; she laughed with her excessive amazement at the joy in his proximity. His huge, sound, harmonious bulk clad in white; his large, ample, slow rhythm; his gentle, dark, beaming smile that flooded out from wide-apart eyes and permeated all his flesh so that his hands smiled when his face did; this was medicine she needed, and without hesitation fell upon.

"He's great, Mabel," she repeated to me, shrilly. "You realize it?" I did.

She rented the studio called Tony's Studio, over on his land across the Acequia Madre, and it was not long before she had painted a large picture. Ella Young and I went to see it when Georgia told us it was finished, and we were speechless before it. We did not realize that she thought she had just been painting rocks. What I saw was a background of burning blue sky, with a sweep of Tony's vermillion blanket against it, and an enormous dark, strong, bulking shape as big as a world, against which seemed to crouch a small, weak, paler form, somewhat rosy in contrast to the darker depths of color. Just two amorphous objects hurled together on the floor

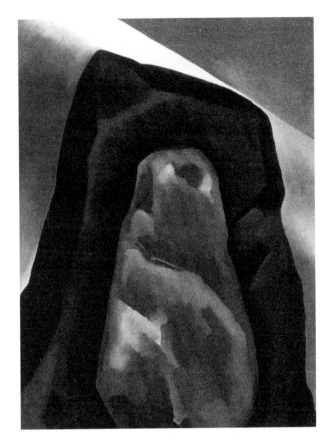

Figure 11 Georgia O'Keeffe, *After a Walk Back of Mabel's*, 1929. Oil on canvas, 40" × 30". Private collection. Copyright 2012 Georgia O'Keeffe Museum/ Artists Rights Society (ARS), New York.

of the desert featureless but expressive; so expressive that Ella Young said: "How the little one is howling!"

"Oh! Is it *howling*?" Georgia cried with pain in her voice. She did not want it to howl, though she didn't know why. "Why, yes. Look." We looked. I saw the small, nebulous thing swim into a more recognizable form. It took shape and became embryonic, became the fundamental monad; not, however, in its customary contemplative attitude, but with the tip raised, the unformed mouth opened; the cry issuing from the unborn; agony pressed from the rock, from the slowest vibration in matter; from the speechless, sound coming; birth in a cry. "Premature birth," I thought, suddenly. "It's not ready." And I felt disheartened.

Though maybe Georgia did not know she had painted her impression of Tony and herself; I knew it and I could not have it so.[19] To dissipate her attention that was turned upon him for nourishment in the world into which she had suddenly been born, I took her into shady spots and told her how Marion [Shevky] and he had flowed together the winter before in California, when Mrs. Wickes had insisted I live alone in New York for six months, to work upon my recalcitrant ego. The little blue-eyed psychoanalyst had certainly scared me when she caught me here.

She had spoken of mysterious separations that were growing between myself and the people of my world, and of a self-sufficiency she felt in Tony that he was building to compensate himself for lacks in me. Intuitively, she said, she felt it. "A man finally must protect himself from the animus-ridden woman," she said. And it seemed to me she was right. Love hadn't flowered in me for any of them, not for my mother or John, and perhaps not even for Tony, I thought. Not real, unselfish love. That small woman took a stopover between California and New York and came driving up to this hill and said things and left in two days.

The night she left, I had two dreadful dreams. In one there was a peach tree growing in the patio of a convent place. A nun came to gather peaches and though they looked fair and ripe on the outside, they were brown within. That faded and I saw a lovely rosebush with roses blooming on it. When I went up to it, the roses were withered and the petals blighted. When I woke up in the morning, I telegraphed Mrs. Wickes I would come to her the first of October, and I wrote her of these dreams. If she had understood psychoanalysis deeply enough, she would have sent me to a specialist for a physical examination, for the dreams were true and tried to tell of organic changes that could have been halted. But no one thought this was going on; and the roses dried and withered further, and the peaches moved to deeper decay during the six months she kept me on the rack, while Tony sat on Mt. Tamalpais passing the time and singing Indian songs for Marion, while Richard watched the stock exchange reports in San Francisco.

I sat alone and did penance in my apartment at the foot of Fifth Avenue. I confessed my sins and received absolution. Like others before her, Mrs. Wickes tried in every possible way to bring to the surface some evidence that I didn't really want Tony—but without success. It seems I did want him. However, had there been any possibility of separating us, it would have been accomplished that winter, for Marion grew dependent upon his strong, warm presence, grew to love him, and he loved her. Which was undoubtedly evening up accounts, for I had leaned away from him to try and subjugate one and another, left him at one side once in a while when I was busy proving my power to myself; feeling justified because I knew he had sometimes turned back to Indian women. So most marriages go, lives running parallel with occasional detours away from each other.

But this relationship that grew and knitted together between Marion and Tony when I went to New York, was the most serious that ever happened. When he finally came to New York and I saw he was different, though I was the same (but, I hoped, less "animus-ridden!") and I asked him about it, he told me a good deal, though it did not seem much. No one had taken my place, no one ever would; still, he loved Marion. I couldn't stand it. I tried to drown it in tears. It wouldn't drown. It seemed to me perfectly unendurable. I couldn't accept it.

I came back to Taos feeling vanquished by life. I cried and stormed and stayed in bed ill. Tony sat by me in silence. He looked grieved and occasionally heaved deep sighs. He stroked my damp hands and brought me drinks of cold water, but he couldn't say he didn't love Marion. All he could say was she didn't have my place, and that he couldn't live or love anyone if he didn't have me. But she was his friend; he would always be hers. As well try to pull down the sun as shatter Indian loyalty. It can't be done. No influence reaches it, and it is beyond their own disposal. My six-months discipline was meeting its first test; the ego, newly trimmed and pruned away, had a fine new chance to burgeon! It did.

Then people I had invited for the summer soon arrived. Georgia and Rebecca Strand were in the Pink House, while Ella Young was alone in the Big House. Tony and I and Una Fairweather were in the St. Teresa House, for workmen were busy putting a furnace in the Big House and I couldn't bear the noise. When I took Georgia aside to tell her some of the story about Marion, she leapt with excitement and said we could change it. Instead of putting her off and making her feel he was completely occupied, it gave her an excuse to be attentive to him! She was able to feel she was doing it to help me, and she applied herself. It gave her an excuse to go after him, to take him in the new Ford car she was learning to drive behind the house in the desert, and to focus upon him at the table. In fact, her unconscious wish completely defeated my effort to get her thoughts off him!

Time passed that summer, then, until a day came when I had to go to Buffalo for an operation. It seemed natural to go back there for it, and I thought John and my mother would wish it. Alice Corbin went with me to help me on the train, for I was feeling queer and ill, not only from what ailed me, physically, but from a combination of all the other things. All the way she encouraged and cheered me, for it is in her nature to be helpful. Tony's face kept coming back to me as I had seen it at the last: so concerned, so truly full of cherishing love. Why did I leave him behind to go to be near the others? Just a convention, I suppose, to think they would want me to have it done near them. . . .

Then Georgia's letters! She wrote me often and always about Tony. She thought she was giving me news of him. She was. I read of their trips to the Navajo country, and of all their good times; she was exalted with joy and vitality and her happiness spread over the pages. A little box came addressed by her and in it I found a small heart cut out of some smooth, semi-transparent, brown stone, a simple, ancient talisman that was instantly congenial to me. Tony sent it to me, wrote Georgia. They had come upon it in an obscure trading shop on the Navajo Reservation and she had seized upon it, loving it. But Tony had taken it out of her hands.

"I want that," he said. "You must send it to Mabel for me." It looked just like him. I wore it on a fine chain and later on that year I lost it. Someone took it out of my room.

Georgia wrote and wrote about Tony. She tried to tell me of the tone of his voice when he spoke of me, but all the things she wrote did no good, when what I needed was something that she was absorbing from his presence which is always healthful, always nourishing, for there is no medicine in all the world like the healing he radiates.

Then Stieglitz's letters and telegrams! The poor old man was distraught. He read between the lines of her letters to him and was horrified at her exuberance. Perhaps he had never known her to be so happy; anyway, it turned him upside down. He telegraphed me (me: chained to a hospital bed with my fainting heart scarcely moving!) that I must return to Taos: "You are needed there," he said. He wrote me how he suffered, though he did not say just why. I, in my own unhappiness, which was so complex that it seemed positively fantastic at the moment, had now reached such a point of saturation, combined with low vitality, that I was mostly numb, but very clarified. Pain was getting beyond the high-water mark where it becomes impersonal. I telegraphed Stieglitz loftily: "All suffering is ego suffering." This discovery, important as it might be, had hardly any comfort in it for the panic-struck man. He continued to insist that I get up, and go home, and how I wanted to!

Somehow our life centers on the heart. Mine was weaker than I knew when I got back to Taos, and though Tony helped, he couldn't make it right all at once. It seemed strange to find my house full of happy people, and difficult to rise to their level of vitality. It was as though I were watching the movements of a bright flock of birds skimming over the surface of water in which I lay submerged, fathoms below them.

At our long dining table, Georgia raked Tony's impassive face with her long, intent eyes. . . . "We did have a good time on our trip, didn't we, Tony?" But Tony, aware of my observation, was non-committal.

One day she held out her loose white belt, that no longer bound her waist, but sagged: "Look at that! That's *your* fault," she cried to him, recklessly, in front of us all. Ella Young's Irish leather face crinkled with elfish amusement and her large, cold blue eyes wandered over our faces, evidently finding Tony's impersonal composure delicious. I hailed him to the upper bedroom of the St. Teresa house and plied him with questions.

"What is between you? What does she mean?" I implored.

"I don't know what she mean. She a little crazy, that's all."

As we talked, she wandered into view in the desert behind the house. We saw her from the window flitting aimlessly about, her instinct instructing her in the methods of a magnet. Presently she was climbing the outside adobe stairs that led to the upper rooms, and at this Tony hastily tiptoed down the inner staircase with no word of explanation—but none was needed! There was in his silent celerity, the age-old masculine "Sauve qui peut!" Georgia appeared at the door of the room where I lay on the bed, looked her unconscious surprise at finding me alone, took no trouble to enter into any conversation with one so flaccid as I, and departed. . . .

~~~~~~~~~~

The Writing and Publication of *Intimate Memories*

In the winter of 1924–1925, while she was living in New York and undergoing therapy with A. A. Brill, Mabel wrote and published several articles for magazines about Taos, along with the first hundreds of pages of her memoirs. It was a triumph of creative "sublimation" that allowed her to exorcise the demon of syphilis and find balance in her marriage to Tony—at least temporarily. In spite of her crisis in 1929, it would sustain her through thirteen years, during which she published her four volumes of autobiography and her idyllic hymn to the ideals of her domestic life with Tony, *Winter in Taos*. As she explained to Alice Corbin Henderson: "Brill has started the machinery in the way I wanted him to do—& now to keep it going! As I've never worked in my life I have to actually learn a new life—& that means make new tracks in my brain so that it becomes a matter of course to slide into the motion of writing. . . . I find I *love* it but not as much as living in 'pure form'—but as no one can live so forever, I accept the substitute . . ." In the same letter, Mabel wrote that Brill and Tony liked one another and understood one another "perfectly." "Brill says Tony is the best *man* he's ever seen me near." For Mabel this was a wonderful coming together of her love and her work, especially since Brill had warned her sternly not to consider marriage with Tony when he heard rumors that she was thinking about it.[20]

By the late 1920s, "the substitute" had taken over her life. She sent the manuscripts of the first two volumes of *Intimate Memories* to Harcourt, Brace in 1929, originally intending, as she writes in "Family Affairs," to have the manuscript "lay moldering in his safe until I should be dead and gone" because of what it "had cost me so much to write and would the family so much to read." She initially planned four volumes of memoirs, accompanied by corresponding volumes of related letters. By the time she donated her papers to Yale, she had twenty volumes of autobiographical materials. In October 1932, she agreed to publish her first volume because her mother had given permission, after Alfred Harcourt had urged Mabel to publish them. In three weeks she and Spud Johnson, a Taos poet and journalist whom she had hired as her secretary in 1926, were correcting proofs. But that winter Sara wrote Mabel that she didn't want her to put anything in her book about "me and my affairs. . . . Why don't you write about all those crazy people in Florence. If you do I'll write the publisher I won't have it and that he's not to sell it." But it was too late.[21]

Writing her *Intimate Memories* made Mabel feel free and alive, as she notes in a wonderful passage she wrote about why she "had" to publish her memoirs, where she quotes from Herman Melville's *Moby Dick*: "'Canst thou pull up Leviathan with an hook?' Thou not only canst, but must, if made like I am! This could banish the sense of futility and the horrible melancholy that came from the suspicion that life is a trap beginning and ending in nonsense." She had tried this by living through people. "That was why I swam off into them, one after another, 'not for love or money,' as they say! But so as to endure living, and it made it endurable. But the emptiness was greater when the illusion was worn out, as it always was, sooner or later. My tempo was up and down, with the dull pause in the middle! I loved Tony, but he didn't always save me from myself, even when he was here."

Mabel's mother didn't seem to complain about the book too much after it came out in 1933, but she became ill shortly thereafter, and her husband, Monty, felt that its publication hastened Sara's death. When Evangeline and Leopold Stokowski visited that summer, Evangeline asked Mabel a pointed question to which she did not have an adequate reply: "How far do you think a person is justified in going in art, if it sacrifices other people?" When Monty called, Mabel writes, "It struck me cold. I had no conscious love for my mother, but we were one blood and indivisible." Mabel flew to Buffalo after her mother died and went to see the body, surprising herself with her reaction: "All of a sudden I heard myself saying, inside me: 'Forgive me, Mother, that you couldn't love me!'—and the voice shook me and made me cry." After the funeral, Mabel lunched with Brill in New York City and asked him if he thought she had hurt her mother. "No. I think it tickled her, and satisfied her hate for your father. . . . After all, she triumphed."

CHAPTER FOUR

The Statue of Liberty

A Story of Taboos

> But as it was all about the Indians and myself, I could not show it to anyone, not even a publisher. I put in it all I know of the Indian life & culture, secret things I had picked up. It was called 'The Statue of Liberty' & the sub-title was 'miscegenation.' Some book! As I believe that most women including myself are symbolized by that great hollow stone image holding up an artificial light at the entrance to this great deluded country!
>
> —MDL to Edmund Brill[1]

MABEL ALWAYS HAD to write *for* someone, most typically one of her doctors. In July 1946, when she was suffering a bout of depression that her Taos doctor, Ashley Pond, did not seem to be responding to, she turned to Dr. Eric Hausner. An internist who practiced in Santa Fe, he continued her "writing therapy" as a means for her to work her way out of her times of despair. Even at age sixty-seven, she insisted that women "are not selfstarters": The thing is, she wrote him, "that I can only do it when someone *orders* a thing, or *suggests a subject*. . . . one can write about anything if it is required."[2]

Hausner was both an extraordinary man and doctor, who ministered to the elite among the writers and artists of Santa Fe and Taos, as well as devoting his time to anyone in need of his help in the communities of northern New Mexico. In a 1959 obituary about Hausner published in *The New Mexican*, "Doctor Considered Link to Life," the reporter noted that "Respect for Dr. Hausner Knew No Cultural Bound." The same seems to have been true of his much more than professional devotion to the lives and well-being of his patients. Born in

Czechoslovakia in 1905, Hausner was Jewish; he came to the United States in 1935 and joined the staff of the Mayo Clinic. After serving in the army, he moved to Santa Fe, "where he became one of the community's leading citizens." Hausner was a friend of Igor Stravinsky, who dedicated a concert at Santa Fe's St. Frances Cathedral to his memory.[3]

Mabel's first idea to work her way through her depression was to turn her home into a "retreat" for creative men and women, something like the McDowell colony, and have a friend of hers run it. She had tried this in the summer of 1929, when she turned over her home briefly to writer Elizabeth Shepley Sargeant, although that had been more of a business proposition. Now she proposed "a place to rest for superior people of admitted achievement." None of the men in her life—Tony, her son, John, or Dr. Hausner—thought this was a workable idea. Mabel often felt negatively about Taos when she was in a depressed state. But after World War II, with her star in decline, and what she saw as the over-development and commercialism of Taos, she felt even more displaced. In "Recapitulation While Waiting," an essay she wrote in 1946, she says that she still wants to see herself as a "pioneer": "I *am* a pioneer . . . Didn't everyone say I couldn't marry and Indian and 'put it across'? . . . I married Tony and even made Indians fashionable, at least to know and admire and dream about, if not yet to legally espouse! Unless I *die of it*, I suppose anyone would say I made a success of miscegenation; and I do not intend to die."[4]

Mabel's attitudes about her marriage to Tony, as we know, veered wildly over the course of their forty-four-year affair and marriage. Publicly, she did "put it across" as a model for the possibilities of interracial marriages between white women and Indian men. In 1932, Mabel told a reporter for the *Denver Post* that her marriage foretold the future of Indian-white marriage and that "the races may amalgamate and the Indians be the ones to save our race." In an article on the interracial marriages of the Eastmans and the Luhans, Margaret Jacobs has noted that while "The symbolic power of their marriage may have sustained Mabel through hard times," Mabel also expressed her fears in private, including to her friend John Collier, that marriage between Indian and white would "ruin the Indian race," and that the Pueblos needed to be insulated "from the 'corrupting' influences of modern white society." She was clearly of different minds about "miscegenation."[5]

The profoundest gulf between the Luhans was due to their unbridgeable personal and cultural differences. In my last visit to the Luhan papers at the Beinecke Library, I found a letter in Tony's handwriting that I could barely decipher. His published letters were probably dictated by him to whomever was serving as Mabel's secretary at the time, although his written English may well have improved over time. This particular letter, probably from 1919, starkly demonstrates the difference in their written literacy: "dear Mabele," Tony writes, "I going right to you to night. . . . you no I can right mut bery well I don't know if you ondar Stend My boor righting."[6] Tony was an articulate, passionate, and persuasive man, and a noted singer, whose effective oratorical skills did much good on behalf of his own and other pueblos. For many of Mabel's creative artist and writer female friends—in particular, Mary Austin, Willa Cather, and Georgia O'Keeffe—he provided an alternative kind of manhood, undoubtedly strong and masculine, but also gentle, undemanding, and sensitive, an admired guide who led them to insightful understandings of the physical and cultural landscapes of northern New Mexico.

But Mabel was a talker and a writer, in constant need of intellectual stimulation; she surrounded herself with men and women for whom reading, writing, and other forms of cultural production were the ways they communicated their ideas about the world in which they were engaged. Tony was mostly silent; he didn't seem to "do" anything; and Mabel was well aware that not all of her friends admired him. He felt that he didn't need to talk to communicate with Mabel; he spoke to her, as he was fond of repeating, "in his heart." While she could never be at rest, he was "full of an even living," and did whatever he did with ease. But she sometimes wished, as she writes in "Family Affairs," that "he'd get up every morning and go to a job."

Mabel came up with many schemes to employ Tony, some of which were advertised in the Taos newspaper, including having him give guided road trips to tourists. She felt tremendous guilt, as she expressed in one of her letters to Jungian therapist Frances Wickes, that she had ruined his life by taking him out of the pueblo, and that she had spoiled him and several of his family members with her largesse. There are poignant moments in "The Statue of Liberty" where Tony expresses his losses and gains in marrying Mabel, and it is clear that she was both keenly aware of and empathetic to his pain.

Undoubtedly, the most important connection Tony made through Mabel was with John Collier (1901–1980), who Mabel knew as a social worker in New York. Under Franklin Roosevelt, Collier created "The Indian New Deal." He was the first Commissioner of Indian Affairs to enact legislation that returned sovereignty to Indians. His activism on behalf of Native Americans began almost as soon as he visited Taos Pueblo, in the winter of 1920, when he first visited Mabel. For Collier, the pueblos became a lifelong model for reform of American culture. Tony partnered with Collier in the 1920s to organize Pueblo tribes against legislation that would have deprived them of their land rights and cultural practices.[7]

While tribal leaders lauded Tony publicly in the 1930s for the political benefits that he brought Taos Pueblo, he was, at times, a man torn between two worlds. But he also had a great deal of independence during his marriage; he spent much of his time at the pueblo, and he built his own separate "Tony House" on Pueblo land, across from the "Big House," where he entertained his friends. He had two ranches north of Taos, and he oversaw the building of the "Big House" and most of the guesthouses on the Luhan property.

Mabel called "The Statue of Liberty" her "Indian book." It was the intended sequel to *Edge of Taos Desert* that took her thirty years to write. It is clear from reading the manuscript that she had already gathered much of the material by the time she decided to complete it; but there is nothing secret in it about the Indians that she reveals. Mabel had published her best writings related to Taos Pueblo during the 1920s and 1930s as magazine articles, journal essays, and short fiction, and in her published memoirs. "The Statue of Liberty" is most interesting as a portrayal of those aspects of her marriage she would not reveal in public—the frustrations, hurt, physical and psychic damage that Mabel and Tony caused each other between the time they became lovers in August 1918 through September 1947, when Tony began to leave home on a regular basis to spend time with the glamorous socialite, fashion designer, and heiress Millicent Rogers.

Mabel had written to both Frances Wickes and A. A. Brill about Tony's drinking problems, which had at times led her to threaten to leave him. When Mabel once again thought of leaving Tony, this time because she assumed he was having an affair with Millicent, Dr. Hausner convinced her to write another memoir instead. The depth of Mabel's anger can be measured by the fact that this is the first memoir in which she writes about her encounters with venereal disease. As such, it stands out as one of the rare and important documents about the impact of syphilis on its times. If it is true, as Mabel asserts here, that she ended sexual relations with Tony after she contracted syphilis from him, we can better understand both Tony's sexual infidelities and the depth of Mabel's anxieties about them. He was the third husband to threaten her with death, and the only one of them that she loved.

Mabel does not say when A. A. Brill "discovered" Maurice's second stage syphilis, but she does write that he did so before they married. The increasing shame Mabel felt over Maurice's syphilis may well have been one of her motivations for sending him out West by himself on "their" honeymoon, two days after they were married on August 18, 1917. She asked him to leave again, sometime after his return in September, when she suggested he join Santa Fe's art colony and wrote letters of introduction for him. By October, he had established a studio there. In "The Statue of Liberty," Mabel writes that Maurice was receiving Salvarsan treatments in New York that had to be continued when they moved to Taos. She makes no mention of whether he was being treated in Santa Fe for the three months he lived there alone before she joined him in late December. (Sterne went to Santa Fe with a doctor friend who might have administered his treatments.)[8]

Mabel suggests that one of the factors that drove her to her daily visits to Taos Pueblo, and into Tony's arms, was her disgust with Maurice's syphilis. "By contrast," she writes, "they seemed so clean and wholesome and free of the sin and decadence of the world." The ironies of Tony's infecting Mabel with the disease that she had feared for much of her adult life are manifold, as is the shock of hearing her write about it in the Victorian discourse of sin and (deserved) punishment. On the night he returns to Mabel after having had intercourse with his corn brother's wife, Mabel recognizes her "doom"; then, and not for the first time, she embraces it. Just before she accuses Tony of betrayal, and he makes love to her to assuage his guilt, she writes: "the smell of seminal fluid was evil, and destructive for me."

Eshref and Marion Shevky were at the Luhans' home during their syphilis crisis. Marion administered their first Salvarsan shots. Shevky (1893–1969) was born into a prominent political family in Istanbul; he came to the United States with his wife Marion, who was a physician, to work at Stanford in the field of experimental medicine. Shevky had first arrived as a friend of John Collier from San Francisco during the first winter that the Colliers lived at the Luhan house. According to a letter that Collier wrote in March 1921, seeking a doctor who would come to northern New Mexico to work with Indian health issues, Shevky had already uncovered syphilis in the pueblo and was treating it. (Shevky was a physiologist, not an MD.) Mabel wrote to Collier about Shevky's continuing work on the problem in November and December 1922, the month after she dreamed up her "new world plan" scheme to save the land and culture of the Pueblos, and bring their ways to the white world. She told Collier she had offered one thousand dollars for Wasserman tests for all the men and women in the pueblo. Some of the Indians were suspicious of why she was doing this, including Tony Romero, who had been the go-between during the Luhans' marriage, and whose wife purportedly infected Tony with syphilis. Mabel expressed to Collier her wish that the Rockefeller Institute would take up VD in the pueblos because the Bureau of Indian Affairs refused to help.[9]

In "The Statue of Liberty," Mabel stated that Tony was the first to take the Wasserman test, as an example, and he came back clean, as she expected. Sometime in the spring or summer of 1923, Tony infected Mabel. Afraid to seek treatment from "Doc Martin" in Taos because of his notorious lack of confidentiality, Mabel sought treatment in Santa Fe with Dr. Frank Mera, the director of Sunmount Sanitarium and a major force in the arts and cultural institutions in the city. In the fall and winter of 1923–1924, she lived with Tony in Mill Valley and they went to San Francisco for further treatment, which included a black mercury salve that they had to rub over their bodies.[10]

As for why Mabel named this memoir after "The Statue of Liberty"—and refers to "her" as a "hollow woman"—it may have to do with her ongoing complaint that modern Anglo-American women who thought they were "free" had little in the way of emotional satisfaction to show for it. She had repudiated her "new womanhood" when she married Tony, and she had invested her public life in touting the ways of a conservative tribal culture. She could never, of course, have lived in accordance with Taos Pueblo gender norms, which had strictly defined roles for men and women, even if she had been given the opportunity to do so.

Mabel subtitled *The Edge of Taos* "An Escape to Reality." She had always written publicly about Tony as the man who freed her from her "epoch" and awakened her capacity to love. In "The Statue of Liberty," Mabel describes their marriage as a "fatal attraction" and herself as trapped, which is how she always felt after she married. Nevertheless, although this is the memoir in which she writes most despairingly about her marriage to Tony, Mabel continues to express her love for him, along with her need to protect what they had come to symbolize to themselves and to the world at large.

~~~~~~~~~~~~~~

Foreword

MISCEGENATION

Edge of Taos Desert was about Tony and myself from the time we met until the last day we lived apart on the threshold of real intimacy. The last words in that book were: "He bent a firm, gentle look down upon me and held out his hand and I took it."

"I comin' here to this tepee tonight," he said, "when darkness here. That be right."

"Yes, Tony," I answered, "that will be right."

And it was right. These words were spoken in Manby's garden, thirty years ago, and since that time I have never felt like taking up our story where we began to live together. I have written of other people and myself but little of Tony and myself. I have written another volume of "Intimate Memories" called "Family Affairs," which is about how families behave, but how Tony and I really behaved and what our affair was like I have avoided. I have never felt like writing *our* book, or all that came after we took that step or union at last, unbreakable as we had both foreseen it would be.

But I did not know why I had never been able to tell it. When people asked me as they did so often, begging me to continue and write the next volume— friends and strangers waiting to know how our life turned out, I have always put them off saying: "I cannot. It is too close yet," until finally thirty years passed and were gone. But only now I really know what has been holding me back. Only now today!

For a week I have been trying every hour of every day to begin the new volume because the doctor persuaded me it would be good for me, and more than that, it could have a value if I wrote it truly. Did he know, I wonder, when he talked to me that day, did he know more than I knew myself? I did realize I must do something to save myself, to heal myself, as each one of us must do if we need to be saved. No one else can do it for us. In that hour in the white office, while I watched the young branches moving green outside the window, and I vaguely understood: "Work and go free. Nothing but work can help if one is made as I am. Work to know, work to tell what you know. Work to find the truth."

Very well. I accepted that and I left there determined to begin the very next day, to tell the happy story, the great love story we had lived. . . .

So every day I have been trying to go back into our early life together, the days that followed the night when I crossed the great gulf between us on a bridge that went with me and was gone when I reached him, as I had foreseen it would be, and told him. An irrevocable step! To pass across from one's race to another is an irrevocable step.

I looked down at the clean paper before me and I tried to remember the past, to remember the happiness I must have known, but there was no memory of happiness. The happiness had all been before that night. . . . I could not write of happiness. There had not been much happiness in our painful existence. It had been "more wrestling than dancing!" It had been stormy and full of conflicts, not only with the world but also with each other—a long, formless, uneven searching for peace. An endless adjustment, a perpetual effort to meet one problem after another and solve it with scarcely any rest between whiles, a buffeting wind forever beating.

So, I thought, I cannot write this book. I cannot find us where I thought we had been. After that first night there had been no rest. Excitement yes, all those problems to be met, the world to conquer, terrible issues to accept and overcome and ourselves to conquer and overcome! Only one thing had been sure and certain, we could never get away from each other. We had shared a strong conviction neither of us understood, and this was that we had been brought together for some cosmic purpose unrevealed to us, for the accomplishment of some ulterior necessity that was beyond our knowing. "God wants it," was the way Tony summed up our relationship.

We had each seen the other plainly in waking and sleeping dreams before we ever met. ("Only your hair was long," Tony told me reproachfully!) We had recognized each other then and afterwards the first time we met. It was only natural for us to feel our union was powerful and significant in spite of hidden meaning. And also it was almost imperative for us to believe in this significance, for we made each other so unhappy!

Yet this was not altogether a rationalization that we invented to console ourselves, for others felt the same about us and told their belief: that we had been brought together for some purpose. More and more the most real and true aspect of our relationship forced itself upon us. We were bound together. We could not break away from each other no matter what we did to each other, no matter what the world did to try to separate us.

This, then, had been one of those rare "fatal attachments" I had heard about and once or twice observed in others but had never experienced myself. I had been so free until I came to Taos, never caught, never rooted in this universe. At last I had been trapped. I was still trapped! Now, again, I thought as I looked back on the unfolding of it all, it must have been for some good reason, but I knew it was too soon to know yet what the reason was. Only thirty years! And I saw that all this must have been as true for Tony as for me. What has he gained in our life together to compensate him for the loss of his health, his hereditary position as head of his clan in his tribe, his satisfying religious ceremonies and his culture?

We have injured each other—torn each other apart, inhibited each other and removed, one from the other, the legitimate satisfactions of our so different *mores*; and what is left to us, then, is the necessary consolation of each other's continued presence, for I believe neither of us can remain here on this earth without the other.

We cannot bear it unless we are together in our strange, bleak separation from each other. (Yesterday I told Tony our lives are so divided from one another by different interests and activities that we do not pass an hour of the day or night together. That is the way the pattern has formed itself. He linked together the fingers of both his hands, and trying to tear them apart again, he groaned: "I can never get away from you. Every minute no matter where I am, my heart is with you."

And I said: "I know it. All day when I am wearing myself out doing all kinds of things you don't even know about, and keeping this place going, and getting so *tired* there is no satisfaction in it for you are always away doing your things—your farming, your animals, your family—all those boys you are teaching."

"What would I do here? These people—what are they to me? What would we do if I stopped working and you stopped doing your things? Maybe we die. I guess we are together no matter what we do.")

So the peculiar marriage goes on. It is a wonder we are both alive for, though the depredations we have inflicted upon each other in our unconscious preying on the powers and faculties of our rich natures have not been intended to destroy, yet they have destroyed all but the unbreakable union. The changes we have inflicted upon each other are in the *values* of what we were born to. Tony says he can never "go back" to the Indians; I feel I can never have an essential interest in the interests of my race. We are each divorced in spirit from our own by each other; yet we have been turned back in our outer life to the forms and movements that our own employ. This exchange makes a peculiar strain. Its antidote and relief comes only when we return to each other's presence for sleep and rest, to mitigate the everlasting loneliness of the shift in our lives.

At least our life together has been an unexampled challenge to the spirit in both of us. Though battered and broken we have grown strong, and always we are alive. Neither of us would have left undone what we have done even if we could, nor would we ever go back on what has been. Facing this unsuspected past, now I can try and write of what has taken place since I can see it at last differently, but perhaps more truly than I have always maintained it was. And who knows, perhaps such strong persistent living and wrestling is a kind of happiness, though not known to many!

Chapter I

There was a great darkness lifted from my life when Maurice finally went away from Taos and left me free to give up to Tony.

In volume four of "Intimate Memories" I avoided referring to the terrible secret that underlay our marriage, but I have come to realize that nothing can be truly understood about people and the cause of their behavior unless the inescapable facts of their flesh and blood are known. After all, the body is the physical basis of life and the spirit-of-life, and it is the most influential of all human factors. All my years I have been victimized by the mysterious fatalities of the flesh and by the ignorance of these in my generation. I have been made helpless and shamed and unable to determine what to do to save myself or another by unnamable horrors.

No one ever named them. When I was a child I never heard the words syphilis or gonorrhea. I had been aware of people whispering sometimes with their heads together, about disasters in our town of Buffalo. When a young man that everyone knew hung himself in his bedroom, naked save for a pair of white gloves, I heard my mother and a neighbor mumbling about it, sitting in the shaded drawing room in their summer silks:

"He had. . . . you know!" my mother said and drew down the corner of her mouth.[11]

Sometimes when I grew older the girls I knew would say: "Look out. There's something the matter with him: They say he has *IT*—that awful *thing*!" But I hardly knew what it meant except that it was connected to doing *THAT*—the unspoken that had to do with having a baby!

Early when I was only eight or ten I had been impressed by the sinfulness of having anything to do with little boys (beyond trying to dance with them at dancing school). For my father scared me every time I was ready to go to a children's party by accompanying me to the front door and warning me in a low voice with a pointing forefinger: "Now remember: You're not to play kissing games." Shaking his finger in my face he would go on: "Remember now: No 'Post-Office,' none of those at all."

I was frightened to death of kissing and of boys themselves. In fact nearly all of us were afraid of each other long ago. So later when I was old enough to be curious about what people "did" when they were married, whatever it was, it was all tied up with sin and forbidden acts and having "that awful thing."

Once I found a big book hidden in my mother's bureau drawer under her French lingerie. It was Boccaccio's *Decameron*.[12] Because it was hidden I was allured to it and I took it out and sat on the floor and read it all one warm summer afternoon. I had not the faintest understanding of what all those characters were "doing" but there was some magic in the lines hidden behind the words that aroused the first delightful stirring of the flesh that lay hidden and ignored beyond my voluminous small ruffled "drawers" and embroidered petticoats. When I returned the book to its secret place something had been awakened in my nerves and blood. But with that awakening there was a dreadful shame and a sense of sin and a feeling of uncleanness.

The verse in the Bible or the Prayer Book about the sins of the fathers being visited upon the children unto the third and fourth generation has worried me all my life. At the beginning I wondered if my father's sins were visited upon me and if I must die from his wages of sin, the wages of sin being Death! And I was only the second generation—a generation that even now today hardly dares to think and much less to write of the secrets of the body.[13]

These taboos and fears crystallized me into a certain mold long ago so that I was always nervous in sex and still am.

It seems a strange coincidence that both Dodge and Maurice should have had syphilis when I married them, or was it perhaps only that this so-called social disease is very general in our society? Even now these facts are hermetic, the doctors are very close-mouthed about them. Syphilis is still a shameful accident to be hidden from the world.

Edwin Dodge was of an impeccable respectability in a well-known Boston family. A serious young architect would not be suspected to have "THAT"! When we met on the ship and he fell in love with me and told me he was "sick," and told me how he got it in Paris from a cocotte, and described all the details and routine of his cure, it was the first knowledge I had of such a frightening affair. I pretended to be emancipated and not to mind it. He told me he was beyond the phase where he could "infect" me. The word scared me—but I shook my head and tried to shake away out of it the memory of his confidence, but it dropped into my unconscious and festered there. I never could overcome my revulsion to Edwin's body no matter how I tried. I am forced to believe we are strongly ruled by biological influences and that perhaps all sense of guilt is biological.[14] Perhaps nature cares for nothing but the fit—and all that interferes with racial fitness impels us creatures, ruled by the biological destiny, to reject all that interferes with that. We may think we are self-determined and that we rule our lives but I wonder!

With Maurice—well, he did not even know he had "it" until I, pestered by his neuroticism, persuaded him to go to Dr. Brill and be psychoanalyzed. Dr. Brill brought it to the surface from his dreams. He had contracted it in Bali, where he had been living recently for two years [1912–1914]. He had never realized he had anything the matter with him, so ignorant had he been of such esoteric maladies, but when Dr. Brill sent him to a doctor for a blood test he was in the last phase of it![15]

He began his loathsome cure, shots that were continuous and prevented us from ever forgetting *this enemy in the blood* [ED: my italics]. I developed a phobia about spirochetes and their sinister prevalence. In no time I shrank from Maurice and our intimacy lapsed away. There were always ghastly secret things that were happening that must be concealed from people. There was always this nauseous accompaniment to our life, this disgusting and ignoble disease that could never be ignored or forgotten lest death or madness come upon him and we could not avoid our accompaniment of secret guilt and vileness.

We could confide in no one for we were so ashamed of it. Maurice was very morbid about his misfortune and constantly dwelt upon it in his Russian fashion. He was impelled to discuss it all the time and speculate about it, and I was the only one he could talk to, for we both felt no one on earth had it but him. So he never let me forget it for a moment.

When we had first come to Taos one of the hardest things had been to select a doctor, for his treatments must go on and on and *on!* I had heard that Dr. Martin was a great gossip, so we were afraid of him, for we believed if he knew it and told people about it they would look down upon us. Though we liked him and saw him all the time, for he lived next to us and he was my doctor for any small ailments, we decided that Maurice must go to the Indian office doctor—a Dutchman named Dr. Bergman. So Maurice had to go and see him and tell him about his shameful sickness and engage him to give those shots.

Dr. Bergman had to send away for the Salvarsan and Maurice grew more nervous waiting for it to come and fearful that he would have a stroke or develop paresis while he was without it. We knew so little about the whole thing! No one had told us anything. In fact no one knew about the case except Dr. Brill and the New York doctor to whom he had sent Maurice and who had taken care of him before we came away. And neither of these had told us the details of how long and how many treatments must go on. They only frightened us about the risk of neglecting the malady. Madness and death: The wages of sin again, I thought to myself.

Maurice skulked down the street to Dr. Bergman's office, some doors away from Mr. Manby's house where we lived. I could see him trying to appear invisible going in and out, and I could tell that his whole bearing was so guilty and ashamed that anyone seeing him must guess what his errand was in that house. This poorly hidden shame gave me a need to compensate for a feeling of defectiveness and ignominy. So I became aloof to people, seeming cold and indifferent while all the time I was burning with the grief of my misfortune which I felt was undeserved, and almost too much to bear. I felt set apart from other people and I was very lonely—shut into myself with this pariah feeling. Life could have been so wonderful but I could never experience it; I could only be crippled and marked by being tied to "that awful thing," syphilis.

The only comfort I had, I derived from my acquaintance with Tony and the other Indians out in the Pueblo, which I seized upon in the first days of our arrival in Taos. By contrast they seemed so clean and wholesome and free of the sin and decadence of the world.

Maurice made the situation much harder by his morbidity than I had felt when Dodge had it; and the Indians in their purity made it seem much worse, so that my encounter with it a second time, and having to live with it in that pristine place, seemed much harder than the first one. Then, too, I felt I could not forsake Maurice in his dark hour. I must stay with him and see him through it. In fact, I became identified with it as with some inevitable Fate.

Until I got more interested in Tony. That tore me loose and all my compassion seemed to fade away out of me. Then I just wanted Maurice to be gone—and never to have to see him again. Perhaps I had been too cowardly to leave him and be alone, until that strong good man took hold of my whole being!

But before I got clear of the morass I was stuck in, there were some hard times. One day Mrs. Bergman rushed into our living room, her like face livid and distorted. She looked like a frightened parrot, the pupils or her pale eyes dilated, her tongue balanced dry against her lower teeth. "Come quick," she gasped. "Something is the matter with Mr. Sterne."

"What?" I cried springing up.

"I don't know. He has a kind of fit!"

Everyone must see us from their windows, I thought, as we ran down the street together and into the doctor's office. Maurice was lying back on a couch choking and clawing the air, his brown eyes rolling up. He was unable to speak. I froze at the sight—I just felt very cold and horribly annoyed. What *next*? I thought. I had no idea what to do or how to act, and Dr. Bergman looked helpless and didn't know what to do either. We all just stood around and watched Maurice fight for his life and I thought again—"The wages of sin are Death!"

It seemed a long time but maybe it was only a minute and then he came out of it. He calmed down and lay still. The sweat was running off his face and he had a dreadful color. Soon he took a long breath and said faintly. "Oh Dar-r-r-ling: I nearly died!"

"What *was* it?" I exclaimed, turning to the doctor.

"I think I got a bubble of air in my hypodermic!" He did not seem at all embarrassed. Now that it was over he looked a little annoyed at Maurice. "Well, I think you may go home now," he added. We crept down the street, Maurice mopping his forehead while I held myself as straight as I could and felt that sunken, pariah feeling all through me.

I felt still more estranged from Maurice after this and more and more drawn to Tony, so I went out to the Pueblo nearly every day and over to the place he had persuaded me to buy on the edge of the sagebrush desert, next to the little place he had also persuaded the Young-Hunters to buy.[16] He had helped us both to get them. There the work was going on tranquilly and gaily and I felt a great relief in getting away to it from the dismal atmosphere at home. . . .

Chapter II

When Maurice returned to New York [in August 1918], Tony and I gradually moved away from our homes and stayed together at my new place east of the town, on the rising land where the desert swept up to the hills.

The new "studio" was finished and we had the four old rooms attached to it that I had found there. These were under a very fine long portal Tony had been working on all summer. It was built of pale grey beams that had been cut in the fall before and had been weathering for a long time, and Tony put it up in the old manner of building by pure construction—with not a nail—but calculated by weight and measure and overlapping the edges. The corbels were cut out by an adze and the cross beams squared by the same tool. No metal, no mill work in it. It reached to our front door in the large living room and went on down past the old rooms, ending in a sixty foot well where we hauled up all the water we used then.

Above the living room the Indians were building a sleeping room now and a large square sleeping porch outside it overlooking the fields and across to Manby's place and beyond to the western skyline. While I watched the Indians at work I was thinking how lovely it would be at night to hear the running water that curved around the orchard and the fields below. What peace there would be! So I left Manby's house where I had spent nearly a year with Maurice and John Evans, Alice [Thursby] on her frequent visits back and forth, Elizabeth Duncan and Agnes [Pelton].[17] I let them all go now and took only John with me to the new house.

Tony came down every day to work and gradually stayed at night. He just edged in, leaving his family group, his wife Candelaria and all his relations. He had told me, in the first days I was in Taos, that I must need a studio, as all Anglos did, so now I had one and he was in it. I imagine it was some time before people in Taos realized our situation. They probably thought Tony was just building for me and helping me run the place. He had associated himself in their minds with building the Harwood's house and others; he had always worked in the town, even far back when he and Mr. Manby planted all the big trees on the Pueblo Road that led out of the village. I think they just thought it was "a job," as it certainly was![18]

At first the Indians, too, looked upon it in the same way. Tony had always been coming and going, away on trips, off hunting, building down in Taos. He had worked a long time, with his friend Antonio Martinez, on the Harwood house and this summer they worked together on my house. That was all, they thought, but this simple belief could not last for long. Soon the unprecedented . . . truth must ooze out.

The house was full of light and life given to it by the Indians who came and went all the time. They were always singing while they worked and making jokes and they were full of fun and laughter. Whenever Tony was in the house he had a drum standing on the floor between his knees and he sang, sang day and night. The Taos Indians were great song makers and they traded songs with the Apaches, Navajos, and the Oklahoma tribes, and Tony knew hundreds of these songs with varying themes and rhythms. Sometimes, in the evening, the Indian boys rode down on horseback and spent the evening sitting around Tony, all singing together. I learned a great many different beautiful songs and have never forgotten them and often dream of them.

One afternoon an Indian rode down to the house on horseback to see Tony in our happy home. He talked for a while to him in his room, the third room down along the portal where he always received his friends, where the Indians who were working left their serapes in the morning, and where they foregathered in the late afternoons to wash and chat before leaving for the night. When this visitor rode away galloping back to the Pueblo through the sagebrush, Tony came in and said, "My brother say Candelaria sick. Better I go and see what." . . .

He did not love this woman, and had not, since years before when he had caught her among the trees in Glorieta up in the canyon, lying with her lover, whose arm Tony had broken with a powerful blow. When I had questioned him in my terrible, gnawing jealousy of her and her claim upon him, and of her beauty, which I had not, he had told me, "She is nothin' to me any more. Only a nice lookin' woman I own like my good saddle." Now she did not look nice but he treated her the same as he always did, nice or not. Courteously. . . .

Chapter III

While the work was going on upstairs Tony and I slept on a couch in the alcove he had built in the living room, and John slept in the old room called Tony's, down the portal. These ancient rooms were clean now and freshly whitewashed with Tierra Blanca from the pit beyond Ranchos de Taos. The original doors and windows had been painted blue and white and the ceiling boards were painted blue too between the age-darkened beams.

When Tony was a little boy he had helped his father make these doors and windows for Jose Trujillo, from whom I bought the place. They were set in rather crookedly but had the charm of all hand-made things. It was nice, to Tony's mind, to be using them himself with us. We ate our meals in front of the large fireplace at the end of the living room. Here, in an arched niche, a Virgin of Guadalupe stood. This was a fine bulto, painted in faded tones of blue and red, her robes flowing below her clasped hands, her head on one side bearing a tin crown, with high points upon it.

An Indian girl that we called Big Frances, to distinguish her from another, little Francis that was somewhat demented, came down from the Pueblo every day and cooked for us and cleaned the bare house. She cooked on a small wood stove in the adjoining room that later became the Book Room, and a preacher, who was also a carpenter called Old Man Thomas, who lived down our road, was building a tiny staircase up out of it to reach the bedroom where the Indians were working. . . .

Upon looking back I am surprised to find there was not a perfect harmony in our life just because we had each other and our love. In fact, gratified desire seemed to have released exasperations that heretofore had been patiently controlled, so that sometimes I grew angry among the Indian workers where before everything had been so idyllic. . . .[19]

Chapter IV

One morning in that first autumn Tony and I got up at half-past five in our dark, cold unfamiliar early morning house, and made fires, made a pot of coffee, hitched up the horses and went out into the iron cold darkness of the desert when the sky began to grow pale behind the eastern mountain range. We drove out to the Pueblo. There was to be an Indian dance of young men just when the sun rose.

How strange our sleeping little town looked when we drove through it! No one about, only the faithful milkman going on his rounds, leaving milk at all the closed doors. The world seemed new. When we left the town behind and went along the empty country road there was such a miraculous beauty in everything we saw! First it was muted, then the whole white snow-covered earth began to shine with a pale glow; every twig and blade of grass was frosted, and the trees with all their trunks and branches stood still and glistening in the trembling green light, for there was no rose color yet. A few cows and horses were in the fields, and even they were coated with silver all over their fuzzy winter hides.

Ahead of us the high Sacred Mountain loomed over the Pueblo, black and heavy at the bottom, with the snow cap on the top shining like white steel where the high light struck upon it. The sky was rapidly growing warmer; the blue behind the peak was warmer than the green that had first showed when we started.

Along the sharp steep ridge up there we saw white smoke rising like the fumes of a volcano. It was the wind that moves over the mountains in all the seasons of the year, now blowing off the deep drifts. How strange it is to find the same aspects in nature coming from the utmost extremes, and whether from the fiercest heart, deep down in the earth below, or polar cold of midwinter freezing, to see the same effect! . . .

From every Pueblo house long streamers of white smoke unfurled, all bent the same direction from a west wind. The light changed very fast now and in a flash the sun that we could not see struck the white peak and turned it into a rosy flower. The mountain moved and stretched like a great animal as the light descended upon it, revealing all its curves and canyons. So the sunshine came down through the upper levels of the sun until it shone in our faces even while our feet on the earth were still cold in the shadow. When the sun lighted up the mountain peak, the old governor of the Pueblo went up on his housetop and called out some words to the people. When he finished and came down and joined us where we stood beside his house, the little church bell in the belfry of the tiny Catholic church close by, gave three child-like peals. It was a young voice in this old village. The walls under it furnished a guesthouse for the royal visitors who had been introduced here three or four hundred years ago, the infant Jesus and his mother and their friends, the saints. I asked the governor what he told the people and he replied:

"I told them if they are willing, they might come to church today, for it is San Pablo's day. If they are *willing*, I said," he repeated, giggling a little.

Then the young men could be heard coming up out of the kiva, up out of the womb of their clan, at first with a sound of silver bells, then with joyous shouts, and presently we saw the long line of them crossing the snow covered open plaza, crossing the molten metallic river on an ancient foot bridge made of squared tree trunks. Their bodies were naked save for a short ket or hand-woven Indian cloth, with long sashes of colored ribbons; on their feet they wore moccasins, on their heads three tall feathers from eagles and macaws and peacocks. Each one carried a rattle gourd with pebbles in it and a sprig of evergreen pine. They had strings of shining bells bound to their limbs from waist to ankle; and around their knees a cluster of shells carved from turtles, for this was the Turtle Dance.

Thirty-six young men came padding across the snow, silent all but the bells and shells. As they passed across the background of the eastern mountain, they were black silhouettes against the smoking columns or the chimneys, with the sun full up behind them. As they passed us one by one, a fine, strong, assertive force went by. They lined up in front of the Catholic church (it is customary courtesy for the Indians here always to dance first for the visiting mother and her child and the saints!) and then they wheeled to face the sunrise and raised their right hands in a sharp salute of gourd rattles and began thumping a strong slow salva, *right*—left, *right*—left, and raising their eyes and their voices in the solemn sun chant.

Only a few moments of this welcoming song to the creator, slow and soaring, then they broke into a fast rhythm. Their feet rose and fell with their voices, rapid and joyous and in perfect unison. One of the chiefs, wrapped in his purple blanket and holding a great bunch of long feathers in his arms, moved sideways up and down in front of the dancing line with tiny steps and so soft and even were his steps he seemed to inch along as though floating over the snow. The young men chanted, eyes on the golden sun that rolled rapidly up the side of the blue eastern sky. Their teeth shone in the light, the bright warm light that made every feather and streamer or ribbon look surprisingly intense as it was borne up flashing out of the dim morning twilight. This all seemed like a birth. To have known for once the dark cold early morning earth, and to have shivered as we did and known the strange unearthly immobility of the hours before sunrise in January, and then to have experienced the immense kindliness and beauty of sunshine, not only to see, but to realize the warmth of it, the fulfillment of it in the bones and flesh, yes, this was like being born onto the earth.

It was so rich, so sumptuous—what worldly riches, what house, or palace, or church, affords such brilliance and such beauty? Why, I thought, do we put up with mere imitations of this magical natural world, going *inside*, staying *inside* so much of the time when all this lies about us all day and all night long? . . .

Chapter V

How I envied tribal life! Although all my life I had made every effort to break away, and successfully, away from my family, my schools, my group of girl friends, and finally away from one husband after another, yet my longing had always been for some kind of social unity. Somehow to escape the solitary hours, the *lonesome aloneness* I always felt when I was by myself. . . .

I often wished one of those old men in the Pueblo had been my father instead of the frustrated, tortured man I had known and turned away from in my childhood! And the women! They did not think about being free, nor did they try to be free. They were free. We think we are free. We fight for emancipation, for every liberty. American women are strong to endure; they have learned to overcome the male and dominate the environment. They are, anonymously, running the country, and there is a woman behind every man in every office and high post in the land telling him what to do. And he is doing it. But where does it get these women? To be impersonated by a great stone statue at the entrance to the port of New York? A hollow female statue bearing an artificial light upraised! How shall we learn not to be this Statue of Liberty?

My life seemed empty when I looked back upon it, empty and meaningless without the poise and dignity these Indians had from sharing a common reservoir of power to which each contributed and upon which each one drew his strength. They did not rely upon their sex life to make them whole and satisfied. None of them would look at a woman and conjecture as Dodge did, saying, "She has it" or "She has not got it," when he sized up a pretty woman in a restaurant. A satisfactory sex life was the last of the Indians' needs, I thought. There was that greater satisfaction upon all those Pueblo faces. Oh! These happy people!

"This will be mine," I thought when I crossed the barrier between Tony and myself, and I sought in every way to become like one of them as I turned away from my own kind. I wore a shawl and moccasins, and I sat upon the roof in the sun and adopted the repose and the calm of the Indian women. At night, I almost arrived at the fulfillment I had missed, though it was not through the act of love. That was all right and far happier than it had been with those others I had left behind. Love was simpler, easier for me now, though I still had frightened flesh, and it relaxed more freely with Tony's gentle body near.

No, it was after it was over, when lying beside him or curled against his strong protecting wall. Then at last I had that feeling of *home*, of having arrived, of having reached the unknown contentment all through, peace and healing from his wholesome, fresh and clean body. This became of the utmost value to me and nothing in the world should deprive me of it. But everything tries to! It was not long before the worlds began to interfere with us. Not just my world, but all the worlds. The Indian world, the world of friends and family and last my own inner world.

A letter from Dr. Brill [1919] came after some time. It was not calculated to influence me! He wrote:

My dear Mabel:

I have not written to you for a long time because, as you know, I am very busy and I really had nothing to write you. What induces me to write to you now are all kinds of rumors that I heard, which I am inclined to lend credence to. You may not like my butting in but I know that if you will realize you will know that my doing so is purely in a friendly spirit and that I have no other interest in the matter except my friendly regard for both you and Maurice. Incidentally I wish to say that I have not seen him until last Saturday when I asked him to call on me so as to see whether he could give me any information. He was in very poor spirits and as he put it:—'all I hear are rumors. I am the last man to whom people would come and tell things.' But from my own information, I feel that you are making a great mistake, and as you know me to talk straight from the shoulder, I shall talk frankly to you, realizing fully well that you are *not* going to take my advice.

Now don't you think that you ought to have some regard for the future and give up all that ridiculous mystical Indian business? Everybody thinks you are crazy and if everything that I hear is really so, as an alienist, I would agree with them; the game is too dangerous if not altogether crazy. I again wish to assure you that I am telling you that in the friendliest of spirit, and am very anxious to hear from you if you will take it as it is given. On the other hand, I will feel that I have done my duty to an old friend.

Very sincerely yours,

A.A.Brill. . . .

Chapter VI

Awareness is the most important faculty for the development of consciousness and there have been several people along the way whose influence heightened my awareness, the awareness of what my life had been, what it had become in me, and where it might lead me next. Thus from fortunate contacts one learned gradually to get on to oneself. The major influences were like strong searchlights thrown upon one; they were suggestive of Michelangelo's great painting where God the Father leans toward the sleeping Adam with the index finger of his outstretched hand pointing, as though to awaken him with a creative touch. . . .

Tony was one of these influences. He had the sun in his heart. Coming upon the arid desert within me when my heart seemed turned to stone, it was terribly sweet to feel it open outwards and breathe once more when he awakened in me a feeling of responsive affection and good nature, the warm loving-hearted way of being that had slept in me so long that it seemed like death. For not since a discouraged baby, born ready to laugh and live and who, instead, had been thrust back into isolation in a loveless environment, had that atrophied heart lifted itself spontaneously to beat in response to another's heart and to give its life to another's life without self-seeking or calculation. Tony gave me his fire, the fire of love that is like rich oil rising from the deep well of the psyche, burning in the darkness of the body. . . .

Chapter VII[20]

In the empty rooms of our new house in the desert the days were golden and quiet that autumn, and the yellow leaves fell from the big cottonwood along the ditch occasionally, one at a time very slowly. In the nights, there was a fresh thin edge of ice in the air and the stars bristled in the blue-black sky. From the orchard below a winey smell of apples ripening filled the house with a lovely smell. There was so little in the rooms that the air moved free and easy, always sweet with sage and cedar wood smoke and fruit. For every morning and evening a fire of pinon burned in the living room fireplace, and the logs lying out on the adobe hearth ready to be added to the embers grew hot, and their perfume was like incense. Sometimes the fire smoked a little and this threw a thin blue veil of color across the room. It was like the ethereal haze upon the mountains, and the sun [coming] in from the east windows made it drift slanting in broad bands dreamily.

The new life was gradually shaping itself, developing its features of change and test. I had relinquished nearly everything that had surrounded me in former years and I had been so glad to do so, feeling free and unburdened in the emptiness, so little furniture—few books, pictures, *things*. I felt free and open to new values and the simpler ways I was learning from Tony, and for a while there was a euphoric zest and delight in every day and night, and the pleasure of living filled the empty cells of my body as well as my heart and spirit and renewed them.

At first I did not question, but just lived and did not bother to know why; but alas! One of the most fundamental needs in me had always been to know *why*. At first, in the first months in Taos, I had paused to ask myself *why, why*, what was the reason for the radical alteration in the whole pattern of existence, what had compelled me to its acceptance, *why* was Tony chosen to initiate me into a completely new life.

This life now had a new content. The artists with whom heretofore I had spent so much time had talked a great deal about "significant form" but it had seemed to me that this phrase was often a mystery to them. Life itself as the Indians conceived of it now really had this significant form, but the significance of it remained undisclosed to me no matter how often I pondered upon it. It was always good to sit with them and one felt nourished by their company. But to accept this and not to understand it was not enough for me after a while, and the old habit of analysis began to move in me again, and I started to try to feel my way into their mysterious mode of being, to try and comprehend it. There was something unfathomable about it; one could share their well being, but the source of it remained hidden.

It sometimes seemed to me they blocked the way and refused to let me pass to their deep center of being. When they felt me try to penetrate it, even in silence, I always came up against the secretive Indian silence. And never would they answer any questions. It was evident that they hated the white race's habit of probing and interrogating. They themselves never asked me any questions, and it seemed they had none to ask.

"Why did Manuel go to the mountain?" "Why does he change his hair today from braids to a knot?" "Why?"

And the utmost response would come, taciturn, from Tony: "Secret."

When did this begin to be a torment? Gradually it ceased to be enough to share instinctively his simple strong direct life. It was no longer enough to have, through him, judgment without thought, living without apparent productivity, living without the need to make and have *things*. Then Tony would repeat, "God told the Indians they must not have *things*. The white man can have things but the Indian can only have what he finds in the mountain."

Certainly, in the reaction away from the old life, it had been a relief to get away from things. There was only weariness in the thought of old tunes, sculpture, books, furniture. I thought I was through with them forever; discarded and abandoned, I was free of them, I thought. All I wanted, all I sought now was to exchange the endless futile activity over objects that preoccupied the whole white world for the mysterious activity of the Indian, concerned only with the occult and deeply religious inner Indian life, and I wrote:

The mountain, the arrow, and the star your symbols are;
The flag, the cross, and the dollar sign,
These are mine!

I had been ready to give up everything, customs, beliefs, nationality, and income if my family became upset over my situation, in exchange for the new life Tony brought me into. But now I wanted more. I wanted to know the secret of the Sacred Mountain, the secret of the Indian's sufficiency and their innate scorn of the white man's customs. What did Jesus Christ know that the Indians did not? He came to give more abundant life, but the Indians had that, not us for whom, apparently, He died.

What knowledge and what dream lay behind the strange lined brows of the Indians gazing into the sunrise over the eastern range? No puerile creed or compensating philosophy had molded those strong stern features, nor caused the deep eyes to glow with the persistent flame.

The questioning mood was intermittent when it first began to come upon me, for the days were always filled. There was work to do. I was learning to cook, and Tony was helping with the work on the house, and simple needs were more or less slowly attended to. When it grew cold we went rabbit hunting and duck shooting, either on horseback or driving an old horse and buggy. Tony was always teaching me something new: how to see farther than I ever had before, how to distinguish the winds and their portents, when the moon held water, why the owl hooted.

He taught me to distinguish the difference in the sound of the stream after midnight and how to taste food with more relish. But he never explained why he could walk straight up a hillside with no more effort than when he went down it, nor why he had no large, hard muscles like other strong men, nor why an Indian woman would pick up a large child or a hundred pound sack of wheat and sling it onto her back with no physical strain. He never taught me anything about the quality of Indian strength.

But sometimes he would talk about Taos in a way that was difficult to understand. He would stare at the Sacred Mountain for a long time and then he would say:

"Can you feel the power coming out of the mountain?"

Once he said: "Taos is the beating heart of the world. Do you know that this world *lives*?"

When he spoke so I felt a strange vibration of life pass over from him through me, and I almost understood something hidden from me. But I gradually realized he never told me anything definite about the Indian religion.

It was soon after Tony and I were living together that I woke up in the dark in the middle of the night and saw him pulling on his clothes in the dim room. It was cold and black and still and I was afraid.

"What are you doing?" I asked him sitting up.

"Dressin'," he answered. "Goin'."

"Going *where*?" I exclaimed.

"To the mountain. You know I told you I must."

"Oh Tony: *Why*? What for?"

"Secret," he told me in a short tone, hurrying. "Indian work to do on the mountain."

I couldn't bear this. Though I knew the Indians had their unexplainable customs, their curious ways the white people knew nothing about, we had grown so close and intimate I couldn't bear this sense of separation from his life and having to be cut off from his activities. He had told me before that the Indians had to go each in their turn all the year round up the big mountain on some kind of errands for the chiefs of their clans, but what errands they were were inconceivable to me;

I knew that even the Indian women did not share these religious secrets and that only the men were involved in the mysterious activities of the ceremonies.

Now that it was brought home to me I could not take it. A quick suspicion flooded me like a habitual poison. I began to think he was fooling me, that it was somehow concerned with a woman—perhaps he was going to see a woman out in the Pueblo under the cover of the night. Maybe this was the penalty of my own secret life with him, the result of our hidden happiness together, that forced me to suspect him of the same conduct with another; or perhaps it was a consequence of the conventions or my race, that prevented me from being able to imagine any reason in the world for getting up in the night and hurrying out into the darkness other than a clandestine one concerned with secret love. Whatever it was that conditioned me to this commonplace assumption, I was instantly possessed of it so that I couldn't control myself.

"No! No! Don't go: I won't *let* you go."

He gently removed my clinging hands. "Please," he said quietly, and went on with his preparations.

Now I was under the influence of a certain heroine type that I had encountered in books and plays, the high-spirited passionate creature that requires to be handled like a lively racehorse. I understood that men found value in such violence of feeling, in such highly-strung, nervous emotions; that they enjoyed the sensation of power they experienced in gentling these wild, extravagant and even dangerous females. I naturally supposed that Tony, so strong and capable himself, would love to meet strength in me and overcome it, that he would like a combat, a physical test between us, and that the satisfaction of dominating me in my frenzy would be melted in love, and he would be unable to leave here at this moment for anything, no matter what. Other men would have been stimulated by this strategy, but not Tony. Perhaps he did not need to test his strength. Anyway, when I threw myself upon him and began to try to drag his clothes off him in a hurricane of passion, he only remarked mildly:

"Don't do that. You tear my trousers."

This was an instantaneous douche of cold water that banished my simulated mood quicker than if he had thrown me on the floor. Naturally, I had not felt as much anguish as my action had portrayed. No one does. But I had felt the need to prevent his mysterious escape, and I had taken the means to deflect him that was considered irresistible, according to the teaching of the period I was brought up in.

He finished dressing and bent down and kissed me where I lay perfectly deflated upon the bed. "Don't worry. I come back pretty soon. You sleep," he said cheerfully and went out the door, and I must admit I comfortably slept and I never again tried to draw him into a wrestling match with me, for I had learned it was of no use to put on an act of any kind with him. He always somehow saw through it. But I continued to pester him.

"Where have you been, Tony? What have you been doing?" Jealously I begged him for an explanation without getting any answer. Sometimes I cried with exasperation and he let me do so without making any effort to satisfy me or even to stop me. After a little while he would go again just the same.

Once I said, "*Who* ties your hair up like that for you?" but he did not answer.

"Why can't I tie up your hair?" I cried. He only laughed.

It seemed to me the Indians were always going on mysterious errands to the Mountain. Tony would mention that Lupe had had to leave our building work and go get a weed on the mountain.

"What did he do with it?" I queried.

"He gave it to the war chief."

I didn't have the slightest idea what it was all about. Once in a while a faint feeling of scorn rose in me for this constant activity that did not seem very important. It was the usual feeling that people have for what they do not understand and cannot estimate in terms of their own customs. But it did not assail me often for I always saw that the Indians were keen, ready and full of enjoyment, and that their life made them so. Besides, I realized they were grave and serious and centered, and supported in an unfailing equilibrium that no outside circumstance had thus far been able to upset; and always there was the perpetual glow in them, a kind of still radiation.

One evening this was particularly apparent when several of the Indian boys came down to the house and danced while Tony sang and drummed for them. I had a few people come and spend the evening to watch them. The Indians sat cross-legged beside the fire when they were resting, and the white people sat in chairs around the room, and suddenly I saw that the Americans were like cold ashes and the Indians like glowing coals. Why? Why? Would I ever find out? . . .

There was no name for the relationship that grew between us. I had used the word love in the past, and now I realized that I had made it a cloak for many abuses, abuses of powers and potentialities. It had been a mask for greediness, for self-expression and what we had called sex-expression! Trivial outlets to assuage the persistent groping of the spirit that did not assuage but only defeated it. The world of science and of art had been full of such lovers, and it had been a world reduced to compromise and failure, a world well lost indeed!

I slowly learned by loving to stop thinking and talking about love, about sex, or even about life. But alas! I could not stop looking for the reason! The Reason.

The reason *why*. And that old habit clung to me until it began to poison me in the garden of life. . . .

There was an additional reason for the conflict that was going on in me. The time was approaching when he would have to leave me and go away, down into the earth in the underground kiva for six weeks. He did not tell me anything about it, but I saw it had a great importance in the ceremonial life. It was the turn of his clan that came around every ten years to absent themselves in that way; the men emerging only a few minutes night and morning to attend to their needs and to stop in their houses long enough to eat the specially prepared food they ate during that period. I wondered if this was a way of having a rebirth, refreshment from nature whom they worshipped and called mother. Later Tony told me his part in the ceremony, but when it was imminent I knew nothing, and I dreaded his absence, having him go so completely away from me, leaving me alone in ignorance. It was like a death.

When he saw how I felt about staying alone without him, he persuaded me to go away to New York for the time he would be occupied by his duty. I did not want to do that either, but he told me he felt I should and that perhaps it was *necessary* for me to go. He seemed strongly impressed with this idea as though it were a voice in him trying to advise me so, and when he was moved in this way, he was very strong and hard to oppose.

When he went down to the train in Albuquerque with me just before I left, he revealed to me that at the end of the period in the kiva he would be made the head man of his clan, the one to take care of the young boys during their year and a half of training and initiation. For a year, he said, he had been preparing his "things" for this, the objects he would use, the medicines and herbs he would need, and the "things" that had belonged to his father.

He was a little uncertain, at that last moment, that he would get through it; for, he admitted, the old men had been antagonistic to him lately on my account and because of Candelaria. He asked me to write a telegram for him to send me if anything went wrong, a telegram saying: "I am out."

~~~~~~~~~~~~~~~~~~~~~~

[In chapter VIII, Mabel tells the story of her returning to New York City in April 1919 and meeting the occultist Mrs. Lotus Dudley, who prophecies her and Tony's mission of serving as a "bridge between cultures" between the white and Indian worlds.]

Chapter IX

At home, now, I felt a new significance in my life with Tony. Had I really been prepared for some cosmic purpose? I wondered how the new old truth would pass over to me without word or mouth from the Indians. Would I recognize it? I looked deeply into the eyes of old Indians when I met them in the lanes and along the highways. Would they recognize me and pass something to me across the invisible airy path?

But they only continued to look at me as they always had before, deep and observant, but blocking something away from me, always letting down a shutter between us. They went continually on their way to and from upon the mountain, up its steep flanks lightly and easily and unendingly, but they never gave a sign that I could take for a sign. Neither did Tony give me any particular training or teaching. Living by his side began to modify me in some ways, but not deeply enough.

I could not accept those strange occasions yet, when at unheralded times, he still seemed to abandon me. He would just suddenly go away in the night and stay until morning, or if he was already away he would not come back until too late for dinner. . . .

These interruptions to our good life were infrequent and the following day, after such a fearful night, would be serene and cloudless, and gradually they lessened, for Tony hated the break in our tranquility. He began to give up. When he was summoned, he neglected to go, though he looked thoughtful and was silent in an evening when I knew he was expected up there (for I learned to recognize the messengers who came to remind him of his duty). He would not say anything. He would sit by the fire and tap his drum without singing. And he would avoid my eyes. Then I would break in upon his silence and complain of his inattention and accuse him of "going away" from me inside himself.

He would shake his head and say, "No. I never leave you. I just thinkin' about my brothers in the kiva all so happy and glad doin' their work. That's all. Prayin' for the world together."

I would feel sorry and glad at once, to have him there with me, but I wished he could be away too, at the same time. I suppose I wished I could share his life, but that I never could do. There was always, always that Indian life that I never could share: "Oh Tony! I am sorry! I spoil everything for you!"

"No. I don't want to go much any more. The old men put me too far down. I lost my place. I don't care like I used to be."

"My fault again?"

"No. That none of their business what I do. I take care my duty in the work, I reach my place. What for they bring you and Candelaria in, for?"

"Oh! It's all so hard, isn't it?"

"It is," was the fervent reply.

"Isn't there some way you could get back in again, Tony?" He shook his head.

"Only if I would go and spend one whole year in the kiva." . . .

Chapter XII

I believe now I never realized what Tony went through when he failed to keep up his age-old custom and duty in the kiva. He did not talk about it to me again. He has never talked much to me. Perhaps I was too obtuse to notice his feelings and too wrapped up in my own then. And also perhaps he himself was unaware of what went on inside him.

It did not enter my head to wonder how Candelaria was getting along without a man to keep her and take care of her. I simply put her out of my head. Who brought her wood to keep her house warm? Who took the grain to be ground into flour? The men always took care of the fire and the women of the water, fetching it in ollas or buckets from the river—wonderfully balanced on their heads, one arm stretched up to hold it. I never wondered how she managed with the balance of her life broken.

I knew that when sometimes he had to have his hair tied at the back for ceremonial reasons, instead of in the two long braids on each side, he went to his mother's house to have her do it for him. I had tried to do this once but the long slippery hair slipped out of my hands like a snake and I could not manage it. Tony laughed and pushed me away and I never tried it again.

I knew after that he went to his mother because I had forced it out of him when I nagged him and pummeled him about it: *Did* he go to Candelaria's house? *Who* tied up his hair for him? *Did* he have anything more to do with her? No, no, and *no* he always replied. Finally about the hair I dragged the reluctant words out of him, "My mother." So low voiced, so unwilling: "My mother." It seemed to me finally that he changed in a way from the time he had been lowered in rank in the kiva, and gradually went there less and less. It was as though he lost some interest in life. He sat around the house more; somehow he let things slide. . . .

"Why don't you ever go out to the Pueblo any more?" I began complaining soon.

"I don't feel I got anything there anymore. The old men took away my religious things and gave them to my younger cousin. I don't feel I belong anymore. Guess I belong here!" He ended with a wry sweet smile, raising his eyebrows at me.

Perhaps because there wasn't enough going on, perhaps because I instinctively wanted to get Tony interested again in something outside, some reason I have forgotten led me to begin building another house across the fields. Tony always liked building and soon had a bunch of Indians down making adobes, laying rocks for the foundation. They worked all summer and the Two Story House got built [1920]. That is what everybody called it then and they still do. In those days there were only one or two houses in Taos with a second floor: Old Lady Gusdorf's and the Harwood's. The new house was finished by late autumn. Made without any plan drawn to scale, just from a little drawing I made, and the rooms paced out on the ground and marked off by wooden pegs. It has been a lovely house to live in all these years. And how many people have passed through it!

The first to come were the Colliers [in December 1920]. John Collier had resigned from the People's Institute in New York, and Lucy, the children, and he had been living in California since I had left New York. He had no new job yet, but she had one in Child Welfare work. I wrote and asked them to come and spend the winter. I had a vague idea, scarcely a thought, of getting him interested in the Indians in the hope that he would suggest some way to help them. They were friendless and innocent. They had been betrayed again and again, and I was afraid of something any day. . . .

No matter how the Indian Bureau pretended to protect them and their rights, the *protection* always seemed placed more on the white employees of the Bureau than upon the Indians! I also hoped Tony could cooperate with him in some kind of Indian work and have a new interest and activity. Together they might discover a way to preserve the pure ancient culture of these people, I thought. Had not Maurice written to me from here when I was still in New York that I must come out and "save the Indians"?

The Colliers arrived with the three little boys, and the night they came, it was cold and the children were chilled from the daylong ride up from Santa Fe. They took off their shoes and stockings and sat in a row on the big couch before the fire, holding their red feet out to the blaze, their brown eyes shining with excitement at the strangeness of everything. Early the next morning Tony and I were awakened by the youngest, little John, peeking in at us from the sleeping porch, up which he had climbed from the ground. The family fitted perfectly into the Two Story house and we had a nice winter together. . . .

The children made friends with the Indians and spent much of their time in the Pueblo, often sleeping out there with their small friends. Big John [Collier] spent hours sitting with the older Indians and hearing about their problems. They liked him and sometimes invited him to their council meetings in the governor's house, and more and more I hoped some idea would occur to him whereby he could be of assistance to them, as well as supplying him with a job to support himself so he could stay here and offer them some adequate protection.

Though Tony no longer took part in the religious ceremonies, he did attend the council meetings, for they were concerned with the administrative life of the village, its communal activities and the behavior of the people. The governors were newly elected every year by a system of voting of which I am still in ignorance, though I have heard many camouflaged stories about it from the Indians, who are skillful about suppressing the facts about their life. Sometimes they said it depended upon who won the September relay race at San Geronimo [harvest] fiesta, the north side or the south side of the Pueblo; that one of these winners would choose the governor like Democrats or Republicans, only these were Summer People or Winter People: However, I don't know.

The sixth of January, the day of the new governor's election, all the young men and boys dressed up in the evening in masks and the costumes of other tribes and they visited the houses of the new governor and those of his chosen officers, as well as those of the new War Chief and his men. They made fun and mimicked the stranger tribes, and showed up their queer ways of dancing and singing, and one had no trouble in recognizing Navajos, Apaches, Comanches and others, for they are natural actors in the Taos Pueblo and their parodies are inimitable. As they left each officer, the woman-of-the-house gave round loaves of new wheat bread and cakes sprinkled with sugar, and the boys tossed them in the gunnysacks carried for that purpose. At the end of the evening these would be full to the top.

The winter wore along, and in the spring, John sighed and said he must be on his way back to California to look for a job that would take care of them. I was disappointed but I said nothing.

Chapter XIII

A year passed and then a real bomb seemed about to burst upon the Indian people [1922]. . . . We learned now that a man named Bursum was trying to pass a bill in Washington proposing to take the Indian land and allot it to individual Indians and allow them to sell it if they wished. In this manner, the government could buy it back and convey it to the returned soldiers by a loan system, or rich Americans could buy it up and build fine ranches and farms upon it. . . .

When this Bursum Bill popped up I sent a telegram to Collier about it. Before he received it, I had a letter from him saying he had tried to stay away from the Indians and work but he could not forget them. He didn't know anything that could make him as happy and refreshed as to sit for an hour with the old men in council and share their quietude and strength. He could not find any work he believed in as much as he did in the noble, just, and balanced way of life these people had, and that they must lose it sooner or later unless someone interposed for them with the government of the United States.

He had thought it out and he believed he could form an organization to be called "The American Indian Defense Association," and that he could gather together a large enough group of influential, sympathetic people who would work with him. He went immediately to work on this plan, constituted himself the Secretary and soon had the whole thing under way with a number of other organizations connected with it. For instance he had interested Mrs. Stella Atwood, the president of the Federation of Women's Clubs of America. (Practically all of them Statues of Liberty!) She was one of the directors of the new association and she alone represented three or four million voters. . . .[21]

Collier's salary was now assured and he returned to Taos. There was a new kind of humming and buzzing going on around us now. Tony and he were constantly on the move back and forth, for Tony took him to all the twenty-two other Pueblo villages where council meetings were called. He told the Indians there was a great new movement started by the white people to defend them from government fraud and injustice, and they would oppose all political action that was against Indian rights. He would watch for all the bills and lobbying that constantly came up in Washington to deprive Indians of their land and the products of their lands like timber, grazing, oil, and other riches. They would defeat these efforts by publicity and an appeal to the public conscience.

More than that, there would be started a new fight for the health and a better educational system for the Indians. They would protect and insure the continuance of their old customs so their culture would be preserved. Collier had been convinced by his year in Taos, and from hearing many stories and incidents I had told him, that in these minority groups scattered about America, there was the truest spirituality to be found in the United States. "This is [a] haven," he kept saying, "This is the vision without which the people perish."

Tony grew more and more interested in helping Collier and it was gratifying to him to use his influence again and work for his people. Collier listened when Tony told him that long ago the Pueblo tribes used to meet when some attack or danger threatened them and have a pow-wow to decide how to act. Old John Archuleta, Ventura (Candelaria's father), and other older men would travel for days on horseback down to San Felipe and take council with the others gathered there.

There had never been any effort made by any government employees to assist the Indians or get them together. In fact our government policy has always tended towards the British one: divide and rule. So they had had to work many things out by themselves.

Now Collier had one of his inspirations. He told Tony they must organize an all-Pueblo Council that could be called together at any time at some central meeting place like Santo Domingo or San Felipe Pueblos. He said the Indians must establish a great solidarity among themselves and their villages so they could always know what was going on among them and be able to defend themselves, and not be taken unawares. As he and Tony traveled from Pueblo to Pueblo all the way from Taos to Zuni and Hopi land they organized this new political device, and the people took to it enthusiastically. They agreed at once to fight together to defeat the Bursum Bill.

Tony was in his real element now. He had a true social sense and when he was eliminated from the religious group and its activities, he felt wasted of his power and persuasion. Besides the individual strength of his own personality, he had always been respected as one of the Taos Indians who call this village the King Pueblo. I suppose that is because it is at the head of all the others along the Rio Grande. I know that Tony told me that when Montezuma came here before the arrival of Cortez in Mexico, he is said to have told the Taos Indians they were the head of his empire. Montezuma was carried on his own litter by relays of runners, bringing twelve of his courtiers and his little queen called the Malinche. He gave the Taos people his fire and told them to keep it burning until he came again and this they are said to have done, in a shrine high up in a cave on the mountain. He taught them his dance—called now Matachines—wherein he danced with the Malinche and his twelve men, a clown, and a Buffalo. He told them to dance it until he should come again, and this dance they keep alive, as do all the other pueblos where he is said to have passed. . . .[22]

Chapter XVII

[In chapter XVII, Mabel writes about Tony Lujan's decision to divorce his wife Candelaria and Tony Romero's suggestion that Mabel pay her a monthly stipend to get her to agree. Mabel seems to have forgotten that she had already made a contractual agreement with Candelaria in 1920, approved by the Taos Pueblo Council, to pay her a stipend of thirty-five dollars a month for life on the condition that she agree to accept Tony and Mabel's liaison.[23]]

While Tony was interested and active again now, I was left alone a great deal, . . . Once more I grew depressed and unoccupied, I longed for something to do.

I tried to take an interest in what was going on and to contribute to it all, and sometimes I had some useful ideas. I occasionally wrote some publicity, an article and so on, but I was not deeply involved as the others were; Collier because he loved power and enjoyed functioning in his own brilliant Jesuitical fashion, loving to defeat lesser men than himself who were established in sound government positions; Tony who was filled with the satisfaction of an altruistic activity where he could use himself and his faculties for the benefit of the Indian people. All his life he had been a part of a great and ancient organization whose fundamental principle was cooperation. He had suffered the loneliness of the newborn individual whose previous habit had been to share the group spirit. Now once more he was working for and with his own people in a new way.

And I? I was neither one thing nor the other. Neither a cog in a machine nor a gleeful solitary laughing devil like Collier, outwitting the herd by the simple genius within. I had to listen to so many details about Tony's efforts to get the Indians together! I remember now hard it was for him to persuade Antonio Romero to join in the new movement. Tony Romero was a huge, fat, astute Indian who was as clever as he could be within the limitations of his nature, which was warped by distrust and suspicion. He believed in no one, white or Indian. Frequently he proved to be right, other times he was mistaken and lost out by his lack of faith.

Tony said to me, "He is my corn brother. I know him well since a long time. I cannot make him come to the council meeting in the Pueblo and hear Collier tell about that Bursum Bill!"

"Now what is a corn brother?" I asked, for I was struck by the name.

"We spent our months of initiation together. We sleep together a long time. We eat our corn meal together. We become corn brothers then. So I know him all through."

"Do you like him?" I asked.

"I don't have to like him or not like him. Sometimes we not agree about things. But he my corn brother just the same. He run away and hide when Collier talked to the Council last night. Maybe I make him come next time. He got lots of power and influence."

Indeed I knew that. Tony Romero was mixed up in everything that went on around him. When I started to build our living room he appeared immediately and pointed out the iron pegs in the ground marking the boundary of the Indian reservation and warned me against trespassing even one inch over it. I had to obey him then and run the house down a straight line that made the back of it look like a railroad train with the locomotive at the end of the first floor rooms. However, after Tony Lujan and I were married, he took a large piece of the uncultivated sagebrush desert behind us, and we could build out on that as far as I wanted to. For by fencing unused Indian land, any Indians could take portions of it if they needed.[24]

Sometime before, Tony Romero had come down here and told me how much anger and disapproval there was among the Indians on account of Tony and me, and he told me they were going to make trouble for me with their Indian Bureau lawyer because Tony had deserted Candelaria for a white woman. This threw me into a panic and he played upon me until I was thoroughly frightened, and I saw that Tony was worried too.

We began to talk about the possibility of Tony getting a divorce, although he, like the other Indians, was a Roman Catholic, in name, at least. I had already divorced Maurice [1922] and it seemed about time Tony and I should marry and put an end to the threats that were always upsetting us. But Tony Romero forestalled that. He said that Candelaria would get the divorce as we were in the wrong.

I wrote Arthur Brisbane for advice about this and was horrified. He had his sister Alice [Thursby] write me back and tell me I must settle the matter at once in some way that would prevent Candelaria from taking action and naming me as the correspondent. "Arthur says you must not let this go on record and you must be sensible and give it up if you cannot arrange matters otherwise." I could imagine Arthur's consternation at my involvement with one of the "dark races," for his life-long phobia against them dated from his father's effort to free the southern Negro slaves! When I told Tony what Arthur said, he saw it from my side just as Arthur did, and immediately he took a strong attitude about it.[25]

He said, "I see. I got to leave you and go stay in the Pueblo. I got to find excuse against Candelaria so she won't hurt you. I can find it because that woman always have a man. Maybe Tony Romero. I go out and watch." . . .

The next day seemed time enough to Tony, and then he brought in the big, wily self-sufficient man [Tony Romero], who sat down looking like one of the elder statesmen and we talked it all over. He said he thought he could straighten it out with Candelaria if I would agree to support her. That was what she wanted most and needed. "You make a paper and give her a promise you pay her something every month and I make her sign a promise not make no trouble for you and Tony."

Though he seemed to be there to work on our side, I knew Tony believed he had been telling Candelaria what to do all along; but anyway this plan was agreed on and I had a paper drawn up. It said that if she agreed not to take any legal step against Tony, I would agree to pay her . . . ("How much?" I asked Tony Romero. "Oh, twenty-five a month, I guess." "I'll make it that then," and did so.)[26]

He hesitated on the threshold enquiringly as he left. "Guess you need something for your trouble?" inquired Tony Lujan.

"Guess so. You bring me that money every month, now, and I give it to her and make her act right," he said. I hastily made Candelaria's first check and another for him for twenty-five dollars and he looked gratified and left.

He had told me he was writing down the history of his tribe, that nobody had ever been able to get, and he would show it to me when it was finished. I was surprised at this because there is the strongest taboo about telling or writing down anything about the past. They do not believe in telling things nor putting them into words except once a year when for three days and nights, the boys' initiation period ends with the old men telling them their history: where they came from and when and many other things, as the names of all the animals on earth, and all the things that grow. This history then is handed down by word of mouth and only told once, for they believe that the power goes out of anything that is talked about or written about. They warn the boys that the punishment they will get if they *repeat* all this is madness or death. (Like the wages of sin!) The greatest sin then for the Indians is losing the Truth of things by talking or writing about them.

So of course Tony Lujan looked upon what Tony Romero said as a crime. He told me as he had before, "No white person has ever been able to get it! But now Tony Romero expects to get *money* for it from you. Perhaps he die for that." . . .

Chapter XX

For publicity Collier and a group of Taos Indians went to San Francisco and stayed a few days and he arranged a few public engagements for them to dance there. Tony went along to lead the singing and play the drum. No one there had seen these dances and everybody was most enthusiastic and surprised to find them so beautiful, and the Indians so attractive to know, poised and self-possessed. After the dances were over, each time Collier gave a short talk to the gathering and told how the Indian Bureau wanted to put an end to dancing and singing in the Pueblos. He raised a great deal of indignation about it and much support among prominent people, for the protection of a culture that produced so fine an art.

The Indians were entertained and made many lifelong friends on this first visit. One night they were taken to a symphony concert and sat in a couple of boxes, dignified and calm throughout the evening, wrapped in their white sheets. This was the first time any of these Indians had attended such an example of our type of amusement, and I never did hear what they thought of it, but when the concert was over they were taken behind the stage to meet the conductor, Dr. Hertz.[27] The governor was introduced first and when he shook the perspiring maestro by one hand, he bowed slightly and said, appraisingly: "You are a very good dancer, Doctor!"

By this time, Collier had engaged Dr. Richard Shevky to go to Taos to make a survey of the amount of syphilis that existed in the pueblo, for he had a suspicion there was a fair amount of it there. I protested strongly against this belief of his for the Indians seemed so wholesome and healthy and apart from that depressing feature of civilization. But Collier insisted. He introduced me to the Shevkys and I liked them at once. Richard was a Turk who had studied medicine in America, and he had a charming way of smiling, and his wife, Marion, was a sweet girl. His real name was Eshref not Richard, but she had renamed him to avoid the complications of always spelling out the unfamiliar syllables to her friends.

At Collier's suggestion, I invited them to stay with us because Tony was going to help him by accompanying him to the Pueblo and introducing him slowly to the people, and also he would help persuade them to agree to what seemed to them a witchy performance—giving up their blood to this stranger for goodness knows what purpose. First of all, it was hard to persuade Tony about this. It was completely foreign to him and only his faith in Collier finally made him accept it without understanding the first thing about it. Undoubtedly it was associated in his mind with some of the Indian beliefs about witchcraft. . . .

No one of them ever allowed any portion of themselves—hair, fingernails, anything of the body—to remain carelessly strewn about to be used by witches. Everything human was destroyed by fire or water. Tony had complete faith in Collier. Anything he said or did was right. It must have been a great conversion in him that enabled him not only to give his sample of blood but also to persuade the other Indians to do the same. Since he was the head of it, he began with his own family and made them all go through the fearsome ordeal.

The Shevkys were living with us now and on certain days Richard and Tony went out to the pueblo and gathered up a few samples of blood and these had to be mailed to Albuquerque where one special day a week the Wasserman tests were made at the state laboratory. Then they have to wait for three or four days to hear the results by our slow mail. I thought nothing of Tony's examination. I knew he was beyond corruption. So that for him to have a test was only to help the morale of the other Indians, and of course I was right. His report was negative.[28]

Chapter XXI

In spite of our pleasant life all together downstairs, upstairs at night, Tony and I often had great disturbances and trials. Though he worked with Richard in the morning, or sometimes drove about the valley and into the canyons with us on picnics, at night he would disappear after dinner and generally came back very late when we were all in bed, the others asleep in the end of the house, I lying awake in a panic. I could not stop suspecting him of being with other Indian women. Always, he always denied it. Calmly, dispassionately, solidly he denied it.

"Then where *have* you been?" I would cry, "*What* have you been doing?"

He would reply differently each time and always diffidently: "I been talkin' with my family, or I been with my old friends." And once he said: "I been at Tony Romero's house. He has a watermelon and we eat it." . . .

Chapter XXII

It was midnight and I lay sleepless in the wide bed upstairs. The oil lamp burned low and I stared at the soft ruffled ceiling where thick white wash over the saplings had wiped out every edge and left the look of drifted snow. I was waiting as on so many nights for Tony to come home, for I could never sleep until he was safe beside me. My heart, as always, beat with the hard sickening thump of apprehension. I who had never known fear now learned to be afraid at night on his account. Finally I heard the door close down below and soon his moccasins padded on the stairs.

I sat up in bed and turned up the lamp beside me higher so I could see his face when he came in. He entered without a word, looking dignified and calm as he always did. "Tony, why are you so late? I get so scared!"

"Scared why?" he asked, bending down to take off his moccasins.

"'Cause I always think something has happened! Where have you been and what have you been doing?"

He raised his head and looked at me. It seemed there was a colder, less affectionate expression on his unreadable face. I got out of bed and began walking up and down in the warm summer night. I felt like crying but I did not know what do.

"Oh *dear*!" I murmured.

He rose in bare feet, unwound his white sheet from about his loins and threw it down on the bed. "Seems like you always got to act foolish!" he said in an unfamiliar voice.

I did not answer. My eyes were fixed upon the wrinkled end of the sheet lying there with the lamplight shining on it. I stared at the dampened border that had tiny red veins of blood streaking through it. Without conscious thought I raised the cloth to my nose and smelled it, and a wave of sickness swept over me. That odor! That unmistakable smell of the male seed, fresh and new, the semen! I threw it on the floor with a cry and fell over on to the bed and threw the pillow over my face. For a while I was unaware of everything outside that smell that lingered in my nostrils like a doom. And hard upon that, an old memory rushed back to me.

There was a dream I had had years ago . . . , a dream [that] was overwhelming, yet it was only about an odor, a strange unknown effluvia that assaulted me with menace and threat and it was accompanied by a voice I had never heard before that uttered meaningfully: "That is the odor of evil." . . . even to recount it now revives the terror and despair it gave me.

So on that night, lying in the darkness beneath the pillow, I lived again caught up in the same terror and despair of the first dream experience. For I recognized then for the first time what the nature of that odor was, a recognition I had never known, an association I had never made before in waking life. For me now the primitive, physiological character of the smell of the seminal fluid was evil, really, and destructive for me. All I knew when I struggled back to full consciousness, then, was fear, real fear and despair, as though life was over, while I was still alive.

"Tony! Your white sheet!" I cried in horror, for the white sheet of the Taos Indians is their insignia of privilege and honor. . . . At any Indian settlement a Taos Indian has always had a special welcome from a traditional influence it bears, patriarchal and ancient, and that dates back to a former age when it consisted of a wrap of finely tanned white buckskin. The deer man! How many times I had seen an Indian on a housetop seize his sheet, stretching it out wide behind him in his two hands, then draw it about him closely as though enfolding someone within it against him! A passionate gesture to some woman, watching through a tiny window far across the Pueblo: And how many times Tony had bound it about me likewise!

"Alright. I did it. It don't mean anything," I heard him say, his voice seeming far away and muffled. He took the pillow away from my face and lifted me up.

"Who?" I murmured, questioning as always within me the memory of this black anguish.

"Christine," he responded calmly.

"Who is Christine?"

"That Tony Romero's wife." His corn brother's woman!

"Now you have broken everything between us. It can never be the same again."

"Oh yes. It will always be the same between us. You know it. We are together for always. You know it."

Yes alas! I knew it. For better or for worse, in the deepest sense, we were together for always and I did know it. I remembered now he had expressed this once, standing by this same window up in our room and looking over to the eastern hills. "You can't ever stay away from me now. Even if you go far off, far as New York, and I go up on these hills and play my flute and call you, you will always have to come back."

No, I could never get away. I would always have to come back. This thing between us was the unbreakable bondage, although in all these years since then the white people have muttered together and said I could not get away even if I would, for "the government" would not let me divorce him, or they murmured, "She is afraid of him; she dare not leave." So they have rationalized this lasting union that seems to them so unsuitable, so illogical, so inexplicable, never guessing at a simpler explanation.

I lay back very weak on the bed while Tony sat beside me. There was no fury of jealousy in me as there had been before at the suspicion of the betrayal. No, now in the reality there was no anger, no jealousy, only a deep, terrible realization of an end of something, the end of our innocent happiness and completion, and the beginning of tragedy.

"Do not be mad," Tony said in a low voice, putting his hand on my shoulder.

"No, I am not mad," my breath came sobbing for my heart was beating so fast in its fear.

"That Christine waiting for me when I come out her house in the dark. She want it. That's all."

"All," I thought. "All." ("The woman tempted me and I did eat!")

"That *blood*," I murmured turning my face away.

"Blood?" he asked.

"There is blood too," I answered.

"That funny. I don't know what for blood."

"Oh Tony!" I couldn't stand his cool indifferent mood when for me it was incomprehensibly the end of our world. Since I could not control my weeping and it seemed it would never stop, he rose and lay beside me and tried to comfort me in the age old way a man takes when his woman is hurt by him, and thus he sought to restore my contentment to me and after a while we slept.[29]

Chapter XXIII

When I woke up the next morning I realized I carried a new burden inside me like nothing I had ever known before. It was the weight of a *new* life, different from anything I had experienced in my whole past life. I was reborn into another world unfamiliar and painful to move in, and with no landmarks to show me the way I must go. A totally strange and difficult road lay ahead of me; that was all I knew, and I knew it in some deep unconscious manner, just the fact of it, but nothing else. From now on I must grope ahead step by step, never knowing where my path was taking me. . . .[30]

Tony rose serene and poised as usual. He had weathered the storm and taken up his daily work as on all other mornings. I dressed and prepared to meet the people downstairs as before. The Shevkys were gay and smiling and waiting to go to the Pueblo with Tony. Nothing could have showed on my face for they did not look at me in surprise or with new sympathy. Human flesh is strangely slow to change, is unsusceptible to the upheavals of life, does not register anything immediately, but only very slowly. So life went on as before, while I carried my secret grief and apprehension beneath the surface.

All that week passed in the usual fashion except for me and my nameless fear and the sense of change and the realization the past was gone and future held something new and not good as that past had been till now.

At the end of the week Tony went on one of those trips with Collier and Alice Henderson came to stay as she had often before. John Evans and little Alice had married months before and gone to Europe on their wedding journey. . . . Not long now and they would be coming home, and I had prepared the "Tony House" for them to live in for the Lawrences were up at the ranch. So her mother came to stay with us for a few days . . . and all that time I had to pretend I was as before and no one saw any difference. I was glad when she went back to Santa Fe and only the Shevkys were here, for they were away from the house much of the time.

The following week I suddenly felt a sharp pain when I was in the toilet, and each time after I had to pass water, until it grew unbearable and I found I had a sore swelling that the urine burned. So I had to tell Marion Shevky about it for something had to be done to relieve it. She asked me if I would like to call Dr. Martin, but I said, "Oh no! I don't want him for that kind of thing. Maybe I better go down and see Dr. Mera in Santa Fe." He was a nice man, the Henderson's doctor and head of the Sunmount Sanatorium.

We got in the little Ford and started down the long, slow drive over that frightful stony road and every little while I had to stop and get out, and the dreadful burning brought tears to my eyes, and Marion looked worried and said: "Poor thing! Is it so bad?"

"Awful," I told her. "What do you think it can be?" But she only shook her head and answered: "We must wait and see what Dr. Mera says."

When I went on the table in his office and he examined me he looked grave and did not say anything until I asked: "What *is* it anyway?"

"It looks very much like a chancre, I am afraid."

"What is *that*?"

"It is—well—frankly this is the first symptom of syphilis."

The strangest darkness came down on me shutting out the light, the room, Dr. Mera and everything. It was like a stroke of black lightning. Then it lifted.

I said: "Syphilis? *Me*?"

"I am afraid," he said regretfully.

Afraid! The fear of a whole lifetime was in my heart. "Can't you *tell* for *sure*?" I stammered.

"No. Not at this stage. I cannot make a Wasserman test until this has passed. Perhaps in ten days or two weeks."

"And I have to wait, not *knowing*, all that time?"

"I am sorry," he said in a low voice.

He was busy putting some yellow ointment in a white jar. "You keep putting applications of this on it and come back in a fortnight." I took it in a daze and went out to join Marion and we went out to the car not saying a word until we left there.

"He says he thinks it's syphilis," I told her.

"I was afraid of it," Marion answered and put one hand off the wheel over on to mine.

"I can't believe it. I have been scared of it all my life, horrified, and a nightmare to me—and then to get it. I can't take it," I said.

"Oh yes, you can. Richard and I will take care of you. No one need ever know."

"I will know," I cried.

Chapter XXIV

Now I hated my body for the first time. I had had illnesses, I had had a baby. I had gone through most of the things women have to sooner or later, but I had never felt unclean as I did now. And I could not forget it night or day, for I had to keep putting that ointment on myself, and I continued to feel pain.

Marion had told Eshref (or Richard as she had renamed him) and he did not act horrified or anything but rather matter of fact and practical as scientists always do.

"As soon as Tony comes, I will give him another test," he said thoughtfully.

"*Again?*" I exclaimed.

"Well . . ." he smiled and raised his eyebrows.

Of course. I had forgotten. Now I knew when it had happened and from where it come. His corn brother's wife and did Tony Romero have it too? Without explaining anything to them I asked: "Did you ever examine Tony Romero?"

"No. He was one of those who refused. Tony was working on him trying to persuade him," Richard told me. I had a flash of hatred in me as I thought to myself: yes, and working on his wife too! But I did not tell them what I knew.

I cannot remember how that week passed, only the misery and horror of it and the everlasting effort not to betray my feelings. . . .

Tony and Collier came back late one evening—too late to sit down by the fire and talk all together, thank God. Late enough and tired enough to say hello and make for the bedrooms. I climbed wearily upstairs to join Tony after I had put the lights out and said goodnight. I did not know how I was going to tell him that thing. But as soon as I reached our nice room he said in a low voice, as he continued to undress:

"I got a little trouble. Kind of sore place *here*," and he motioned to it.

I burst into tears. Was I always going to be crying in this room?

"Oh Tony! Don't you know what it is? You have got that sickness from Christine and you gave it to me! I have been sick all this week!"

"What sickness?" he queried innocently.

"Don't you *know*? The sickness you and Richard have been looking for all over the Pueblo. Syphilis!"

"Who me?" he exclaimed with a frightened look.

"Of course."

He got up and came over to me with a sorry face and put out his arms as though to protect me from something, but in that instant when I wanted comfort more than anything else, and he was the only one in the world who could console me, something in me froze up and would not be touched by him. Not my heart, for I was not angry and I loved him as before, but my nerves, my blood, the biological, racial self that must repel all harm.

He gave me such a terribly wounded look I couldn't bear it. I had never been aloof from him before, but now I was dead to him. He sat down heavily on the bed and rubbed his hand over his forehead. "What we do now then?" he asked.

"I don't know," I sobbed.

Then he said, "I guess I sleep here in my blanket," motioning to a corner near the fireplace where the embers were still red.

"Oh *dear*! Everything is spoiled for us. I have felt it ever since *that night*."

"What night?" He asked dully.

"Oh that night . . . when I found that on your white sheet."

"*That?*" he said unbelieving.

"Of course."

"I don't believe it," he muttered.

He had not the slightest understanding of cause and effect. Indians did not reason that way. I remembered that the women never calculated the periods between their love acts and the birth of babies—never any sense of cause and effect and it was so with Tony. He slept on the floor, losing consciousness quickly and easily as he always did, but I did not sleep that night for wondering what our life was going to be like from now on.

I had to tell Marion about his condition in the morning. It seemed to me there was nothing left on earth to think about, to talk about, but this horror we carried with us. She was matter of fact enough but she looked sympathetic and sorry, if not surprised. "Of course it is no use giving him a test yet. We will have to wait . . ."

Wait! Wait! That was all there was left to no now. And then what? Marion said: "I think we should tell John Collier and he can advise us. After all, there will be the treatments and it must be decided who you want to have give them, for you will both take a couple of years before you can be sure you are negative, and Richard and I can give you the shots for a while, but we are leaving soon, you know."

Tony came in to the room, having eaten his breakfast. "I told Marion," I said. He gave me a hurt look as though I had betrayed him. "I had to tell her, Tony, and we will have to tell Collier. We have to find out what to do."

"All nonsense," he replied. "I don't believe this stuff." I had a sudden realization of how hard everything was going to be. He did not *believe* in white people's sicknesses nor their doctors and medicines. He swung his blanket about him and left the house cold as a stone and hard, and I knew felt separate and apart from me and all my kind for the first time.

Chapter XXV

The days were dreadful and the nights were dreadful and the life was unpleasant![31] I had never had to go through such turmoil, such an agony of distaste, and such a longing for escape.

When the time came, Richard gave us each that Wasserman test and sent the little bottles away to Albuquerque as he had sent the others from the Pueblo. Of course they were both positive. After that Tony and I were more estranged than ever because we had to persuade and persuade him to have the injections of Salvarsan, and he continued to reject all belief in his condition and almost refused to take the medicine. Added to our sadness of separation (for now he slept downstairs alone) and added to my disgust at myself and my own state of being, was the fear of what could happen if he would not undergo the loathsome cure. Madness or death! The wages of sin are death, I remembered again.

As was my habit, I concealed my thoughts and feelings when I was with people downstairs, but in my empty room at night I lay awake and gave way to horror.

In that strange irrevocable way of scientific people, Richard continued to go among the Indians looking for "cases," and Tony continued to go with him, persuading them to submit to what in his own mind had assumed the characteristics of unreality and "nonsense" with which Indians all too frequently cover up uncongenial situations or facts. Richard particularly insisted upon having Tony work upon Christine and Tony Romero, which somehow seemed to me the extreme of human frightfulness and irony; and Tony, unabashed, did his utmost to persuade them to undergo the drawing of blood into little bottles, forgetting, apparently, how he himself had all but refused that test.

But with them—nothing doing. They could not be induced to agree and laughed at the idea. To terminate that element in this record and not have to refer to them again, I will say now that Tony Romero died about seven years later without benefit of white physicians. So no one can say what killed him, and his wife Christine died about nine years later. Only the Indian medicine men were in charge of them both.

Taking those shots either from Marion or Richard was nerve-wracking, for she was a bacteriologist, and he a research man, and neither of them were practiced in finding the vein so hidden, so invisible below the surface in the bend of the elbow. In and out again—probing under for the wall of the vein was painful and exasperating. Going down to Marion's room at the far end of the house in stealth, the door closed and locked, so no one should surprise us, watching her wrap up the small empty vials to dispose of them later, locking her syringe and her electric sterilizer in her suitcase—all of it was contrary to everything in me and to the habits of a lifetime.

I who had never believed in "secrets"! Now I had this shameful one that hurt me with every breath I drew and made me understand at last something of what poor Maurice had gone through. I remembered how irritated I had been at having to help him, at being in any way associated with such a business, and now disagreeable I had often acted about it. I was truly sorry now. And how unsympathetic I had been with Edwin Dodge, unfeeling and mean. I remembered now, when he had to go to Aix Les Bains in the summer for the cure, I had coldly refused to leave Florence. "Just because you have to go off there and take that nasty water I don't see why I should have to." I had said that and hurt him, and now I was sorry for that too.

And Tony kept away from me as much as he could. We were never alone together anymore. I felt he had the same revulsion towards me now that I had involuntarily shown towards him that night. Everything was ghastly around us and between us. I wished I could die or escape.

One sunny morning I was dressing. I had on one shoe and picked up the other and couldn't remember what it was. "Shoe," I said to myself, and went downstairs with it in my hand. Marion was sitting in the living room alone reading and I walked up to her and smiled. She smiled back. I held it out to her and inquired: "Shoe?" And at that instant I escaped.

I was upstairs in my bed and the sun was shining on me. Alice Henderson and Dr. Mera stood at the foot of the bed looking at me.

"Hello darling," Alice cried smiling at me. There were tears in her eyes.

"Where have I been?" I asked her. She shook her head and could not answer.

I moved a little and saw Tony sitting cross-legged on the other side of the room with his white sheet over his face. I knew he was praying. "Hello, Tony," I said and even he did not answer me.

Marion had been standing behind me and she came beside me now. "What's the matter anyway?" I asked her and she had the sense to tell me.

"You've been unconscious for three days, Mabel. We were worried but you're all right now." She smoothed down my hair and went on smilingly: "You never lost your lovely color all that time."

Dr. Mera took a deep breath. He was a nice man with kind blue eyes but he never did have much to say. Now he said to Alice: "She will be all right now. I would like her to go down to Albuquerque though, soon, and have that spinal fluid tested. Just in case." He collected his bag and some things lying about and he and Alice went down the stairs. Marion made a sign to me towards Tony and she went away too. So I was left lying there, and Tony still had his face covered up, so I said: "Tony—please speak to me."

At that he rose and threw his sheet back and came over and put his arms about me and laid his face beside mine. "You been dead three days," he said in a low voice and his tears wet my face. "I pray and pray all the time till I bring you back. And now you back! Thank the God!" he said.

At the touch and closeness of him my good life started to flow back through my heart again, and I felt our love coming and going back and forth between us again, and everything was all right once more. We never were lovers as we had been, never at all during all these long years, for we had suffered a bodily shock from which neither of us recovered. So that was gone for good. But we were never separate or cold or lost to each other again. We have truly always loved one another and nothing can come between us—not even death. I am sure.

Chapter XXVI

Although we were able to console each other at all times and were never essentially lonely, still it was true I had entered upon a new life and a new road to cut as I traveled ahead.

Almost at once I was up and dressed and looking for Marion downstairs and asking her what had been going on. She told me that when I lost consciousness and fell at her feet, she and Richard got me to bed and telephoned Alice Henderson to come. She suggested sending for Dr. Mera to come up for none of them here knew what to do, and they did not want to call Dr. Martin for I hadn't had him when I was taken ill. Marion had to tell the "history" she knew of Maurice's disease and even of Edwin's case, and she told him that I had never been infected. But he was not certain that I was suffering only from amnesia for, he said, possibly I had been infected early and never known it and that I had a latent case of syphilis that had been stirred up by the Salvarsan and was now showing in a brain condition. That was why he insisted upon my having the spinal fluid tested.

Oh Misery! Would there never be an end to horror? There was not, for a long time.

In Albuquerque I made the acquaintance of Dr. Lovelace, who has been our friend for all the years since then. He sent me to the hospital and of course, he too had to hear this whole foul story. He did that test and it was, of course, negative.

John Collier, who was staying with us off and on, now knew all about all this. It was not any secret anymore! I began to feel *everyone* knew it, and I looked for signs of disgrace and sometimes found them! For instance, we all went up to have a picnic with Frieda and Lawrence on the ranch. . . . I tried to act as though nothing had happened, and as though all was well and our life not broken in half.[32]

We were sitting under the big tree, all of us, Frieda and Lawrence and Brett and Tony and I. Lawrence began a diatribe against "society," how decadent it was, how sown through and through with corruption, a "white sepulcher." He lowered his voice and glared around the table and went on: "Only the doctors know the truth about all these 'best people'! *They* know that the ratio of *syphilis* among them is enormous. They are rotten with it. The men have lost their manhood from it, the women their fertility. Our own best friends are filthy with it for all we know!"[33]

No one said anything. We all went on eating bread and jam and drinking cocoa.

Lawrence had the strangest gift of intuition that was always flooring someone. Did he know he was striking at Tony and me? I never knew. Any more than Frieda knew he was consciously writing down page for page in "Lady Chatterley's Lover" what was taking place between her and Angelino during the weekends they spent together, when she was supposed to be with her mother in the Black Forest.

Tony looked directly into Lorenzo's eyes across the table and asked: "What that syphilis? Something like T.B.?"

Lorenzo flushed red up to his red crest of hair. He was extremely sensitive about his weakness. He did not answer but turned to pass the cocoa pot. I couldn't for the life of me tell whether Tony had done this on purpose or not. But I think he did, for afterwards on the drive home he said suddenly: "That Lorenzo too smart sometimes." Then in a moment he added, "Nice man though. Too bad."

So the days passed somehow. Collier had suggested we spend the winter [of 1923–1924] in Mill Valley on Mt. Tamalpais, renting a house near him and Lucy, and in that way we would be near good doctors in San Francisco, and I had agreed to it for it seemed now everything in our life was conditioned by our sick bodies. I could not get used to it—I who had been so free like a bird all my life, valuing my *LIBERTY* above all else. Now I was the prisoner of circumstances over which I had no control. . . .[34]

Chapter XXVIII

[Chapter XXVIII is mostly about the arrival of Millicent Rogers, which I will discuss in chapter 5. After talking about Millicent, Mabel relates a story about Tony losing his singing voice, for which she felt responsible. Tony was suffering from a tumor on his larynx. Because of Mabel's fears that it was cancerous, she insisted that Tony be treated immediately. Tony was given a high and unnecessary dose radiation (for what turned out to be a benign tumor), while his doctor, Richard Lovelace, was away for a month. This was devastating to both him and to Mabel.[35]]

Tony grew hoarse. He never sang again; our house has been silent and empty of singing ever since, and his drums are put away. After a little, his beautiful thick glossy hair began to fall out. What remained was slashed with white, and his two thin little braids hurt me every time I looked at them.

Finally, Dr. Travers, who was giving him some prostrate gland massage, told me . . . that I was too 'virile' to live as I did and should do something about it. "But

I don't know how," I protested. "Tony and I haven't lived together for a long time and I don't know how to start that up again!"

"I'm afraid you could not even if you did know how. I believe Tony is impotent now. But you could do something else." I told him I could not go seeking a man for therapeutical reasons. . . .

How many times since then he [Tony] has told me: "When I am in my ceremonies or out with the boys singing and I can't sing no more I feel like cryin'. Hurts me inside." And lately we were in Embudo and he had come from a big gathering in Oklahoma where he heard singing day and night. He sat by the table tapping with his fingers, and then he said: "I think I got those songs in my veins. They sing in me all the time! I wake up at night and been singing in my sleep."

What a loss for the man that Tony is. His greatest pleasures have been singing and loving. Can I help feeling it is *less suffering* for me to see him have a little fun with Millicent, than to feel lonesome, knowing he is away some where with her. . . . And if only this does not hurt him in the end, when Millicent finds out how he is. If only he could continue to love me and not shut me out when he is in this thing with her. And if only this *old fashioned possessiveness* about him would die and cease tormenting me so I could love him purely and unselfishly and *really* be glad for him! That Adam and Eve in us die too hard!

~~~~~~~~~~~~~~~

But Mabel could not give up her jealousy, and her biblical notions of sin and suffering, even as atonement for her guilt, and even with the knowledge that Tony might be impotent, as we shall see in chapter 5, "The Doomed."

CHAPTER FIVE

The Doomed

A Tragic Legend of Hearsay and Observation

MILLICENT ROGERS (1902–1953) was the most formidable rival that Mabel Dodge Luhan encountered in her years in Taos. She arrived very late on Mabel's scene (1947), fell in love with Taos, and established a home there, where she lived until she died of a stroke in 1953. The granddaughter of Henry Huddleston Rogers, she was known as "The Standard Oil Heiress." Her life reads like a Hollywood version of Mabel's—much more flamboyant and glamorous—as Millicent herself was strikingly beautiful and fabulously wealthy. She contracted rheumatic fever as a child and was always somewhat fragile. A "jazz age" princess who in some ways defied her class constrictions, she ran off to Europe and married an insolvent Austrian count, danced in cabarets for money, and got pregnant by him. But Millicent also left him and came home at her father's behest, a story that Mabel has Millicent tell in the "The Doomed," in a much more dramatic version than the actual (highly publicized) story of her father's "ransoming" of her from the count. Millicent was known for her charm and wit, but she was also an autodidact who was fluent in several languages and a highly respected fashion designer.[1]

Millicent subsequently married twice, once to a wealthy Argentinean aristocrat, Arturo Peralta-Ramos, by whom she had two sons, Arturo II and Paul. She had friends among the elite in politics, film, and the literary world, and had affairs with some remarkable men, including Undersecretary of the U.S. Navy James Forrestal and British espionage agent Ian Fleming. Millicent made her first trip to Taos in August 1947 with Hollywood clothes designer Gilbert Adrian and his wife, actress Janet Gaynor, who were close friends of Mabel's.

Her trip was precipitated by her unhappiness at the end of a nearly yearlong affair with actor Clark Gable. Like Mabel, Millicent bought and redesigned several homes in which she tried to recreate the historic periods, along with herself. These included an estate in Tidewater, Virginia, which she converted back to its eighteenth-century British décor, and a chalet in Switzerland, for which she designed and wore Tyrolean peasant dresses.[2]

Millicent had showed a flair for fashion as a debutante. She developed this into an internationally acclaimed style of dress to which she gave her own creative and dramatic signature, personalizing designs by such fashion notables as Schiaparelli and Mainbocher. In 1948–1949, she collaborated with Charles James on the exhibition *A Decade of Design* at the Brooklyn Museum of Art, to which she also donated close to six hundred of her couture garments and accessories. In 1975, she was one of ten women "featured in the exhibition 'American Women of Style'" at the Metropolitan Museum.[3]

When she first moved to Taos, Millicent chose Mabel as her mentor. At first, Mabel was enchanted with her, as will be seen in "The Doomed," which is deeply flavored both by Millicent's magnetic pull and Mabel's increasing hostility to her. After her first month in Taos, Mabel wrote about her, in "The Statue of Liberty": "She had an accomplished sweetness and an unshakeable poise. She loved our house the moment she entered it, she loved me, she loved Tony, she loved Taos. In fact she loved just about everything in the place."[4]

The most important of these indicators for Mabel, which precipitated her writing of "The Statue of Liberty," was Tony's infatuation with Millicent. He entered her orbit frequently for several months until his young nephew, Benito Suazo, became Millicent's lover and lived and traveled with her until her death. Part II of "The Doomed" is about Benito's traumatic experiences during World War II, Tony's attempt to help him recover, and Benito's affair with Millicent.[5]

From her first week in Taos, Millicent began to take shopping trips, eventually buying over one thousand pieces of Indian jewelry and Hispano furniture and religious art. Some of these were for the home she bought and renovated in Taos, which included the remains of a seventeenth-century fort. Millicent bought the house from Judge Henry Kiker, with Mabel acting as the go-between estate agent, much to the annoyance of his wife, whom he had apparently not told about the sale. Millicent also began to design her own jewelry, based on traditional Pueblo and Navajo pieces, but with a strikingly contemporary flair. She has been credited with the "introduction of Southwestern style into the fashion mainstream." While the house was being prepared for her, Millicent rented the "Tony House" for a year, which Tony had built across from

Figure 12 Millicent Rogers dyeing velvet at Tony Lujan's house, 1948. Photo by Arturo Peralta-Ramos, Courtesy of Millicent Rogers Museum, Taos, New Mexico.

the Luhans' Big House on Taos Pueblo land. In the meantime, Mabel built her last home, "Hill House," in 1948 because she felt that the Big House had been poisoned by Millicent's presence. She and Tony would live there for most of the rest of their lives.[6]

Millicent not only lured Tony away from home, but she also took up Indian affairs, just as Mabel had in her early years in Taos. Within her first month in Taos, Mabel writes in "The Statue of Liberty," Millicent was talking about reopening the Indian hospital at Taos Pueblo which had apparently closed: "Now this," she wrote Mabel, "is perfectly unnecessary. I have telegraphed for a very efficient girl named Mallary, who was Ann Morgan's executive for all her Red Cross work during the war. She can handle this whole thing. I will send her to Washington to talk to Senators and I know several editors who have told me if I ever have anything I want to *say*, they will publish it. . . . But I *must* talk more to Tony about it all." According to Millicent's son Arturo Peralta-Ramos, Millicent worked with Santa Fe and Taos writer-activists Oliver La Farge and Frank Waters, as well as with New Mexico senators Clinton Anderson and Dennis Chávez, on a bill "for full Indian citizenship."[7]

In late 1952, Millicent had a series of strokes, which left her debilitated. She died on January 1, 1953, just short of her fifty-first birthday. In her last letter to her son Paul, Millicent described her feelings for Taos in language very similar to that of the woman who saw her as her gravest threat: "'Suddenly passing Taos Mountain I felt I was part of the Earth, so that I felt the Sun on my Surface and the rain. I felt the Stars and the growth of the Moon, under me, rivers ran. . . . And I knew there was no reason to be lonely that one was everything, and Death was as easy as the rising sun . . . If anything should happen to me now, just remember all of this. I want to be buried in Taos with the wide sky—. . . .'"[8]

Millicent's funeral, as Mabel notes in her memoir, was attended by many members of Taos Pueblo, including the governor. In 1956, Millicent's sons created a tribute to her and her Taos legacy by working with her friends to create the Millicent Rogers Museum, located north of Taos just off the main highway. The core of the museum was her collection of several thousand pieces of Navajo and Pueblo jewelry, Navajo textiles, Pueblo pottery, and basketry of the western Apache tribes, some of the finest to be found in museums in the Southwest.

Millicent's letters to Mabel, mostly written during her first year in Taos, are filled with love, deference, appreciation, and affection for her and Tony. Mabel was flattered by the former, but she must have bridled at the possible hidden meanings in such comments as (in Millicent's letter to her of September 1, 1947): "Tell him [Tony] that last night there was a Moon Rainbow over the gourge [*sic*] and that it was double. Tell him too that at noon, the day at my house, I saw a white headed Eagle that came from the mountain . . ." I am not certain when Millicent and Benito became lovers, but it's likely to have been in the fall of 1948, after she moved out of the Tony House into her own home, where Benito took up residence.[9]

In her letters, Millicent referred to Benito as Mabel's "grandson," which must have annoyed Mabel greatly, even if she was using it as the "honorific" that was common among the Pueblos for close relatives.[10] The fact that her rival was now having sexual relations with someone who *could* be Tony and Mabel's grandson, at least in terms of his age, must have replayed for Mabel her encounters with the themes of incest that appear throughout her unpublished memoirs. It is interesting to see Mabel blaming Millicent for behaviors she herself had displayed. Mabel accuses her of "ruining" Benito in some of the same ways she believed she had "ruined" Tony and his family. All of them drank too much. Mabel did not have to wait for Millicent for alcohol to become a problem for her and Tony. It was one of the ways that Mabel medicated herself during her depressions, while Tony's drinking had been a continuing issue in their relationship.[11]

There is one letter from Mabel to Millicent in the Luhan papers. It's undated but written after Mabel came to know her "in this year," so it is probably from sometime in the fall or winter of 1948. In it, Mabel chides Millicent for her bad influence on the Indians, her giving them too many gifts. She tells Millicent that "You have somehow spoiled the Indians who are like sensitive children—& you have set them to quarreling and acting unlike themselves. Presents & all that do not help them. Altogether I feel we should not see each other now because actually we belong to different worlds, have different aims, & only alcohol seems to blend us. . . . Whether Tony & you continue to see each other is up to him; naturally I cannot do anything about that. You can see him at your house, or before at Manuel Suazo's house . . . or anywhere else. But not here. . . . I have too deep a distrust of you to be happy with you."[12]

Beneath her patronizing voice, one hears pain of a betrayal that may have been the most serious Mabel experienced since Tony infected her with syphilis. While it is highly unlikely that his relationship with Millicent was sexual in nature, it was devastating to Mabel. It brought her to write about her lifelong fears and experiences with syphilis, as we saw in chapter 4, as well as to take (written) revenge on the woman whose life seemed to shadow, mimic, and then outshine her own.[13]

~~~~~~~~~~~~~~

Part I

MILLICENT

Judge Kiker, my longtime friend and lawyer, asked me to try and sell his Taos land and house for him.[14]

"How much do you want for it," I asked him.

"Twenty-five thousand dollars, and commission, six percent," he replied.

I was allured by the idea of the commission. Money plays a part throughout this story. So I wrote to Adrian and told him about it. An adobe house with four goodish sized rooms and a hall running between them. The land consisted of a large number of acres with the finest view in Taos Valley, looking toward the Sacred Mountain and showing the crescent of the lesser hills running to the north and northeast. A wide handsome view on all sides with the property backing on the long mesa that cuts through that tableland.

There was a pond below the house that was fed from a spring. It was full of bullrushes and ducks and other wild birds kept up a continuous chatter there. A row of enormous cottonwood trees were lined up on the road that led from the gate and across the porch of the house. A beautiful place with real possibilities.

Adrian was attracted to my description of this opportunity and it was not long before he arrived in the cold springtime, bringing Janet and a friend of theirs from Hollywood, Millicent Rogers. . . .

"Mabel," Adrian began, in the low important voice he used to discuss business and financial matters, "Janet and I have talked [it] over and while she is mad about the place, we both feel the view is too much like our view at home in North Hollywood—you know, the fields and cows and horses and mountains. So, we have decided against it, but Millicent wants to buy it." My heart sank and I would have forgone that commission then and there, but it was too late.

"And Mabel," Adrian went on, "you may be sure that if Millicent gets it, she will make something beautiful out of it. She has wonderful taste." A pause and he added, "And lots of money to do it." So it was settled and they all left that day, Millicent planning to return shortly with her dachshunds and her personal maid and accoutrements, to stay at first for a while with the Dicuses, where they had specially recommended "Paying Guests" and excellent food.

They came over to say goodbye before leaving Taos, and Tony was there for it was early after lunch. Janet looked relieved and refreshed; Adrian looked the same as he always did; and Millicent was brilliant and glowing, her painted mask, newly made every day, was illumined and its delicate tints shown. Her hand in Tony's, she cried, "Will you help me build my house, Tony? You have made such a beautiful one here for Mabel!"

"Yes," Tony answered gravely, holding on to her hand, "but it take a long time."

"That's all right. I don't care how long it takes," she replied. . . .

It took some time for the Kikers to pack up and leave and store all their things, and settle the deal with a lawyer. So much down and the rest to be paid later. I thought I would never get that commission. . . .

Millicent had her car and chauffer at the Dicuses, and she used to drive over to see me. At first, she came about four o'clock but when she found that Tony usually returned either from the ranch at Tienditas, where he kept his cows, lunching in the pretty little cabin we used to stay in overnight once in a while, or when he would come back from the ranch on Indian land at Arroyo Seco where he raised crops and kept pigs and other animals, at about five o'clock. She changed her own habit imperceptibly, until her appearance at our house coincided with Tony's return. . . .

Over the bridge of the Acequia on Indian land is the Tony House. It has quite large rooms, but only five of them, and two bathrooms. It has an unbroken, sweeping view of the Sacred Mountain across three miles of fields bordered by wild plum bushes. There are two garages, one large studio with "facilities" downstairs and one upstairs studio with only a lavatory.

"Oh! Why can't I rent *this*? I don't really like the Dicus place very much!" cried Millicent, before she had even been in the house.

I felt reluctant at the suggestion, but I knew Tony would like the rent, which was always large. The rent always went to him because the land was Indian and the house was built by him and his uncle, Joe [Suazo], and some Indian boys and I put the plumbing in for him. So presently she moved in for a year with all her trunks, her car and chauffeur.

But Millicent got along all right. She engaged Dixie Yaple to be her housekeeper and secretary, and soon she had two Indian girls, Rafaelita and Isabel, for cook and housemaid. They were with her for quite a while, until she moved over to her own house, and after that for a little while. Then, they got tired of the confusion and irregular hours and left and came to me. There was always confusion around Millicent, though she herself was very quiet and good-natured, never cross or cranky. There was great sweetness in her and a certain languor. When she walked, which was seldom, her left arm hung down stiff and as though it did not belong to her.

"Oh, I am so happy in the Tony House," she told me soon. "It has a lovely feeling in it. I was very unhappy in Hollywood in Annabelle's house. It was very dark and sad." . . .

Lisa wrote me from Beverly Hills that Millicent had had a love affair there with Clark Gable that was ended by him telling her that she was the stupidest woman he had ever known, and by her answering him that he was nothing himself but a ham actor. . . .

[Tony] drove us through the village and over to Ranchitos to the Kiker place. It was really hers now. She had paid the first payment on it and I had been given part of my commission. Nothing could stop things now. In the empty house, we sat on the deep windowsills and Millicent took off the leather bag she always wore over her shoulder on a long strap. She took a flat bottle of whiskey out of it and some folding paper cups and poured it straight. We took it from her and she said, looking straight into Tony's eyes, "Here's to my new house and to what is coming!"

So we drank and between Tony and her something seemed to pass, something secret and strong. The house was empty and forlorn and had no dignity, nor charm, but she did not seem to notice its barrenness. She was gay and satisfied and happy as a lark.

On the way back, I asked her if she and Paul [Peralta-Ramos, Millicent's youngest son] would like to have dinner with us. I had other people coming but she might like them. In spite of the uneasiness I felt about her and Tony, I almost loved this woman, for she was always winning and alluring and, in fact, loveable. . . .

Our friends had arrived and we had cocktails together, and we were seven or eight at the table. Millicent did not bother much with the newcomers. At the right hand of Tony, she talked to him in a low voice through the meal, he answering her with an occasional look across the length of the board to me, apparently to see if I observed their intimacy, which I did.

After dinner, coffee served and disposed of, Millicent drew a straight-backed chair up in front of Tony where he sat in his usual corner in the big armchair. She had her rear to all of us and seemed to forget everyone but Tony. Together they talked in low voices, while I got madder and madder. Forever after, when she came, it was like that. There was no one there for her but Tony and he did not, as usual, close his eyes and pretend to sleep, or really sleep, I never knew. Anyway, he was not bothered by the buzzing of the flies as he had so often called our conversations.

When she and Paul got up to leave, he ahead of her getting into the front seat of the automobile, I followed her and Tony to the outside door. He was ahead, holding it open, and as she passed him, she breathed the word, "Tomorrow?" to him, and he lowered his head.

One morning I ran across the fields to the Tony House at ten o'clock. I wanted to ask her about something—I forget what—and had not remembered how late she appeared, coming down from the upper bedroom as late as eleven or after. I went into the sunny house and Isabel was dusting around and no one else was there. So I went to the foot of the stairs and called up, "Millicent, may I see you a moment?"

"Come up," she called down to me. "I was just going to fix my face."

I went up and she was walking around in an Empire nightgown of the sheerest mull, gathered in at the high waist in tiny pleats. She appeared so girlish I could not believe my eyes until she passed close and flashed a satirical glance full at me. I was horrified. Her dark arched eyebrows were white, her long black eyelashes were purest white and her large brown eyes looked small and hard. There was not a trace of color on her face and her usually large, full red lips were thin and grey. I would not have known her if I had met her in the street.

I had never been up in that bedroom where Tony and I had spent so many hours, since she came. Now, the dressing table had dozens of small jars on it and rows and rows of cosmetic pencils, lipsticks and little instruments. The twin beds were gone and in their place was an enormous high-backed couch with deep mattresses on it and rosy silken sheets bordered with lace, while many pillows of all sizes, silk covered and inset with lacy insertion, were scattered all about.

Now I knew what an artist she was. Her makeup was never too obvious or high-colored, but all of her yellowed skin was daily covered with the most delicate shades and shadows, her eyes enlarged and her mouth fabricated out of nothing. There was no basis for what she created, nothing underneath; it was all made new every day. I had never seen her use a lipstick in public, never a compact. Her materials must have been of the most durable.

She laughed her deep laugh, for I must have looked queer. I forgot what I had come for and had to invent something and get away as soon as I could. I did not tell Tony anything about this experience because the intimacy I felt between him and Millicent had established a coldness between him and me, and I never discussed her with him but once and he was then so silent and aloof, I did not attempt it again. . . .

By this time, Tony was wearing something new. Millicent had given him her father's watch with a gold wristband. It was a small old-fashioned watch with an inscription in it from her father. Tony put it on and didn't mention it to me until I asked him: "For Heaven's sake, where did that come from?"

"Millicent gave it to me . . . It was her father's."

He has worn it ever since, though it does not keep very good time. It was just a symbol, and for these several years it gave me a pang every time I saw it. But lately, it does not bother me, and I even remember to give it to him when he forgets and leaves it in the bathroom. . . .

[Millicent went to New York City for the winter of 1947–1948, returning to Taos in the spring.]

I had noticed people watching her [Millicent]. She was always so striking looking, one could hardly help it. But it was more than her looks. The village was curious about her, her vast wealth they had heard of, and also about her unconcealed interest in Tony. I knew they had been talking about that for several people had asked me right out, "Is Mrs. Rogers after Tony?" And "What is she trying to do with Tony?" I laughed it off, of course. Though actually I was wondering as much as they were and was as much in the dark about it.

One evening, Walter and Bill Goyen came for dinner and she was there.[15] Walter had his rebellion up in him and looked at her critically all through dinner. She did not seem to notice him. She was always unconcerned about other people and taken up with her own affairs. Before we had finished dinner and our coffee in the living room, and before she had drawn up her chair as usual in front of Tony with her back to the room, Walter suddenly broke out:

"What are you doing here in Taos, Millicent? You don't belong here. You are not like anyone else here! Look at that diamond butterfly you have on! Three inches across. Nobody else here has stuff like that! It doesn't belong. *Why are you here,* anyway?"

Tony was in his big chair as usual with his eyes closed, but he was not sleeping this time, I knew. Millicent smiled gently. She never got angry. She answered: "Do you really want to know? Well, I will tell you. When I was a young girl, I was sick in bed in my father's house. I had rheumatic fever. I only saw the servants and the nurses. My parents were always away, busy building a huge house on a big piece of land on Long Island. They had named it the 'Port of Missing Men.'

"One day I got tired of my prison and got up in the evening and, in spite of the night nurse, I called a cab and went to a nightclub. There I met a man who interested me. He was older than I and he was distinguished looking and a European—the sort I had never met before. His name was Count Salm. We spent hours together and he asked me to marry him and go to Paris. He was leaving in a day or two. I agreed. It was an escape for me, you see. The next day I went to my father's office, to his surprise. He thought I was sick and safe. 'Father, I am going to marry a man I met last night,' I said. 'His name is Count Salm.'

"'That you are not going to do. I know all about him and he is no good.'

"'I am going to Europe with him tomorrow,' I told him.

"'That is ridiculous! Impossible! If you do such a thing, you will no longer be a daughter of mine.'

"I got up and went away and I telephoned Salm to meet me in the morning. I got my jewels together, the things my mother and father had given me through the years, and I met him at a restaurant and gave them to him. 'I am going with you. Get me a passage on your boat and save the rest of these to pay my expenses abroad.'

"So I sailed away with him and we got to Paris. Soon there was no money. We went to Germany and lived in a cold-water flat with a steep flight of stairs. He gambled and I danced in cheap cabarets to support us. It was not long before I knew my father had been right. He was a bad man. To keep going, I drank too much. I would come back to the place we lived in, in the early morning and hang over the ash cans at the door, until I could climb the stairs. After some time, I found that I was going to have a baby. So I stole some money out of his pocket while he was drunk asleep, and I sold a few rags I had left, and somehow I got a third class passage on a boat and ran back to New York. I went to my father's office—so rich and comfortable—Colonel Harry Rogers, President of Standard Oil. When I went in, he just looked at me in horror. I must have looked dreadful!

"'You were right, father,' I said. 'He is a bad man and I am no longer your daughter. But I am going to have a baby. Will you help the baby?'

"He took care of me and when Peter was born, he developed a great fancy for him. In fact, when he died, he left a large portion of his fortune to Peter and also, 'The Port of Missing Men.'" She paused and every one was silent. She went on: "That is where Peter lives now."

"After that, I married Ramos, an Argentinean and we had Arthur and Paul. Then, I married another man—nothing came out right, though. Finally I was in Hollywood and alone and very unhappy. I did not like Hollywood. I did not like any place.

"Then it happened recently that I read all of Mabel's books, and all about Taos and the life she had made there after leaving New York, and I thought, well, if she can do it, so can I. I can go out and make a good life, too. So here I am." She stopped and smiled again at Walter while she lighted a cigarette. "Now I am tired and going home," she said, getting up as we all did.

I put my arm around her and kissed her on the cheek. She was so surprised, she looked at me with her brilliant smile. Tony got up to take her to the door as usual, and I followed. Halfway there she stopped and put her hand on my shoulder. "You kissed me," she whispered. At the door, she flashed her look at Tony and said something low I could not hear. He took her to the car and the waiting chauffer. . . .

I do not recall any of the events that followed. She was, as usual, often out in the afternoon—where I did not guess. When the autumn came, she left for New York, meaning to return to the Tony House and move some furniture into her new house and live there while she added a couple of rooms and made a garden and a patio. So far, nothing had started there. She seemed to be waiting for Tony to build it, but I had said two or three words to him, which had seemed to halt that.

Soon we left for Mexico for the winter. The first season of this unexpected and unexplained annal was ended. I never spoke of her to him, nor did he mention her to me, but the night on our drive to Tamazunchale where we spent the night, I inadvertently opened the small drawer in his night table and there I saw two fetishes I had never seen before—a turquoise bear and another small jade animal. At once I knew she had given them to him and I broke out in a tempest of rage and disgust. He was perfectly silent and paid no attention to my disturbance. He just shut the drawer and said, "That is not your affair. Please leave me alone."

We passed an easy, pleasant winter in Cuernavaca and I almost forgot all my worry and watchfulness of the long summer. It was gone until we returned again to Taos in the early spring [of 1948].

Millicent returned to the Tony House to stay until the furniture she had sent to furnish her home arrived and was in order. It was not long before I discovered that Tony often went over to see her before he left for the day's work at the ranch at Tienditas, where the cattle and horses stayed, or over to Arroyo Seco to his ranch on the Reservation where he grew his crops. Once I asked him why he kept going over to Millicent's in the morning, when he saw her as usual nearly every afternoon at our house. He went out of the room without answering me.

I felt dismal and alone in the Big House and I suddenly accomplished two radical acts. I wrote her a letter and told her I didn't want to see her anymore, that she did not belong to my group and that she did not fit into my life. This woman I could have loved, for she was lovable and gentle, had poisoned my life and my house.

The other thing I did was to buy some acres along the ridge we lived on but beyond the St. Teresa House. I planned a small house for two people—along a hall, two bedrooms, a bathroom, a powder room near the entrance under a porte cochere, and a large living room that faced south and west and would be gay and full of sunshine. There would be a tiny kitchen on the hallway and just opposite the large double doors of the living room. On top of the living room and kitchenette, I planned a large open porch, roofed and supported by pillars. Up there, where a winding adobe staircase would reach it from outside, one would be able to see the whole countryside from every direction.

Tony was away so much, and we were so little together for talk, that he did not know anything about this plan until it was well started. I had no architect or contractor but made the plans myself, having first a bunch of Mexican boys and later, when they began to get slack on the job as often happens, a bunch of Indian boys trained by our best contractor, Elmer Montgomery.

Millicent replied to my letter in her usual forthright manner. She said she didn't know what I meant, but that she would carry out her rebuttal in her own way. Thus, our communication ceased, but she told Tony about it, and he became colder than ever. One morning before he left I said, "Wait a minute, Tony. I need some help. I didn't tell you but I am starting a small house over beyond."

"What for?" he asked me.

"Because this house is poisoned for me. I don't want to live here any more."

He looked rather dazed.

"Will you walk over end see what I am doing?" I asked him. "I need some vigas now. I want to cut them up at Tienditas and you will have to help me."

He went over with me and the boys were glad to see him come. I suppose they had wondered why he never showed up there, but perhaps they didn't, after all. Everything in Taos is quickly known by everybody else. I heard from Frieda [Lawrence] that Millicent had hastened out to show her my letter. "Well, I can't say I blame you," shouted Frieda. "Just so much and no more, Ya?"

"Yes," I answered, "No more. Finished."[16]

I did not see Millicent any more. But one day I had motored down to the Kiker's in Santa Fe and there was plenty of talk about her and Tony from Kathleen. She said I should divorce Tony and she went with me to see Dr. Hausner, who was my good friend, and to whom I had told all about this. She told him that she thought I should leave Tony and he looked very grave and said:

"No—after so long-lasting a marriage that would be too much of a shock. After all, Mabel does not know that anything significant has happened. She only thinks so."

I wept and said I knew all I needed to know.

I was spending the night with Kathleen [Kiker] and in the late afternoon, the front doorbell rang and our foreman, Max, came in supporting Tony who was staggering. He had a bloody bandage tied around his head.

"What happened?" exclaimed Kathleen.

"He was driving away from Mrs. Rogers' house and he ran into a tree on the back road from her house. The radiator is smashed and he hit his head on the wheel and the windshield. I thought I should bring him down here."

I hastened to get Dr. Hausner on the telephone while Kathleen got Tony on to a bed. Dr. Hausner said he would be there immediately. While I waited sitting beside Tony who seemed half unconscious, I heard Max say to Kathleen in a low voice:

"The lady is waiting outside on the street in her car."

"*What* lady?" gasped Kathleen.

"Mrs. Rogers," murmured Max.

The doctor came soon and untied the bandage and attended to the wound. I could not look. I think he washed it and put in some stitches. Then, he undressed Tony and put him in the bed and gave him a shot of something.

"It is not too bad. Bring him to my office in the morning."

All that happened after that I have forgotten except that Dr. Hausner said evidently Tony had been drinking. Drinking! Always drinking! Always bottles of whiskey around Millicent.

Soon she moved out of the Tony House to her own house, now furnished. I did not need to be afraid of seeing her any more. She never came to the Big House until long later when Henrietta Harris brought her to see what she would buy, for I had put all the furnishings in Henrietta's hands for sale. When she went into the empty place full of lovely things, she had no fear to meet me, for by then we were living at our new home, the house we are in now, called Hill House. . . .

Millicent had a fantastic habit of buying things. She spent all her income collecting all kinds of objects, some good, some bad. She started soon after coming to Taos spending money on silver and turquoise. She had twenty-five silver and turquoise belts with all sorts of conchas on them, some modern and bastard, many antique and beautiful. She bought rings, squash blossom necklaces, wide and narrow bracelets—every variety of Indian jewelry. Once she said to me that she was getting it all together to return to the Indians who had made them. . . .

Following my example, she started giving Indian dances in her house, but they ended in confusion because she did not give the boys grapefruit and orange juice to drink to refresh themselves between dances. She allowed them to help themselves to the profusion of bottles that always stood about, and they did. Sometimes her chauffer had to take them home to the Pueblo.

And always I was unaware for certain of what went on between her and Tony. I knew that he did not as before spend the weekends with me at our rock house down at Embudo—River House with the Rio Grande in front of it and the Embudo River behind. This place we had always loved to come to after the week's work—no telephone, no unexpected guests, but a perfect hideaway among the cottonwoods full of the singing birds.

When Tony did not come and join me there, at least, he had always told me where he had been. "At the Fiesta at Picuris."

"Who was there that we know?"

"I didn't see much people. Rogers and Paul were there." He always called her Rogers now. . . .

The work at the Hill House went on through the weeks and now—in the autumn, the plumbers, the electricians and carpenters were working inside the house. The weekends were a little lonely at the River House and would have been more so had it not been for the book I was working on.[17] Tony usually turned up late at night and went to bed quietly without a goodnight, though he must have seen my light burning under the door of my bedroom. . . .

The River House was a lonely, lovely place. Mr. Galt, who had built it of the lava rock that strewed the ground from the two pointed volcanic hills that stand to east and west of us, had used it as a hunting lodge. All kinds of game were there, wild and abundant. Fish in the rivers, ducks floating down them, pheasant passing before the house and bears in the night time evidently! And there were beavers at the edge of the water. Across the river in front of the house, I could watch from the porch swing wild horses and burros making their way down the steep ledge of lava, to drink at the brink of the Rio Grande. Above this ledge the wild land stretched for miles and miles and I only could surmise the life upon it, never seeing it. Every morning a long line of white goats passed along the edge of the river, eating the willows that grew there and in the evening, they returned, beautiful in the twilight. It was like early Greece, I always thought. But Tony and I were not.

When November [1948] came, Tony and I left Taos. The Hill House was completed inside, the hardwood floors sanded and waxed. All it needed now was furnishing. . . .

I did not drive out to the Pueblo as I had used to. . . . I did not go anymore, for twice when I went out late in the afternoon, Millicent's car was parked beside Tony's outside his family house. So I knew now how they met but said nothing to him. There was no use. I couldn't do anything about it.

I could imagine her sitting inside the sparsely furnished room with Tony's favorite niece, Sofina, and all her children coming and going. She had six sons and one little daughter. What Tony wanted, she accorded to him. He was the head of the family, as is the eldest brother of the sisters, in their system. I could imagine Millicent like a gay, exotic flower among the ascetic Indians, all dressed in her Navaho finery, like a souvenir.

Soon, however, the nephews began to lose their faded shirts and drab leggings, wrapped about with old blankets. When I saw one of them, he was dressed in silk in the summer and in cold weather, the boys all had jackets with silky outsides, but they were warm with fur linings and collars. She was increasing her madness for buying, buying people with gifts. She bought more and more, now. The girls were busy all day long with the inventories!

When I had Hill House in order and furnished, we moved over there [December 1948]. It was all white inside. White walls and white organdy curtains at the windows of all the rooms of the long hall, except in the bedrooms; I put dark velour curtains to keep the dawn out—very dark garnet in mine, and in Tony's, deep purple, his favorite color. The windows and doors had deep embrasures and the darkness of the velvet threw shadows upon them. . . .

[Mabel had three parties to celebrate her new home: for her intimate friends, for "old timers" from Taos, and for the workers.]

The summer [of 1949] passed very quietly in Hill House. Tony was not quite himself but he was all right. I only found out later, why.[18]

Millicent decided to have an Indian dance on the mesa behind her house, and when everyone was up there and a big bonfire burning, but no food visible yet, it started to rain. Tony and I had [not] been invited to this gathering. We just heard about it.

When the rain started, Brett suggested that every one come over to her studio and have the supper and the dance. They had to move a large cauldron of stew that had been simmering and all the plates and things for Brett had very little in her house. They ate and they drank, and especially the Indian boys drank, so the dance was rather confused. Benito went about with a bottle of whiskey in his hand, pouring drinks and drinking plenty himself. When all the drink was gone, the Indians sort of caved in and discontinued the singing and the drumming and the dance was over. Millicent's chauffer took them all home in a comatose state in her station wagon, and Brett said she would drive Millicent home all the way across the valley because she thought Benito was too drunk to drive her in her own car.

They did not leave until all the Indians were gone, including Benito, but when they did, they came across a telephone pole down along the side of the road, and in the ditch Millicent's pretty blue car turned over, and Benito under it unconscious. Somehow, they dragged him out and got him over to the hospital. Millicent got a private room for him and took the one next to him for herself. His room was the one dedicated to my mother and had her name on the door.[19] His injuries were minor, but they kept him in bed for several days.

I said to Tony, "Did you hear about Benito smashing Millicent's car and now in the hospital himself?"

"Yes. I heard it," Tony replied, noncommittally.

I saw he wasn't going to do anything about it, and I thought one of us should show a sign of being human, so I sent over a bouquet of flowers to him from our garden and the next day I went to the Holy Cross Hospital to see him. Millicent was sitting beside him and the perfume of phlox and stock filled the room.

"How are you Benito?" I asked. "Do you feel all right?" He smiled and did not answer. Millicent smoothed back his long, silky black hair on the pillow. "He will soon be up," she murmured, lovingly. On the table beside him were medicines and mouthwashes, Lavoris and Listerine, and perfumes. I did stay but a minute. There did not seem to be any point in it. . . .

[Mabel and Tony went to Millicent's house for coffee, after Thanksgiving dinner, in November 1949. Millicent brought her to see Benito's room.]

She led me across the hall into a bedroom that had once been Mary Kiker's. "This is Benito's room," she explained . . . "And here is the bathroom," she went on, leading me into it. Yes, there hung his dark blue silk dressing gown, his furry slippers beneath it, and, on a shelf beside the lavatory, all manner of toothbrushes, lotions, and little cream jars. . . .

On the way home, Tony did not say a word, but when we reached Hill House, he gave a sigh of relief. "I guess home be best," he told me. This was very pleasant to me. I knew now, for good, it was all finished between Millicent and him. . . .

Both Millicent and her mother had some method for controlling the press. No detrimental criticism appeared; only what they wished. When Millicent first moved into her new house, the reporter who at that time wrote under the sobriquet of Cholly Knickerbocker, came to Taos to interview her. His piece, syndicated in a chain of newspapers all over the United States, announced that the beautiful Millicent Rogers had settled in Taos, where she was completing her house. "She has become the social arbiter off this well-known artists' colony, usurping the position hitherto held by the aging Mabel Dodge Luhan."[20]

He ended several columns by quoting Millicent, saying it was so quiet and peaceful in Taos Valley and she would remain there, facing the sacred Indian Mountain. "The Mountain likes me!"

When I read that I remembered Georgia [O'Keeffe], too, had used to turn Tony into the fantasy of the Sacred Mountain. Once she painted an abstraction that, on a huge canvas, was simply a great rock with Tony's well-known vermillion serape around it and an intense blue sky above. At the base of the big rock, crouched a little nondescript rock—Georgia. . . .[21]

Tony and I went to Mexico again for the winter, early in December [1949]. We had the usual agreeable easygoing time there for some months in Cuernavaca and came back to our Hill House and the River House in the spring [of 1950]. After the winter that Millicent and Benito spent with Brett in Jamaica, I did not worry about Tony and Millicent any more. Benito had proved to be the man of the house, and down on the Island he and Brett developed a great antagonism. . . .[22]

[Mabel did not see Millicent again until the spring or summer of 1952.]

The following spring [1952] Dr. Hausner was called in for Millicent and removed her to La Fonda Hotel in Santa Fe. Since January she had been slightly ailing. When I heard that Dr. Hausner had removed her to La Fonda for diagnosis and treatment, I was sure it was serious. We learned that he believed she had developed an infection in the valve of her heart and was giving her vast amounts of penicillin. She had a large suite upstairs on the fourth or fifth floor, three nurses who ate in their own room in the apartment, and they had to constantly prevent Millicent from tearing the large needle out of the vein in her arm—the needle that was carrying the penicillin to the infected blood. It was very painful and sometimes she could not bear it. . . .

I have known a great many doctors, and of all these Eric Hausner was the most completely dedicated man. For a case that was needful he gave his whole heart and mind. At the slightest variation in Millicent's fever or respiration, he flew out of his office, for he was on the telephone night and day for her or any other demanding patient. He would leave his office at the Coronado Building and run out across the streets, past the Post Office to the hotel, his long white coat waving in the cold air of the high altitude and up to her room. There, he would test her heart again and again, take her temperature, her momentary condition, administer a slight medication and return to his office full of patients. They grew weary, I am sure of hearing from the secretary over and over again, "Doctor has been called out on an emergency." This went on throughout the days and nights for months. He gave all he had.

Dr. Hausner belonged to the psychosomatic school of internal medicine. He has never given me much medicine, but plenty of advice, perhaps finding me more psycho than somatic! . . .

Eric Hausner, a Czechoslovakian, left the Prague Medical School in 1935 and was accepted at the Mayo Clinic to do heart research. There he succeeded from the first and received a special diploma from the faculty for his contribution. When the war broke out, he was called to the Brun's Hospital in Santa Fe for war casualties and there in a corridor one day, he ran across a nurse's aide who stared at him and then, ran into his arms.

"Eric! Eric! You?"

They had not seen each other since they were boy and girl sweethearts in the same village where they had been born. He had followed his life's devotion to work, particularly on the heart. She had gone to schools and, finally, in Paris had met the man who became her husband and the father of a boy and girl. He was an appraiser of jewels and a merchant in these. After some years they became divorced and she came to America and settled in Santa Fe with the children. But he had the children summers, and she was forever taking them to him in Paris or California with the old nurse they had from their birth.

It was inevitable that Suzette and Eric should become lovers. This was a true romance. For two years they were together in his spare moments and hours, and always she tried to persuade him to marry her so she could take care of him but he always refused. His life was given to his work and always would be. He could not be a husband to make any wife content. However, she persisted and he finally succumbed, for he was devoted only to her outside his office. So they were married. . . .

[Millicent continued to be ill and bedridden for much of the rest of her life. She died on January 1, 1953, while the Luhans were in Mexico.]

Part II

BENITO

There are many beautiful Indian children but the most adorable little boy I ever saw was Benito. He was serene and composed with long, slender limbs, great black eyes, fringed with long lashes and always a gentle, sweet expression. His mouth was wide and thin and his skin a clear olive.

Brett painted a portrait of him pulling a little wagon his father, Manuel Suazo, made for him out of a box and a long stick. In this painting, he wore his tiny moccasins, long red cotton leggings hanging half way up his dark legs, and a blue shirt that covered his small bottom. He looked back over his shoulder with a wistful expression that one often saw later on his face.[23]

Brett was infatuated with him and often had him with her up at her cabin on the Hawk's ranch on Mount Lobo. "Benito! Bambino mio," she often exclaimed and he would respond with his soft, slow smile.

I did not see him often when he was in the Pueblo Day School and rarely, when he left for the Albuquerque Boarding School.

Tony was very fond of him. Maybe he was his favorite nephew, at least, among Sofina's six boys. So it was sad for Tony when Benito was drafted for the war just before he graduated. Since he had to go, he wanted to be a pilot, for he had a particular feeling for mechanical things. But they put him into the Infantry for training and taught him to attack great swinging bags with his bayonet. No one heard from him while he was away and suddenly he was sent home, looking quite altered in the three or four years of active service.

Something had happened to him, but he would not talk. He lay on his pallet in his Mother's dark room, silent and unheeding. Or one saw him standing in the corral beside the Pueblo entrance, staring at the ground, not moving for hours. Once I tried to get him to speak, and I said, "Wasn't there anything you liked over there, Bennie?"

For once, he smiled a little and replied, "Those beautiful lakes . . ."

After he had been home for some weeks, he began to go out at night to the nightclubs at El Prado and other places and then he would drink. As soon as he had a few drinks, he would suddenly launch an attack on a harmless Mexican and try to kill him. Tony had to bail him out of jail several times.

Eventually, I persuaded Tony to take him down to see Dr. Hausner, who was so sympathetic and understanding. I went along and the three of us went into the office, and after the doctor had given him a physical examination, he told us, "He is in good shape—nothing wrong. I would like to talk to him a little alone." So we went outside to the waiting room. He was in there a good while, the usual patient patients hoping for their turn. Then, Dr. Hausner came to the door and beckoned us back to his office.

He said: "Benito cannot forget the war, the killing, the horrors. The only way for him to get over the combat shock is to work. To work hard out of doors, to work so hard he will fall asleep in the evening as soon as his head touches the pillow. He can work off his memories like this."

"I will take him to my ranch at Arroyo Seco ten miles from Taos. Lots of work there, hoeing, plowing, irrigating—a big ranch."

"Good," said the doctor. "Will you do that Benito?"

"Yes sir," he replied and we went out.

"Remember now, no drinks!" said Eric as we left.

"No sir," answered Benito.

It was not for a long time that we ever heard about Benito's life in the army. He remained as silent as before, but little by little he improved and became himself once more. When the harvest time was over, he was able to return to his mother. He looked wonderful. His skin glowed and his long black hair shone and the smile had returned to his frozen face. The little children loved him and clung to him and he pulled them along as they clung to his hands.

Yet we never knew what happened until much later. Millicent related it to Brett to make her understand him again. All we had known was that there was something queer about his discharge and that when he had returned to the Pueblo, he pulled medals and stripes out of his pockets and gave them away contemptuously to the pretty girls who admired him.

I imagine in the long dark nights, the story gradually emerged. He had been a good soldier and the head of his squadron, sometimes under a fine officer, sometimes under a stinker. Battle after battle, while all the time the killing sickened him. He loathed his bayonet; he loathed the sight of the falling boys he had to exterminate while not feeling any enmity. Before action, he was given a stiff drink and ordered out.

One day it grew overpoweringly disgusting. His officer on that occasion was the lower type. "Here," he ordered Benito, "get your squadron together and go out and kill—kill—understand?"

Benito looked at the man and said slowly: "I don't want to. *You* do it," and he knocked the smaller man down. The officer got to his feet and made a rush at the boy. He tore off his medals and stripes and threw them on the floor.

"Now, you get a dishonorable discharge from the army of the United States."

Benito smiled and picked up the trifles from the floor. "That suits me fine," he said, "but up to this minute, these are mine."

So he was sent home and relived for a long time all the horrors he had committed. The only time he forget them was when he got whiskey at the nightclubs. Then, he was in the war again.

After Tony had rehabilitated him with the hard ranch work, Millicent met him one day at Sofina's where she had motored out to have a chat with Tony in the late afternoon. That was the end of Benito. She found that he was an expert chauffer and engaged him, . . .

It was gradual and took time. She was remodeling her house and unexpectedly made over the room next to hers, which was one of the new ones she added to the house. Eventually, Benito was installed there, instead of coming daily to drive her about.

We did not see him then but Tony heard he was drinking a good deal again. Wherever she went, he went with her—to New York, to Jamaica for the winter in the lovely old reconstructed sugar refinery, built of stone and the water lapped against the walls under the windows. . . .

Benito, established in his room and bath next to Millicent's, enjoyed it all at first. Plenty to eat and lots to drink. But he grew restive and needed some occupation other than motoring her about the country roads, so she bought him over a hundred hens and several roosters and a bunch of thoroughbred ducks that enjoyed the pond below the house. He was supposed to raise ducklings and gather the eggs to sell, but he paid little or no attention to them, and the foreman, Ralph, took care of them. Then, she gave his younger brother, Jimmy, now in the army, four fine little pinto ponies, but kept them on her place so they would get good care and they browsed in the fertile meadows beneath the porch. But Benito paid no attention to these either.

The rows and quarrels between him and his lady increased. At night, the household was kept awake by the tantrums and shoutings. Benito wanted to return frequently to his cronies in the Pueblo, and Millicent could not bear him out of her sight. She had heard a rumor of a girl Benito was interested in out there and finally forbade him his visits away, allowing him to go only Saturday nights, when he stayed very late, while she lay awake listening for the car. Often he brought his special friend home with him, both very drunk, and all who passed through his room to Millicent's could see them sprawled in torpor on his wide bed. . . .

Benito was very bored, but since she had opened a bank account for him in the First National Bank, he had plenty of money to buy whiskey and pretty clothes, and maybe that helped. . . .[24]

[After Millicent's return to Taos from her several month stay in the hospital in Santa Fe, in 1952, Benito told a friend, "I *love* Millicent." "And I believe he truly did," Mabel writes. The night of Mabel and Tony's Christmas Party in 1952, Millicent fell down and hit her head in her tiled bathroom. Her nurse found her unconscious the next day.]

She had been unconscious since her fall—possibly she had had a stroke. Eric was in a terrible quandary. He knew she must be operated upon by the Albuquerque specialist, but he also knew that her heart was too weak to stand an anesthetic. He finally was left no choice. An operation was all that would save her and bring her out of the coma. On the table, she rallied, very faintly, showing signs of life, opening her girlish eyes, moving her fingers slightly. Then, she sank and died.

The surgeon immediately shaved her whole head and made an exploratory examination of her brain. A tumor the size of a pecan nut was found in the back of her head, and beside the clot that he had found during his operation, two or three clots were discovered on the other side of her brain. If she had lived, she would have been completely paralyzed beyond hope of recovery.

When they brought her home and lay her in her great yellow bed, Dixie dressed her for her coffin, the tears streaming. "Two or three times in December, Millicent said she smelled death," she said to Benito who was looking away out of the window. "While I was smelling whiskey. Army whiskey," he said bitterly, for he had never tasted whiskey before the army gave it him to urge him to go out and kill.

Dixie dressed her in her favorite dress, a pretty soft thing and wound a lace scarf about her poor defaced skull. . . .

The funeral was beautiful. Very few Taos people came to it, but quite a large number of Indians, dressed in their bright serapes. The Governor, Star Road; the dictator, Severino; the War Chief, all were present and many of Tony's relatives.

The pallbearers were her three sons and Saki [Karavas, owner of the La Fonda Hotel in Taos] . . . Dr. Hausner came up from Santa Fe and stood at one side of the hearse. He was an honorary pallbearer. Benito stood alone, too, no kind of pallbearer at all. . . .

Benito was not invited to join the family council when the will was read. He lay all day in a daze down in the meadow looking at his ducks cavorting in the pond. The next morning, Arthur [Arturo Ramos, Millicent's older son] got out of the station wagon Benito had driven Millicent in for long. "Get in there," Arthur commanded him.

The lawyer came to speak to him as he stumbled into the car: "Now after the appraisers have come to go over everything, you must come to take your livestock away that you own. But I fear you will not get the proceeds of your annuity for quite a while." . . .

Arthur drove Benito silently to the Pueblo and dumped him at his mother's house. The next day, Ralph appeared with a great jumble of Benito's clothes and belongings—and that was the end of that.

The poor fellow lay on his mother's bed in a state of shock. This boy had already had one great shock from the army life but that was as nothing compared to losing Millicent. He would not eat nor speak and he could not sleep. For a long time, he partially shared the coma she had had.

When Tony and I came home from our two months in Cuernavaca, he took Benito in charge again. Twice he drove him to Santa Fe to collect the remainder of his little bank account. Then, he kept him with him at Arroyo Seco, out of doors, out of bed, under the trees beside the stream.

One day Ralph came over and said the appraisers were in the house and the following Thursday was Benito's last chance to come for his chickens and ducks and his brother's little pinto ponies. Benito cared nothing for this. He refused to do anything about it, but Ralph, a kind man, arrived with a truckload of fowls and four little ponies.

Tony persuaded Benito to do something about this. He made him put a big chicken roost together in the large ranch corral and made him clean it every day.

The large number of chickens laid eight or nine dozen eggs a day and the ducks were breeding beside the stream. Then Tony bought egg boxes and made Benito collect them every day and then drove him to the Pueblo. As soon as he arrived, many Indians ran to the house to buy the good, fresh eggs. Benito began to take an interest in the money he could get for them and that was the beginning of a new interest. Though very different from his previous life, it was something *to do* and something to live for. He enjoyed giving the money to his mother to buy vegetables and food for the children. . . .

Tony went to Raton and bought a thoroughbred Hereford bull for eight or nine hundred dollars, and with the remainder, two registered Hereford heifers. We took great care of these animals, and Tony had already raised a couple of steers. We kept them winters, before there was any grazing at Arroyo Seco, at our place in Taos. Then, in the summer time, they were moved to Tony's ranch.

Not long ago, San Antonio Day [the Harvest festival] came along and Tony left Benito in charge of all the animals out there because he still resists gatherings of fun and dancing and fiesta feeling. Tony cautioned him to be sure to put them in the corral at night, but to no avail. Benito got a bottle of whiskey at the small saloon as soon as twilight came. Maybe the loneliness came upon him. That night the bull, left out, broke the barbed wire fence between him and the alfalfa field and ate it all night while Benito slept. In the morning, he was dead—swelled up and dead.

That was another consequence of Millicent's influence. We had sold the place and the poor cattle and bought good stock. Now it was no more because she had hurt him too much, given him too much to drink, and Tony had not been there to look after him.

Millicent is gone and most of the time Benito stands in the mud or dust storm among his chickens. His hand on his chest, he complains of the pains in his chest, which have continued since the Indian dance at Brett's [when] he crashed into the telephone pole afterwards. Poor fellow, it may not be long before he joins her in Limbo!

Sometimes, when I lie awake at night, I wonder what became of her hundreds of dresses, preserved since girlhood and when will be the final end to her influence on this earth.

~~~~~~~~~~~~~~~

In Mabel's telling, the circumstances surrounding Benito's not wanting to fight an enemy in World War II that was not *his* enemy recall M. Scott Momaday's protagonist, Abel, in his 1966 novel *House Made of Dawn*, as well as Leslie

Marmon Silko's hero, Tayo, in her 1977 novel *Ceremony*, who returns from the Korean War. Abel comes back to Jemez Pueblo after the war, with his identity and his life shattered. Silko makes explicit reference to Tayo's suffering sustained guilt from having to kill men who looked like himself. Both Abel and Tayo go through healing ceremonies that help to bring them back to a healthier state of being.

On the last page of her Millicent memoir, Mabel writes that it was completed on June 23, 1953. But even with the death of her adversary, Mabel was unable to find the peace of mind that she perennially sought. She wrote one last memoir, "Doctors: Fifty Years of Experience," in which she tried to come to terms with the physical and psychological traumas that marked much of her adult life.

Doctors

Fifty Years of Experience

IN 1954, MABEL wrote her last memoir, which focuses on her adult experiences with medical doctors, including her experiences with venereal disease. It is very likely that Dr. Hausner assigned her this task because she had not yet worked her way through to an understanding of how she came to marry three men afflicted with venereal disease and then found them repulsive to her sexually (or, in Tony's case, stopped having sexual relations because of the shock of his infecting her).[1]

It seems, of course, irrational for a woman to marry—or stay married to—three men infected with syphilis. Edwin apparently told Mabel he was no longer infectious and that, in any case, they would not have sexual relations, which proved not to be true. But the fact that Mabel subsequently married two men who contracted syphilis speaks not only to her own psychological problems but also to salient issues of the time in which she lived. These issues included the prevalence of venereal disease, which was of pandemic proportions before the discovery and widespread use of penicillin in 1946, and the tenacity of Victorian notions of sin and punishment in the modern era, even among so-called new women who embraced "free love." Mabel may well have represented an extreme of self-contradictions in this regard. But she is hardly the only "New Woman" who embraced conflicting ideas about heterosexual relations and marriage, namely, that they were the key to womanly identity *and* an onerous entrapment, and that they were both life-enhancing *and* life-threatening. Indeed, before there was a cure for VD, these diseases were seriously debilitating at best and life-threatening at worst. It is possible that part of

Mabel's (unconscious) motivation for marriage was a form of self-punishment or, as she would have put it, submitting to her "doom" or "fate." It is also possible that she married Edwin, Maurice, and Tony so that she could feel secure without having to continue sexual relations with them, which she claims became fraught—or ended—between her and all of her husbands not long after she married them. Mabel wrote in her published memoirs that she always felt that she needed the legitimacy of marriage, although it never stopped her from having affairs, at least until she contracted syphilis.

There is certainly no doubt that Mabel used writing therapeutically as a means to find a way out of her illnesses, and her own and her culture's contradictory ideas about what real womanhood entailed. In the epilogue, I highlight new versions of events that appear in her earlier unpublished memoirs and that are related to her unresolved issues around sexuality and VD. I begin with her description of her marriage to Karl Evans, with a story about his infidelity that she tells for the first time, ending with a suicide attempt that exactly repeats the one she writes about at the end of her affair with Dr. Parmenter in "Green Horses." In "Doctors" this incident becomes the occasion for her first attempted suicide, which results in her meeting Dr. Parmenter. In her retelling of her affair with Parmenter, Mabel recounts seeing him and her mother having intercourse rather than in the postcoital moment she describes in "Green Horses." Mabel also writes a new scene in which Parmenter infects her with gonorrhea, an incident not mentioned in any of her previous writings.

I can only speculate on why Mabel might have waited until 1954 to write these changes into her life story. She wrote "Doctors" at the age of seventy-five, when she was many decades removed from the experiences she recounts, although she clearly consulted some of her earlier writings. Writing one document focused on all fifty years of encounters with disease and doctors may have led her to intensify and exaggerate her memories, to read back into her life scenes that provided further justification for her physical and mental suffering. But she may also have felt that at this point in her life she could, finally, tell *all* of the truths that she had not yet revealed, most importantly about her earliest encounter with VD. Her final note to Dr. Hausner, however, which appears at the end of my epilogue, leaves lingering doubts.

I have italicized the material that is new or revised.

Prologue

One day Karl burst into the house and said, "Listen, we've been invited to go down to the country and stay over Sunday with the Grants."

"Grants?" I asked. "Yes, Mary and Henry. Wonderful people. We take a train out there—it's only half an hour, I think." He started throwing some things into a bag and so did I.

The Grants lived in a pleasant house and she was a very pretty, active, gay girl. Henry was rather sober and quiet and actually disappeared for some reason soon after we got there. We did the usual country things, took a walk, climbed a hill, came back in the twilight, and Mary served us quite a lot of drinks. We didn't stay up late but went to bed upstairs in a room next to Mary's, which didn't have a Henry in it, and I quickly fell asleep.

I woke a little later to find Karl absent from the bed and vague, muffled sounds coming from the adjoining room. I lay awake with my heart beating fast. After awhile Karl crept stealthfully back and climbed into bed. I turned on the light beside me and exclaimed, "Where have you been?"

He looked quite sheepish and his curly hair stood up on end. "In there," he whispered, motioning toward Mary's room.

"What did you do that for?" I cried aloud.

"Well, she wanted it and I didn't mind," he whispered. That was the end of marriage for me.

When I got up in the morning I told Mary, "I have to go home now." She looked sympathetic but unperturbed, understanding in a way.

I had assumed control of the situation now and Karl followed submissively. I acted very quiet but I felt terrible inside. When we got to Buffalo I said, "Drop me off at Grandma Ganson's, I want to see her." And I let him go back to his job.

Grandma was sitting in the vestibule of her house bowing and smiling to any of the men who passed who knew her well, for the Buffalo Club was on one side of her house and Trinity Church was opposite and the Saturn Club was at the corner. There was always lots of coming and going and Grandma loved it.

I said to her, controlling my voice, "You know, I don't feel very well, Grandma, I'd like to go up to the spare room and lie down awhile."

"Certainly, my precious, you go right along. It's always waiting for you."

So I went up and undressed and took the nightgown out of the over-night bag I had brought and then I went into the adjoining bathroom, poured a glass of water, and swallowed all the strychnine pills I had in a little box (where did I get strychnine pills—I don't know now). Then I lay down on the bed and waited. It did not take long. I was seized in a sort of cataclysm that was tearing me to pieces. I just managed to crawl down the hall to the head of the stairs and bawled, "Grandma," at the top of my voice. Then I suddenly arched over backwards and I fell unconscious.

I opened my eyes. I was lying in a warm bath. Dr. Parmenter, my father's Doctor, coatless and with his sleeves rolled up, was kneeling by the bathtub. He had one hand under my head and the other supported my body. "You're all right, dear," he said. "I want to get you in bed now." . . .

Dr. Parmenter

He became the motivation and the cause for living. He had a big practice and he was on the staff of the Buffalo General Hospital, but somehow he found time to come and see me every day. At the end of each visit I would say, "Tomorrow?" and he would say, "Yes, sure." Then I would say, "And give me a big kiss." Now all my life was wrapped up in these brief contacts with him. I never went out nor saw any of my old friends, never inviting them to the house. It was just waiting from visit to visit. . . .

Parmenter often said ruefully, "I wish we could be together permanently and for good. Maybe I would find time to stay home more then. As it is I am always on the go, one house after another—one woman after another—one man after another—always patching them up." . . .

I did not say anything. For some reason, in spite of my dependence upon him and the security he gave me, I did not trust him. Once I went up to my mother's house and his buggy was at the door and I supposed he was with my father, giving a shot of something. But I crept to my mother's door and it was closed and I heard low voices inside and rashly opened the door as quietly as I could. Parmenter raised himself from the couch upon which my mother was lying and she hastily pulled down her skirts. "Oh, so that's how it is," I said and closed the door upon them and went away. . . .

[Parmenter has just given her the gold cross she writes about in "Green Horses," after they have been lovers for several months. See chapter 2.] A few days later he gave me something else. He came into the room walking rather gingerly and looking a little pale for him. He threw himself down on the bed beside me and muttered, "That damn bitch of Dr. Sherman's has given me the clap." I had never heard this word before and have never heard it spoken since, but he indicated the nature of it by laying his hand upon himself at the damaged point.

Feeling puzzled, but noble, I cried, "Give it to me and I will take it for you," and throwing himself passionately upon me, he did so.

I did not know what I was letting myself in for. It showed up pretty fast and was very painful. Parmenter didn't appear or send any word. In desperation I telephoned his house, for I really needed help. Karl was away and I was alone with the baby's nurse and the other maid. I could not tell them anything. Someone at the Parmenters' answered, "Oh, Mrs. and Dr. have gone to the country place at Rosehill for a few days." So that was that. . . .

Maurice Sterne

I suppose I must add here a bit of Maurice's history which I shared. . . . He seemed at times so nervous and distraught that I persuaded him to go to Dr. Brill for analytic treatment. In the course of this procedure, Dr. Brill found from Maurice's dreams that he had syphilis. He had never known that he had contracted it when he was on the island of Bali, drawing and painting those beautiful people. Dr. Brill gave him have a blood test and it showed that *he was in the secondary stage, so, of course, he had to undergo the necessary treatment. He is very ill at the present moment, after all these years, with cancer of the hip. In the course of my life I have been forced to discover that cancer follows syphilis even after a long period of time. . . .*

Tony Lujan

One night Tony came home from the Pueblo, having had a love scene in the night with the wife of Tony Romero, his old friend, and as he threw his white sheet off I could not but perceive the signs of this event—blood and moisture and odor. I was devastated at the time, feeling that this was Tony's first infidelity. I recovered from this emotional upset, but some days later both Tony and I came down with the inevitable sign of syphilis on the intimate parts of our body. *Three times and out. The third husband who had syphilis, all of them dignified and rather eminent men in their various situations. Is it possible there is so much venereal disease in the world? . . .*

For reasons I have told before here, I could not go to the local doctor nor take Tony to him for the obvious habit of loquacity. So, I went to Alice Corbin Henderson in Santa Fe, who was my friend at that time, and the mother of John's wife, and asked her what I should do. She said the thing to do would be to take a little house on the Camino del Monte and come down to Dr. Frank Mera for treatments once a week. This was quite a hardship as we had to go down over the old road and it took half a day to get there, and we were so tired we had to spend the night and come back the next day. Also I might have done it differently, for Alice Henderson, sweet and kind as she was, was no more discreet in her talk than the Taos doctor. So I suppose everybody knew what was going on.

That was during the summer and for the winter months we went to San Francisco and took a house for the winter on top of Mt. Tamalpais. There we got in touch with Dr. Kilgore, who was supposed to be the best doctor at the time, and we went to his office once a week for those Salvarsan shots. One horrible addition to his treatment was black mercurial salve which we were supposed to rub on our body, chest and back, every day and night. I am afraid we left this off pretty soon because it soiled every-thing—nightclothes, bedding, and so on. I believe that at the end of this winter we considered ourselves cured. Anyway, we avoided by the treatment the other phases of the disease. . . .

~~~~~~~~~~~~~~

Mabel's last note to Dr. Hausner is dated December 7, 1955. It reads: "No—it is no use. I cannot freely express myself in writing any more. Let it remain in the realm of unspoken understanding. I feel you know already anything I myself fight to express. Love, Mabel"

Notes

Preface

1. MDL to EH, n.d. [1952], MDLP; MD to Leo Stein, November 30, 1935?, LGSP. I use initials throughout the endnotes for names of letter writers and their recipients, as well as for the names of archives. A list of the archives appears in the selected bibliography. Mabel produced twenty volumes of autobiographical writing, six of which were intended to be part of her "Intimate Memories" series. She also donated to the Beinecke Library seven large bound volumes of letters (mostly written to her) and seventeen Scrapbooks of print materials about her life, her writings, and her circle of friends.

2. Lois Rudnick, *Mabel Dodge Luhan: New Woman, New Worlds* (Albuquerque: University of New Mexico Press, 1984), 252.

3. See my abbreviated edition of Mabel's four-volume memoir, *Intimate Memories: The Autobiography of Mabel Dodge Luhan* (Albuquerque: University of New Mexico Press, 1999).

4. See Rudnick, *Mabel Dodge Luhan*, 182–85.

5. For a history of the visitors to the Luhan house, see Rudnick, *Utopian Vistas: The Mabel Dodge Luhan House and the American Counterculture* (Albuquerque: University of New Mexico Press, 1996).

6. Ellen Bradbury to Lois Rudnick, September 30, 2003; John Evans to Donald Gallup, April 15, 1973, MDLP. Some of Mabel's memoirs have notes, written in her hand, that they were not to be published until after her death; some leave that decision to the discretion of the curator of the Beinecke Library.

7. See Emily Hahn, *Mabel* (Boston, MA: Houghton Mifflin, 1977), 173; Luhan, "Doctors: Fifty Years of Experience," 22, 44, MDLP; Lois Rudnick, "The Male-Identified Woman and Other Anxieties of a Feminist Biographer," in *The Challenge of Feminist Biography*, ed. Elizabeth Abel et al. (Urbana: University of Illinois Press, 1992), 116–38.

8. Luhan, "Doctors," 22, MDLP.

Introduction

1. Susan Sontag, *Illness as Metaphor* (New York: Farrar, Straus and Giroux, 1978), 58–59.
2. See Allan Brandt's epilogue on AIDS in *No Magic Bullet* (New York: Oxford University Press, 1987), and John Noble Wilford, "Genetic Study Bolsters Columbus Link to Syphilis," *New York Times*, January 15, 2008, D2, http://www.nytimes.com/2008/01/15/science/15syph.html. Alfred Crosby, in *The Columbian Exchange: Biological and Cultural Consequences of 1492* (Westport, CT: Greenwood Press, 1972), 123–25, has done the most extensive research on the Columbian theory.
3. Edgar Allen Poe, "The Masque of the Red Death," in *Selected Writings of Edgar Allan Poe*, ed. Edward Davidson (Boston, MA: Houghton Mifflin, 1956), 174–80. Nathaniel Hawthorne, Herman Melville, and Mark Twain also took on the subject of syphilis in their fiction. Hawthorne, in "The Minister's Black Veil" (see Carl Ostrowski, "The Minister's 'Grievous Affliction': Diagnosing Hawthorne's Parson Hooper, *Literature and Medicine* 17, no. 2 [1998]: 197–211); Melville, in *Moby Dick*, in his chapter on the "Whiteness of the Whale," where he compares the mask of God to the face of a woman whose ostensible physical beauty obscures her diseased body; and in Mark Twain's passage, in chapter 9 of *Life on the Mississippi*, where he compares a brilliant sunset he recalls to the false flush on a diseased maiden's cheek. The seductive young woman whose beauty masks syphilis was a common trope in popular literature and illustrations in nineteenth-century Europe and the United States. See Sander Gilman, *Sexuality: An Illustrated History* (New York: John Wiley & Sons, 1989), 256–57.
4. Claude Quétel, introduction to *History of Syphilis*, trans. Judith Braddock and Brian Pike (Baltimore, MD: The Johns Hopkins University Press, 1990); Arien Mack, *In Time of Plague: The History and Social Consequences of Lethal Epidemic Disease* (New York: New York University Press, 1992), 46.
5. Quétel, *History of Syphilis*, 3, 196; Crosby, *The Columbian Exchange*, 158–60.
6. Congenital syphilis can only be passed on by the mother; it manifests at birth, not later.
7. For information on symptoms and treatment, see John Ledingham and David Warrell, *Concise Oxford Textbook of Medicine* (New York: Oxford University Press, 2000), 1599–1685; for current U.S. statistics on VD, see http://www.cdc.gov/STD/; Theodor Rosebury, *Microbes and Morals: The Strange Story of Venereal Disease* (New York: Viking Press, 1971), 78.
8. See Harold J. Magnuson, et al., "Inoculation Syphilis in Human Volunteers," *Medicine* 35, no. 1 (1956): 76. According to Dr. Barbara McGovern, an infectious disease specialist at Tufts New England Medical Center, transmissions rates from male to female are about 30 percent (although the data is not good); there are much lower rates for female to male transmission. There is a 50 percent chance of transmission of gonorrhea from male to female (phone interview, July 10, 2006).

9. Brandt, *No Magic Bullet*, 40–41; John Parascandola, states that, until 1921, the typical treatment in the United States was for a few weeks; see *Sex, Sin, and Science: A History of Syphilis in America*, New York: Praeger (2008), 78.

10. Quétel, *History of Syphilis*, 134–36; Mary Spongberg points out that by the first decade of the twentieth century, "Sayings like the 'sins of the father are visited upon their children' . . . abounded in the literature on congenital syphilis"; see *Feminizing Venereal Disease: The Body of the Prostitute in Nineteenth-Century Medical Discourse* (New York: New York University Press, 1997), 155.

11. Brandt, *No Magic Bullet*, 8; Brandt made these estimates in a 1991 phone conversation with me, which he reaffirmed in a 2002 phone conversation; see Rudnick, "The Male Identified Woman," 135–36.

12. See Brandt, *No Magic Bullet*, 23–24; Quétel, *History of Syphilis*, 149, 204.

13. Brandt, *No Magic Bullet*, 9–15, 32. In "Progressive Era Revolution in American Attitudes Toward Sex," John Burnham points out that while most doctors in the United States advocated "education of the public and/or compulsory medical inspections of prostitutes," purity advocates often prevented them (*Journal of American History* 59, no. 4 [1973]: 153–54).

14. Brandt, *No Magic Bullet*, 24; Margaret Sanger, *What Every Girl Should Know* (New York: Belvedere, 1980 [1913]), 59, 63. In *The Great Scourge and How to End It*, London: Lincoln's Inn House (1913), Christabel Pankhurst argued for women's right to the vote because Englishmen were infecting their wives, and thus future generations, with syphilis. Like Sanger, she claimed that 75 to 80 percent of Englishmen had been infected with syphilis before they married.

   On the English "New Women" novels that took on syphilis as a theme see Michael Worboys, "Unsexing Gonorrhea: Bacteriologists, Gynaecologists, and Suffragists in Britain, 1860–1920," *Social History of Medicine* 17, no. 1 (2004): 41–59. In Gilman's *The Crux*, the heroine, Vivian Lane, is saved from marrying her VD-infected fiancé thanks to Dr. Belair, who warns her against "biological sin," for which "there is no forgiveness"; see *The Crux*, Durham, NC: Duke University Press (2003 [1911]), 129–30. Upton Sinclair wrote two novels in which women's lives are ruined by VD, one based on a popular play that had been staged on Broadway, based on his translation/adaptation of Eugène Brieux's 1912 *Les Avariés*. Sinclair's 1913 novel is titled *Damaged Goods* (http://www.gutenberg .org/files/1157/1157-h/1157-h.htm); his second novel, *Sylvia's Marriage* (published in 1914), is much more radical in its sexual politics (http://www.gutenberg.org/ catalog/world/readfile?fk_files=1460853).

15. Brandt, *No Magic Bullet*, 122.

16. Brandt, *No Magic Bullet*, 129, 143–44. Connecticut passed the first blood test requirement for a marriage license in 1938. In 1938, The Living Newspaper (part of the WPA Federal Theatre Project) produced Arnold Sundgaard's *Spirochete*, which traced the history of syphilis from the time of Columbus's voyages to the Americas through the device of a young couple who are about to be married and need to be convinced to take blood tests. See Figure 5, and John O'Connor,

"'Spirochete' and the War on Syphilis," *The Drama Review: TDR*, 21, no. 1 (1977): 91–98.

17. Rosebury, *Microbes and Morals*, 146.

18. Representations of syphilis were rife among Symbolist painters, including Edvard Munch, James Ensor, and Aubrey Beardsley, who drew on images of the diseased city as the embodiment of the death of Western civilization. Munch painted two such portraits, one of a working-class woman, the other of a middle-class woman and baby. (See Figure 6, *The Inheritance*, 1879–1899.) Both babies display the red chancres that marked what was then described as a "syphilitic runt." See Sharon Hirsh, *Symbolism and Modern Urban Society* (Cambridge, MA: Cambridge University Press, 2004), 107–16.

   Raemaekers' *La Syphilis*, circa 1916, is perhaps the most misogynistic embodiment of early twentieth century iconography that embodied the diseased female (see Figure 4). Here a Medusa figure holds a dead man's skull in front of her vagina as a symbol of women's power to devour men's bodies. The portrait embodied European fears, raised to a fever pitch during and after World War I, when prostitutes were referred to as "treponema machine-guns." Many Europeans and Americans believed that syphilis would finish off those not killed in the war or by Spanish flu. See Hirsh, *Symbolism and Modern Urban Society*, 131; Quétel, *History of Syphilis*, 6, 176. It is estimated that some 30,000 U.S. women were incarcerated in detention homes during World War I. See Parascandola, *Sex, Sin, and Science*, 57; also Michael Lowenthal's *Charity Girl* (New York: Houghton Mifflin-Harcourt, 2007), a historical novel about the internment of "loose women" during World War I because it was feared that they would spread VD.

19. Roger Williams, *Horror of Life* (Chicago: University of Chicago Press, 1980), 19.

20. On *Dr. Jekyll and Mr. Hyde*, see Elaine Showalter, *Sexual Anarchy: Gender and Culture at the Fin de Siècle* (London: Penguin, 1990), 109–15; on Oscar Wilde, Deborah Hayden, *Pox: Genius, Madness, and the Mysteries of Syphilis* (New York: Basic Books, 2003), 219, who quotes Ellmann; also see Carol Margaret Davison, ed., *Bram Stoker's Dracula: Sucking Through the Century, 1897–1997* (Toronto: Dundurn Press, 1997), 34–35.

21. Kathleen Ferris, *James Joyce & the Burden of Disease* (Lexington: University Press of Kentucky, 1995), 5.

22. Showalter, *Sexual Anarchy*, 199; D. H. Lawrence, "Introduction to These Paintings," *Phoenix: The Posthumous Papers of D.H. Lawrence*, ed. Edward D. McDonald (London: Heinemann, 1936), 555–58. Lawrence's title refers to a series of erotic paintings he created, which eventually found their way to the La Fonda Hotel in Taos, where they are kept behind a curtain and can be seen for a small fee. Mabel was convinced Lawrence knew about her syphilis; see chapter 4, "The Statue of Liberty."

23. Laurie MacDiarmid, *T. S. Eliot's Civilized Savage: Religious Eroticism and Poetics* (New York: Routledge, 200), 338. There are striking parallels between the decaying city passages in T. S. Eliot's *The Waste Land* and the syphilis passages in the cityscapes of William Carlos Williams's first book of modernist poetry, *Kora in*

Hell (1920), with the salient difference that Williams makes no moral commentary on the disease, which must have been quite familiar to him from his medical education and practice.

The year before Williams published *Kora*, he met Baroness Elsa von Freytag-Loringhoven, a Dadaist performance artist who lived in Greenwich Village. According to Freytag-Loringhoven's biographer, Irene Gammel, Williams apparently made "an impromptu love declaration," after which she "insisted on sealing their union with a kiss," suggesting that he needed to "contract syphilis from her to free [his] mind for serious art"; see Gammel, *Baroness Elsa: Gender, Dada, and Everyday Modernity, A Cultural Biography* (Boston, MA: MIT Press, 2003), 264. There are no medical records to support Freytag-Loringhoven's infection at this time (she had been infected and treated in 1896). Gammel believes that her "intent was to shock the obstetrician, perhaps by grotesquely ventriloquizing her father, who had infected her mother" with syphilis, a disease that Elsa flaunted (Gammel, *Baroness Elsa*, 265).

24. On Picasso's early sketches for *Demoiselle*, see John Richardson and Marilyn McCully, *A Life of Picasso*, 11–18, where they discuss some of the images that make the theme of syphilis more explicit (*A Life of Picasso: The Painter of Modern Life 1907–1917*. Vol. II. New York: Random House, 1996). Picasso's early sketches portray women grouped around a sailor while a doctor or medical student holds a book or a skull. Alfred Barr quoted in Leo Steinberg, "The Philosophical Brothel," *October* 44 (1988): 10; for a feminist critique of the work, see Anna C. Chave, "New Encounters with *Les Demoiselles d'Auvignon*: Gender, Race, and the Origins of Cubism," *The Art Bulletin* 76, no. 4 (1994): 605, in which she quotes Picasso.

25. Jose Martinez-Herrera et al., "Dalí (1904–1989): Psychoanalysis and Pictorial Surrealism," *The American Journal of Psychiatry* 160 (May 2003): 855. See also Ian Gibson, *The Shameful Life of Salvador Dalí* (New York: W. W. Norton, 1998). Gibson's biography deals in depth with Dalí's sexuality, which was also influenced by his shame about the small size of his penis.

26. Patrick Marnham, *Dreaming With His Eyes Open: A Life of Diego Rivera* (New York: Alfred Knopf, 1998), 253; Irene Herner de Larrea's *Diego Rivera's Mural* is devoted to the creation of the mural and the controversies it aroused (de Larrea, ed., *Diego Rivera's Mural At The Rockefeller Center*, 2nd ed. [Mexico City: Edicupes, 1990]). Mabel was effusive in her praise for Rivera's murals, which she saw on a trip through Mexico she took in the late 1930s and wrote about in an unpublished memoir, "Mexico in 1930" (MDLP).

27. Quoted in Cynthia Russett, *Sexual Science: The Victorian Construction of Womanhood* (Cambridge, MA: Harvard University Press, 1989), 61; Charles Rosenberg, "The Bitter Fruit: Heredity, Disease, and Social Thought in Nineteenth-Century America," *Perspectives in American History* 8 (1974): 200, 210.

28. Nathan Hale, *Freud and the Americans: The Beginnings of Psychoanalysis in the United States, 1876–1917* (New York: Oxford University Press, 1971), 121.

29. Mabel Dodge Luhan, *Movers and Shakers: Volume Three of Intimate Memories* (New York: Harcourt, Brace and Co., 1936), 506.

30. Hale, *Freud and the Americans*, 138–40; see also, Eli Zaretsky, *Secrets of the Soul: A Social and Cultural History of Psychoanalysis* (New York: Alfred A. Knopf, 2004), which seeks to balance the "emancipatory" and "repressive" elements for women in Freudian analysis.

31. Freud quoted in Hale, *Freud and the Americans*, 13; Elaine Showalter, *The Female Malady: Women, Madness, and English Culture, 1830–1980* (London: Virago, 1985), 199; on Emma Goldman, see Sanford Gifford, "The American Reception of Psychoanalysis," in *1915, The Cultural Moment: the New Politics, the New Woman, the New Psychology, the New Art, and the New Theatre in America*, ed. Adele Heller and Lois Rudnick (New Brunswick, NJ: Rutgers University Press, 1991), 132–33.

32. Steven Marcus, "Freud and Dora," in *In Dora's Case: Freud-Hysteria-Feminism*, ed. Charles Bernheimer and Claire Kahane (New York: Columbia University Press, 1985), 9. Sander Gilman discusses the status of Jewish doctors in *Disease and Representation: Images of Illness from Madness to AIDS* (Ithaca, NY: Cornell University Press, 1988), 192. In his work on the early Freud, *Freud and the Culture of Psychoanalysis*, Steven Marcus has noted Freud's fascination with the relationship between venereal pathologies and neuroses, partially because of their tendency to mimic each other: "Not only was their symptomology often convertible and interchangeable, but they often tended as well to occur coincidentally or in tandem, and in the same person," 7–8 (*Freud and the Culture of Psychoanalysis: Studies in the Transition from Victorian Humanity to Modernity* [New York: W. W. Norton, 1987]).

33. Elizabeth Lunbeck, *The Psychiatric Persuasion: Knowledge, Gender, and Power in Modern America* (Princeton, NJ: Princeton University Press, 1994), 50–52.

34. Phillip Rieff, introduction to *Dora: An Analysis of a Case of Hysteria*, by Sigmund Freud (New York: Simon & Schuster, 1997 [1905]), 12–27.

35. Rieff, introduction to *Dora*, 76.

36. Lunbeck, *The Psychiatric Persuasion*, 209; Joseph Allen Boone, *Libidinal Currents Sexuality and the Shaping of Modernism* (Chicago: The University of Chicago Press, 1998), 68–69; Mari Jo Buhle, *Feminism and Its Discontents: A Century of Struggle with Psychoanalysis* (Cambridge, MA: Harvard University Press, 1998), 38. Mabel's chief sex consultant, Margaret Sanger, shared these beliefs. A "sex romantic," she never challenged "the conventional Victorian structure of sex relations, which . . . rested on male assertiveness and female passivity," as noted by Linda Gordon, *Woman's Bodies, Woman's Right: A Social History of Birth Control in America* (New York: Grossman Publishers, 1976), 224–25.

37. Ellen Kay Trimberger quoted in Ann Snitow, Christine Stansell, and Sharon Thompson, eds., *Powers of Desire: The Politics of Sexuality* (London: Monthly Review Press, 1983), 9; see also Trimberger's essay "The New Woman and the New Sexuality," in *1915, The Cultural Moment: the New Politics, the New Woman, the New Psychology, the New Art, and the New Theatre in America*, ed. Adele Heller and Lois Rudnick (New Brunswick, NJ: Rutgers University Press, 1991); Linda Gordon, *Woman's Body, Woman's Right*, quoting the doctor, in 1905, 171; Paul

Robinson, quoting Ellis (*The Modernization of Sex: Havelock Ellis, Alfred Kinsey, William Masters and Virginia Johnson* [New York: Harper & Row, 1976], 34).

38. See Christopher Lasch, "Mabel Dodge Luhan: *Sex as Politics*," in *The New Radicalism in America (1869–1963): The Intellectual as a Social Type* (New York: Vintage Books, 1967), 118. Only Anaïs Nin has outdone Luhan, in the literary annals of American women, with nine published volumes of memoirs (some published posthumously). Mabel wrote in veiled ways about incest in her unpublished memoirs, as did Edith Wharton (1862–1937) in some of her short published and unpublished fiction. On Wharton, who shared a similar upbringing to Mabel's (including profound deprivation of maternal affection), see Gloria Erlich, who suggests "that the concealed male sins hovering in the background of many Wharton stories allude to a repressed history of incestuous abuse," ("The Female Conscience in Wharton's Shorter Fiction: Angel or Demon?," in *Cambridge Companion to Edith Wharton*, ed. Millicent Bell [Cambridge: Cambridge University Press, 1995], 106).

Wharton and Luhan were Victorian enough to keep the subject couched in mystery. Of a younger generation, and much more invested in openly exploring her sexuality, Nin (1903–1977) was quite explicit about incest in her diaries and novels, such as *The House of Incest* (1958). See Diane Richard-Allerdyce's discussion of Nin and incest in *Anaïs Nin and the Remaking of the Self: Gender, Modernism, and Narrative Identity* (DeKalb: Northern Illinois University Press, 1998), 30–43. There are many interesting parallels between Luhan and Nin, including their fascination with D. H. Lawrence. (Both of their first books were biographies of Lawrence and were published in the same year, 1932.) In 1933, two gay writers, Charles Henri Ford and Tyler Parker, published *The Young and the Evil* (New York: Arno Press, 1975 [1933]). They foreground Mabel's polymorphous sexual perversity in chapter 10, where a "Mrs. Dodge" picks up a Mexican "whip" dancer at a local tavern in Greenwich Village and beds him simultaneously with the gay protagonist of the novel.

39. MDL to HH, November 5, HHP.

40. Paul Eakin, *Fictions in Autobiography: Studies in the Art of Self-Invention* (Princeton, NJ: Princeton University Press, 1988), 8; Susan Friedman, "Women's Autobiographical Selves: Theory and Practice," in *Women, Autobiography, Theory: A Reader*, ed. Sidonie Smith and Julia Watson (Madison: University of Wisconsin Press, 1998), 108; Donald Spence, *Narrative Truth and Historical Truth: Meaning and Interpretation in Psychoanalysis* (New York: W. W. Norton and Co., 1984), 92–93.

41. Leigh Gilmore, *Autobiographics: A Feminist Theory of Women's Self-Representation* (Ithaca, NY: Cornell University Press, 1994), 55.

42. Judith Thurman, *Isak Dinesen: The Life of a Storyteller* (New York: St. Martin's Press, 1982), 283; "noble savage" quoted in Parmenia Migel's biography of Dinesen, *Titania: The Biography of Isak Dinesen*, as cited in Jan Mohamed's "*Out of Africa*," chapter 3, in *Understanding Isak Dinesen*, ed. Susan Brantly (Columbia: University of South Carolina Press, 2002), 138. Dinesen published one very explicit short

story about syphilis, "The Cardinal's Third Tale," in *Last Tales* (New York: Random House, 1957), in which an aristocratic British woman, who has maintained life-long celibacy and atheism because of her disgust with her father's sexual escapades, contracts syphilis by kissing the foot of the statue of St. Peter in Rome, in the same spot where a working-class man had just pressed his mouth.

43. Simon Lewis, *White Women Writers and Their African Invention* (Gainesville: University Press of Florida, 2003), 35; see Sylvia Rodquiguez, "Art, Tourism, and Race Relations in Taos: Toward a Sociology of the Art Colony," *Journal of Anthropological Research* 45, no. 1 (1989): 35.

44. Luhan, "The Statue of Liberty," 13. Mabel wrote on the front page of the typescript that it was not to be published until after her death.

45. See the following studies, among the many that have critiqued Mabel: Margaret Jacobs, *Engendered Encounters: Feminism and Pueblo Cultures, 1879–1934* (Lincoln: University of Nebraska Press, 1999); Flannery Burke, *From Greenwich Village to Taos: Primitivism and Place at Mabel Dodge Luhan's* (Lawrence: University of Kansas Press, 2008); Marianna Torgovnik, *Gone Primitive: Savage Intellects, Modern Lives* (Chicago: University of Chicago Press, 1990); Sherry Smith, *Reimagining Indians: Native Americans Through Anglo Eyes, 1880–1940* (New York: Oxford University Press, 2000), who has the most balanced perspective, from my point of view.

46. GOK to HM [Taos, Summer, 1929], in Jack Cowart and Juan Hamilton, eds., *Georgia O'Keeffe: Art and Letters* (New York: New York Graphic Society, 1990), 189.

Chapter One

1. See Patricia Everett, "Letters in Psychoanalysis and Posttermination Contact: Mabel Dodge's Correspondence with Smith Ely Jelliffe and A. A. Brill," *The Annual of Psychoanalysis* 26 (1999): 330–60.

2. Hale, *Freud and the Americans*, 93, 121–30.

3. Hale, *Freud and the Americans*, 216, 220.

4. Hale, *Freud and the Americans*, 383–85.

5. For Mabel's and Maurice's relationship, see Rudnick, *Mabel Dodge Luhan*, 125–37. Mabel adopted Elizabeth during a moment when she was feeling maternal, although it also may have been motivated by her desire to anchor Sterne's relationship to her. Elizabeth was given Sterne's name and was part of Mabel's household at least through the early 1920s. I have not been able to track what happened to her after that.

6. MDL to UJ, 1938, JC; Ronald Walters, *Primers for Prudery: Sexual Advice to Victorian America* (Englewood Cliffs, NJ: Prentice Hall, 1973), 6–7.

7. See Adrienne Rich, "Compulsory Heterosexuality and Lesbian Experience," in *The Lesbian and Gay Studies Reader*, ed. Henry Abelove, Michele Adina Barela, and David M. Halperin (New York: Routledge, 1993), 227–54.

8. See Ralph Martin, *Jennie: The Life of Lady Randolph Churchill* (Englewood, NJ: Prentice Hall, 1969), 307. According to Dr. Barbara McGovern, Mabel's father's symptoms were consonant with neurosyphilis (phone interview, July 10, 2006).

9. See Luhan, *European Experiences: Volume Two of Intimate Memories* (New York: Harcourt, Brace and Co., 1935), 29–30.

10. See Luhan, "European Experiences," "Making a Life, Part II," dated 1927, MDLP.

11. Dr. Barbara Morgan noted these three symptoms as consonant with gonorrhea (phone interview, July 10, 2006).

12. All of Mabel's letters to Jelliffe are in the Smith Ely Jelliffe file, along with his notes, in MDLP.

13. In an unpublished section of her typescript "Movers and Shakers," Mabel had sex with two of her closest friends in New York, journalist Hutchins Hapgood and painter Andrew Dasburg (with whom, she writes, the act was not consummated), because she felt compelled to as a "free love" advocate. But once was enough, she claimed about these two men, who remained lifelong friends.

14. SEJ to MDL, quoted in Luhan, *Movers and Shakers*, 444–45; Joseph Allen Boone, *Libidinal Currents*, discussing Foucault, 8.

15. Mabel's divorce from Dodge came through in April 1917. It is interesting that she did not divorce either Dodge or Sterne quickly. She was separated from each of them for five years before she divorced them.

16. "Why Bohemia's Queen Married an Indian Chief," *Pittsburgh Post*, n.d., Scrapbook vol. 17, MDLP.

17. Sterne's letter is published in Luhan, *Movers and Shakers*, 534–35.

18. Donald Meyer, *The Positive Thinkers: A Study of the American Quest for Health, Wealth, and Personal Power from Mary Baker Eddy to Norman Vincent Peale* (New York: Anchor Books, 1965), 64.

19. NB to MDS, n.d., MDLP; Beryl Satter, *Each Mind a Kingdom: American Women, Sexual Purity, and the New Thought Movement, 1875–1920* (Berkeley: University of California Press, 1999), 245.

20. Luhan, *Movers and Shakers*, 467–68; ECH to MDS, January 24 and November 11, 1918, MDLP.

21. ECH to MS, May 15, 1919 and January 5, 1921, MDLP.

22. Satter, *Each Mind a Kingdom*, 16.

23. Noted by Edmund Brill on the index to A. A. Brill papers donated to the Beinecke Library.

24. Sigmund Freud, "'Civilized' Sexual Morality and Modern Nervousness" (1908), *Sexuality and the Psychology of Love* (New York: Collier Books, 1972), 32.

25. AAB to MD, n.d., MDLP; "The Quarrel" was published in September and "The Parting," in October 1916; for a discussion of these stories, see Rudnick, *Mabel Dodge Luhan*, 136–37.

26. AAB to MDL, May [1923], MDLP. Brill had diagnosed Sterne's syphilis, and Mabel certainly would have informed him about Tony's and her own. His objections to her marrying Sterne and Lujan may have been partly due to this; he also indicated in earlier letters that her relationships with them were regressive. This letter comes in the month after her marriage to Tony. If the "diseases" to which he refers obliquely here are related to their infection with syphilis, it suggests that the event happened close to the time of their marriage in April. In "The

Statue of Liberty," Mabel situated the event as occuring sometime in the summer of 1923.

27. AAB to MDL, January 20, 1930, MDLP.
28. MDL to AAB, [1938], AABP.
29. MDL to AAB, October 1938, AABP. Mabel wrote a lay guide to psychoanalysis, which was never published (see "On Human Understanding," MDLP). The typescript indicates she had only a rudimentary grasp of many of Freud's analytic terms.
30. AAB to MDL, December 7, 1938, MDLP.

Chapter Two

1. DHL to MDL, April 12, 1926, quoted in Luhan, *Lorenzo in Taos* (New York: Alfred A. Knopf, 1932), 296. Lawrence is referring to an early version of Mabel's first manuscript that is not in MDLP, but it is likely to have included "Green Horses," which is "Part II" of her first volume "Background," in the typescript in the MDLP. Havelock Ellis's praised "Green Horses" as the best part of the draft she had sent him to read, HE to MDL, November 3, 1925, MDLP, "Green Horses," n.d., appears on page 400 of Vol. 1, "Intimate Memories." It is 314 typescript pages.
2. See Luhan, *European Experiences*, 16.
3. *Buffalo Evening News*, June 2, 1932, 38. Parmenter's medical practice didn't end quite so dramatically as Mabel portrays it in "Green Horses" (see head note for this chapter). On May 25, 1930, A. A. Brill wrote to Mabel that he "occasionally" hears from Buffalo patients of John. "They don't know that I know him, and he doesn't know they are coming to me. Everything they say about him and his wife seems very satisfactory." AAB to MDL, May 25, 1930, AABP.
4. See chapter 2 for an analysis of Mabel's relationship with Violet and her lesbian experiences. See also the epilogue, in which Mabel writes a new story, about Karl's infidelity, early in their marriage, which she says ended it for her.
5. Rembrandt's painting is about the civil guard; Mabel might have intended it as a foreshadowing of Buffalo society's moral opprobrium of their affair.
6. Mabel gave birth to John on January 4, 1902; she seems to have conflated the time period between the start of her love affair and her conception of the baby with John.
7. In "Doctors," Mabel writes that Parmenter infected her with gonorrhea sometime after he gave her the gold cross. See the epilogue.
8. Mabel is referring to Madame Defarge in Charles Dickens's 1859 novel, *A Tale of Two Cities*.
9. Mabel would have been reading *The Golden Bowl* (1904), a story of perfidy with deeply incestuous undertones; the Ververs, father and daughter, marry a man and woman who had been lovers.
10. F. Scott Fitzgerald, *Tender is the Night* (New York: Charles Scribner's Sons, 1962 [1933]), 315.
11. Review and letter in Matthew Bruccoli, *Dictionary of Literary Biography: F. Scott Fitzgerald's "Tender is the Night."* (Vol. 273. Detroit: Gale, 2003), 227–28.

Chapter Three

1. "Family Affairs" is dated May 1933; the typescript is 438 pages.

2. Mabel titled this letter "journal intime" and wrote it over the course of three days, from April 15 through April 18, 1923, the day of her marriage to Tony. The letter is in ACHP.

3. In a lengthy letter that she wrote to me on April 15, 1982, Bonnie included this information about her father and claimed that he had incestual relations with her. I chose not to publish anything about this in my biographies of Mabel. A few years before she died, Bonnie tried to publish a memoir about her childhood. In it, she narrated a scene in which her father enters her bedroom, begins to undress her, and fondles her breasts. He stops when her mother, Claire Spencer, walks into the room. It is not possible to verify her account, although another family member suggested to me that it could be true.

4. See Rudnick, *Mabel Dodge Luhan*, 300.

5. See Rudnick, *Mabel Dodge Luhan*, 296–301. Although Mabel never admitted any wrongdoing in this horrific scenario, the Jeffers's departure was followed by her experiencing a deep depression, about which she wrote A. A. Brill extensive letters, discussed in chapter 2.

6. Information about John Evans's time as Superintendant of Indian Affairs in New Mexico can be found in Carol Venturini, "The Fight For Indian Voting Rights in New Mexico" (master's thesis, University of New Mexico, 1993), 136–37.

7. On Wickes, see M. Esther Harding, "Obituary Notice," *Journal of Analytic Psychology*, vol. 13 (1968): 67–69. On Jung, see Andrew Samuels, "Introduction," *The Cambridge Companion to Jung*, ed. Polly Young-Eisendrath and Terence Dawson (Cambridge: Cambridge University Press, 1997); also in the same volume, Sherry Salman, "The Creative Psyche: Jung's Major Contributions," 52–70. There are seventeen letters from Mabel to Frances Wickes in FWP and two from Wickes to MDL. Mabel began her therapy with Wickes sometime in the spring of 1928 and terminated with her by November 1930.

8. MDL to FW, April 20 [1929], FWP.

9. On Mabel's relationship with Toomer, see Rudnick, *Mabel Dodge Luhan*, 227–30. MDL to FW, n.d. Everett was Everett Marcy, a composer of Broadway musicals, who wrote a song about Mabel. Bruce Kellner, the editor of Carl Van Vechten's Daybooks, notes that Marcy was an "ambiguous companion" of Mabel's when she was in New York City in the fall and winter of 1925. He is perhaps referring to Mabel's suggestion, as Van Vechten put it, that "she wants me to have a 'thing' with the beau Everett" (Bruce Kellner, ed., *The Splendid Drunken Twenties: Selections from the Daybooks, 1922–1930* [Urbana: University of Illinois, 2003], 100). All Mabel reveals is that Tony noticed that he "seemed to care for me" and that she cared for him, too. Marcy's name is scratched out, but still visible, in the letter that Mabel wrote to Brill in 1930, about giving him the manuscript of D. H. Lawrence's *Sons and Lovers* to pay for a friend's therapy. Marcy was receiving treatment from Brill in New York at the time. Frieda Lawrence had given Mabel the MS as a *quid pro quo* when Mabel gave

the Lawrences her son's ranch on Lobo Mountain, north of Taos. Edwin Brill sold the manuscript in 1962.

10. MDL to FW, March 20, April 9, April 20 [1929], FWP.

11. See my interview with Larry Torres in the "Epilogue" of *Utopian Vistas*.

12. MDL to FW, May 10 and undated [1929], FWP.

13. MDL to FW, October 7 [1929], FWP.

14. MDL to FW, n.d., FWP.

15. MDL to FW, October 12 [1929], FWP.

16. MDL to FW, October 18 [1929]; n.d. [December 1929?], FWP.

17. MDL to FW, November 25 [1929?], MDLP.

18. For the O'Keeffe-Luhan relationship, see Rudnick, *Mabel Dodge Luhan*, 234–41.

19. Mabel's description of Georgia having a clitoral orgasm is more comic than graphic. She provides a similar but more attenuated description in her memoir about Millicent Rogers (see chapter 5).

20. MDL to Alice Corbin Henderson, February 5 [1924], ACHP. Mabel and Tony were in Mill Valley during the winter of 1923–1924, taking treatments for syphilis. The letter should be dated 1925. It is interesting to note that Mabel's worst moment—her meddling in the marriage of Robinson and Una Jeffers—occurred after the publication of her last memoir, *Edge of Taos Desert*, in 1937, when she found herself unable to write. See note 5.

21. There is a copy of Mabel's 1929 contract in her file of letters to Alfred Harcourt, which states that they shall not be published until after her death. According to a letter I received from Rita Vaughn at Harcourt, Brace, Jovanovich, Inc., 15,000 copies of her four volumes of *Intimate Memories* and *Winter in Taos* had been sold by 1974. Rita Vaughn to Lois Rudnick, July 23, 1974, personal correspondence. Marcel Proust, one of Mabel's chief inspirations for *Intimate Memories*, published seven volumes of *Remembrance of Things Past*.

Chapter Four

1. MDL to EB, August 23, 1949, MDLP. The typescript is 222 pages, dated September 1947.

2. MDL to EH, October 20 [1946?], MLDP.

3. *Santa Fe New Mexican*, July 12, 1959, 14.

4. Luhan, "Recapitulation While Waiting," MDLP.

5. Margaret Jacobs, "The Eastmans and the Luhans: Interracial Marriage Between White Women and Native American Men, 1875–1935," *Frontiers* 23, no. 3 (2002): 44; Mabel quoted in *Denver Post*, August 7, 1932, in Scrapbook, vol. 11, MDLP. Elaine Eastman had met her husband, Dr. Charles Eastman, when he was Supervisor of Education for the Dakotas. Charles was a doctor at the Pine Ridge Agency, appointed in 1890. The Eastmans, according to Jacobs, "held themselves as an example of the assimilating power of interracial marriage." But in her autobiography, Elaine wrote with "unmistakable bitterness" about having to give up her career to become "a traditional wife and mother." Jacobs argues that it was Tony's

and Mabel's living together before they were married that was viewed as "scandalous," not the interracial nature of their liaison, "The Eastmans and the Luhans," 38–39, 43. (New Mexico was one of the few states in the United States that did not have anti-miscegenation laws.)

6. TL to MDS, n.d., MDLP.

7. On Tony's work with and for the Pueblos, see Rudnick, *Mabel Dodge Luhan*, 172–81, 261–65. Also Lawrence C. Kelly, *The Assault On Assimilation: John Collier and the Origins of Indian Policy Reform* (Albuquerque: University of New Mexico Press, 1983), chapter 7.

8. In his autobiography, *Shadow and Light*, Sterne has very different memories about his marriage and his trips out West (as well as on many other aspects of their relationship and experiences); see Maurice Sterne, *Shadow and Light: The Life, Friends, and Opinions of Maurice Sterne* (New York: Harcourt, Brace, & World, 1965). He claims to have planned a trip to Wyoming with a friend and, when Mabel heard he was going, she suggested they get married, and he go on the trip without her. When they weren't getting along after he got back, Sterne writes that A. A. Brill suggested they separate for a while, and so he agreed to go to Santa Fe with a doctor friend, Joseph Asch, to get "some fresh perspective on my personal problems"; see Sterne, *Shadow and Light*, 130–32.

9. JC to Dr. L, March 30, 1921, JRH. Collier mentions in his letter to Dr. Lucas that Shevky stopped in Taos on his way back to Turkey, and when he discovered the problem, "became deeply interested," such that he would stay on until they found a "medical man" to take his place. Apparently that hadn't happened by the time Mabel wrote Collier about the issue in 1922. Collier notes that 12 percent of the Wasserman tests Shevky administered came back positive. Shevky went on to have a prominent career. He directed the 1935 "Tewa Basin Study," which was an important interdisciplinary survey of the Rio Grande Basin that became the basis of a New Deal land reform program for northern Hispano villages. He was also a highly respected urban sociologist who served on the sociology faculty at the University of California, Los Angeles. On Shevky's work on syphilis with Collier, see Kelly, *The Assault on Assimilation*, 120. For a brief biography of Shevky, see the online entry under Eshref Shevky, University of California, "In Memoriam, 1979": http://texts .cdlib.org/view?docId=hb629006wb&chunk.id=div00040&brand=calisphere &doc.view=entire_text. I have not been able to find any other information on his work in Taos.

10. Sunmount Sanitarium was one of several in New Mexico devoted to the treatment of tuberculosis. Many prominent politicians, writers, and artists who moved to Santa Fe had first come to stay there, including Alice Corbin Henderson. In "Doctors," Mabel discusses a black salve that was added to their treatment by the doctor they saw in San Francisco the following winter. In 1921, bismuth and mercury compounds began to be rotated with arsenic preparations and the length of time of the average treatment prolonged from several weeks to a period of one to two years in the United States (Parascandola, *Sex, Sin, and Science*, 78).

11. This incident, which is recorded in Jelliffe's case notes, is mentioned on the first page of Mabel's first published memoir, *Background*, without any reference to syphilis, but as an example of the buried private lives of Buffalo's Victorians. She names the man Donald White in her published memoir, but this is very likely a pseudonym; see headnote to chapter 2.

12. Giovanni Boccaccio wrote *The Decameron* between 1348 and 1353. It is composed of one hundred stories told by ten narrators who have fled Florence to escape the Black Death. Several of the tales are bawdy, which is presumably why Mabel's mother had it hidden in her lingerie drawer.

13. Mabel seems to suggest here that her father may have had syphilis when she says that she is "only the second generation."

14. Mabel spoke like a eugenicist at times; here she echoes Charlotte Perkins Gilman's statement about "biological sin" in her novel *The Crux*. See note 14 in the introduction. Edwin died in 1938, at age fifty-nine.

15. It's very unlikely that Sterne was in the tertiary stage of syphilis. In the epilogue, Mabel says he was in the secondary stage when it was discovered. If Sterne had late latent (postsecondary stage) syphilis, which is quite possible, he would not be infectious (phone interview with Dr. Barbara McGovern). McGovern also told me that Mabel could have been asymptomatic or not noticed the signs. Mabel and Maurice first visited Taos on January 1, 1918; Mabel rented rooms from Arthur Manby, and they moved soon after.

16. John and Mary Young-Hunter bought property next to Mabel's in 1918. John was a British portrait painter who had fallen in love with the Southwest when he saw Buffalo Bill's Wild West Show in England. He painted a flattering portrait of Mabel in 1935 that hangs in the Harwood Art Museum in Taos. Mabel bought her property in June 1918.

17. Alice Thursby was the sister of Arthur Brisbane, the editor of the *New York World*. Elizabeth Duncan was the sister of the more famous Isadora Duncan; she had a Duncan school of dance in Croton-on-Hudson, which Mabel helped to finance, and where she sent her son John for a while, during the two years she lived there between 1915 and 1917. Mabel returned to Finney Farm at various times during the 1920s. It was there that she began writing her memoirs. Agnes Pelton was a modern painter, one of the few women who showed in the New York 1913 Armory Show.

18. Burt and Lucy Harwood were Taos artists and art patrons. Lucy began the town's first lending library, and after the death of her husband in 1923, she established the Harwood Foundation as a public library and museum. The Harwoods were the first to build a home in the Pueblo Spanish revival style in Taos; the Lujans were the second. On the Harwoods, see Dean Porter, Teresa Hayes Ebie, and Suzan Campbell, *Taos Artists and Their Patrons, 1898–1950* (South Bend, IN: The Snite Museum of Art, Notre Dame University, 1999), 266–70.

19. Mabel never seemed to learn that "gratified desire," as she puts it, always led to friction, anger, and jealousy between her and her lovers and husbands. Her reaction was undoubtedly related to her fear of, and continuous exposure to, VD.

20. Much of this and the next chapter is taken from "An Intimation," which Mabel wrote in the 1920s about the winter of her first discontent with Tony, in 1919, when she could not learn from him "the secret" of Indian life. In the original (unpublished) story, Mabel fictionalized them as José and Marcia, MDLP.

21. Collier formed the American Indian Defense Association in 1923, as an umbrella organization for other Indian rights groups with which he had worked; Atwood's organization had about two million members. On Collier and the Indian Defense Association, see Kelly, *The Assault on Assimilation*; also Flannery Burke, *From Greenwich Village to Taos*, chapter 2, whose point of view on Collier is much more critical than Kelly's. For the most thorough and balanced perspective on Collier's work on Indian land reform, see David Dinwoodie, "Indians, Hispanos, and Land Reform: A New Deal Struggle in New Mexico," *The Western Historical Quarterly* 17, no. 3 (July 1986): 291–323.

22. On the Matachines dance at Taos Pueblo, see Sylvia Rodriguez, *The Matachines Dance: Ritual Symbolism and Interethnic Relations in the Upper Rio Grande Valley* (Albuquerque: University of New Mexico Press, 1996), introduction and chapter 2. The dance was brought by the Spanish to the New World and was probably originally performed as a dramatic lesson for the need of Indian subjugation to their rule. Although scholars disagree on its meanings, many believe that one central element, the symbolic killing and castrating of a bull by masked dancers, may represent an indigenous response to the Spanish conquest. The Taos Indians believe that the dance was brought to them from Mexico by Montezuma.

23. Mabel wrote to Collier about this agreement, drawn up by Candelaria's lawyer; MDS to JC, c. 1920, JCC.

24. See chapter 3 for Tony Romero's involvement in the Lujans' wedding.

25. See chapter 2 for Mabel's discussion of Brisbane.

26. As noted in note 23, Mabel agreed in 1920 to pay Candelaria thirty-five dollars a month for life. At the end of chapter XVII, Mabel includes a letter from Tony Romero, dated April 4, 1920, in which he talks about collecting the monthly check to give to Candelaria, although he doesn't specify the amount.

27. Dr. Alfred Hertz was the second conductor of the San Francisco Symphony; he held his position from 1915 to 1930.

28. Mabel is most likely referring to the Wasserman tests she paid for in December 1922.

29. It is not clear why Tony's semen would have had blood in it as a result of having sexual relations with a woman who had syphilis, as blood is not typically a symptom that accompanies the infection.

30. These words echo in reverse the last pages of *Edge of Taos Desert*, when Tony promises: "I give you a new life, a new world—a true one, I think" (Luhan, *Edge of Taos Desert: An Escape to Reality* [New York: Harcourt, Brace and Co., 1937], 331).

31. Mabel is parodying here the opening lines of Gertrude Stein's "Portrait of Mabel Dodge at the Villa Curonia" (1911), which begins: "The days are wonderful and the nights are wonderful."

32. At the earliest, the picnic would have had to have been the late spring or summer of 1924, as the Lawrences left Taos in March 1923 (before Mabel and Tony married)

and did not return until April 1924. Lawrence was first diagnosed with tuberculosis in 1925.

33. See the introduction for a discussion of Lawrence's essay "Introduction to These Paintings," on the psychological and cultural devastation wrought by syphilis on Western civilization. I do not know whether Mabel read Lawrence's essay, but she may well have been correct that he made "literary" use of his knowledge of her and Tony's disease, just as he did with many other aspects of their lives that he borrowed for his fiction and essays. For Lawrence's fictional and nonfictional appropriations of Mabel and Tony, see Rudnick, *Mabel Dodge Luhan*, chapter 6.

34. Mabel, of course, had never been "free like a bird"; this is one of her favorite mantras that she repeated each time she got married. At the end of "The Statue of Liberty," there is a note in Hausner's hand, which he initials, that reads: "I am very happy you did this—only putting objectively one's life before one['s] own eyes can [one] see and understand it."

35. Mabel gives no indication when this incident happened. Photographer John Candelario made a very brief recording of Tony singing and drumming in 1949, in which Tony's voice sounds strained.

Chapter Five

1. See Shelby J. Tisdale, *Fine Indian Jewelry of the Southwest: The Millicent Rogers Collection* (Santa Fe: Museum of New Mexico Press, 2007), chapter 2. Tisdale's book is primarily about Millicent's Indian jewelry collection. See Cherie Burns, *Searching for Beauty: The Life of Millicent Rogers* (New York: St. Martin's Press, 2011), for the first full-length biography of Millicent. See chapters 7 and 8 for the story of her father's negotiations to end her marriage to Count Salm and the media publicity they generated.

2. In her pop biography of Clark Gable, *Long Live the King*, Lyn Tornabene discusses the end of Millicent's affair with him (*Long Live the King: A Biography of Clark Gable* [New York: G. P. Putnam's Sons, 1976]); she republishes the good-bye letter that Millicent sent Gable on 333–35; see also Burns, *Searching for Beauty*, 235–42. Millicent sent a copy of the letter to Hedda Hopper, who published it in her *Los Angeles Times* gossip column.

3. Tisdale, *Fine Indian Jewelry of the Southwest*, 27–28; Burns, *Searching for Beauty*, chapter 11, "Making a Mark in Fashion."

4. Millicent's letters (September 1947) to Mabel are signed with "love" and "devotedly" through December 1947, when Millicent wrote Mabel that she was sending her and Tony a case of good Scotch for Christmas. In an undated letter Millicent wrote after Benito's accident, she thanks Mabel for the flowers she sent and signs her letter "Sincerely, M. Rogers."

5. Once again, Dr. Hausner urged her to write, telling her in a letter of July 20, 1949, that she "must write the book they talked about, about her last two years in Taos." EH to MDL, July 20, 1949, MDLP. He was referring to what became "The Doomed."

6. Tisdale, *Fine Indian Jewelry of the Southwest*, 21–22; Burns, *Searching for Beauty*, 277.

7. APR to ST, May 14, 2005 in Tisdale, *Fine Indian Jewelry of the Southwest*, 41. Millicent may have been working for Indian voting rights. While all American Indians were purportedly given citizenship in 1924, as was true for African Americans after the Civil War, in many states, they were not allowed to exercise their rights. Efforts to correct this major civil rights violation began during World War II, as discussed in chapter 3, "Family Affairs," where I mention John Evans's involvement in this fight while he was Commissioner of Indian Affairs for the Bureau of Indian Affairs in Albuquerque during World War II. Burns writes that there is no formal record of Millicent's collaboration on Indian rights, but that she did pay for a delegation from Taos Pueblo to travel to Washington, D.C., where they met with government officials and created "the groundwork for the Indian Health Center on the Pueblo" (Burns, *Searching for Beauty*, 300).

8. Quoted in Tisdale, *Fine Indian Jewelry of the Southwest*, 186–87.

9. Anna Dooling mentions Millicent's affair with Benito in her article "The Lady & the Legend," *Impact*, *Albuquerque Journal*, July 15, 1987, 4–9, 14. See Burns, *Searching for Beauty*, chapters 23 and 24, on Millicent's relationship with Benito, including her attempts to rehabilitate him.

10. In a letter to Tony Lujan, written just after he was inducted into the U.S. Army, Benito addresses Tony as "grandfather" and refers to himself as his "son," BS to TL, December 1942, MDLP.

11. The artist Cady Wells wrote to Merle Armitage, in December 1949, that Millicent was thinking of visiting St. Croix, where Wells wintered, "and maybe bringing that grim young Indian I thought she had around just for show." Wells then describes an incident from the winter of 1948, that Mabel recounts in "The Doomed," about Benito's attending a part at Dorothy Brett's house, where he quarreled with Millicent, left the party, took her car, and "smashed into a pole, breaking 6 ribs." CW to MA, December 9, 1949, MAP.

12. MDL to MR, n.d., MDLP. This is the only letter of Mabel's to Millicent in MDLP. There are no letters between them in MDLP after September 1948. Mabel's letter was probably written after Benito's drunken smashup. Millicent thanked Mabel "sincerely" for the flowers she sent him in the hospital. Their relationship clearly cooled dramatically after this incident.

13. In his memoir, *Of Time and Change*, writer Frank Waters, one of Mabel's and Tony's closest friends, remembers Millicent telling him: "She thinks I'm trying to steal Tony away from her. How preposterous! What do I want with an aging Indian when there are so many young and attractive men of every kind?" (*Of Time and Change: A Memoir* [Denver: MacMurray & Beck, 1998], 95). The typescript of "The Doomed" is dated both May 20, 1953, and June 23, 1953; it is seventy-five 11" × 14" pages. Mabel wrote on the front page that it was not to be published until after her death.

14. Judge Henry Kiker (1879–1958) was a lawyer and judge in Raton and Santa Fe; he also served on the New Mexico State Supreme Court.

15. William Goyen (1915–1983) was an American fiction writer who grew up in Texas and, after World War II, lived in Taos, Manhattan, and Los Angeles. He is best known for his 1950 novel *House of Breath*. Walter Berns was Goyen's companion, a writer who accompanied him to Taos after World War II, where he worked as a waiter. They were good friends of Frieda Lawrence. See Joseph Flora, "Charles William Goyen," in *Southern Writers: A New Biographical Dictionary*, ed. Joseph M. Flora, Amber Vogel, and Brian A. Giemza (Baton Rouge: Louisiana State University Press, 2006), 163.

16. Mabel and Frieda had come a long way. Mabel had fought with Frieda over D. H. Lawrence, in a series of battles that lasted from their first arrival in Taos in November 1922 through the disposition of Lawrence's ashes, when Frieda returned with them to Taos in 1935. See Rudnick, *Mabel Dodge Luhan*, chapter 6.

17. The River House, in Embudo, was a hunting lodge that Mabel purchased sometime in the 1940s. It was two thousand feet below Taos (seven thousand feet). Because of heart problems, her doctor advised her spending time there. The book she refers to was "The Statue of Liberty."

18. In a letter of August 20, 1949, Dr. Hausner tells Mabel to stop building houses "and write!" EH to MDL, August 20, 1949, MDLP.

19. Mabel had built "La Posta" as a grand Spanish style hacienda in 1929. Her son John, and his second wife Claire, had lived in it for a few months in 1934. Mabel donated the building to Taos in 1936, and it became the community's first public hospital.

20. Cholly Knickerbocker was the pen name of Igor Cassini (1915–2002), the brother of the famous fashion designer, Oleg, and codirector of his fashion company.

21. The O'Keeffe painting Mabel refers to is *After a Walk Back of Mabel's*. See "Family Affairs," chapter 3, in which she also discusses this painting.

22. See note 10.

23. The Honorable Dorothy Brett (1881–1997) was an English painter who D. H. Lawrence brought to Taos in 1925 when he returned for his second visit from England. It soon became Brett's permanent home, where she lived until her death. Brett befriended several Indians at Taos Pueblo and made numerous paintings of them and of Taos Indian ceremonies and dances.

24. Mabel's descriptions of Millicent and Benito quarrelling after they became lovers mirror her own relationship with Tony.

Epilogue

1. "Doctors" is fifty typescript pages.

Selected Bibliography

Archives

A. A. Brill Papers, Library of Congress (AABP)

Alice Corbin Henderson Papers, Harry Ransom Research Center, The University of Texas at Austin (ACHP)

John Randolph Haynes Papers, Department of Special Collections, Charles E. Young Research, UCLA Library (JRH)

Frances G. Wickes Papers, Library of Congress (FWP)

Hutchins Hapgood and Neith Boyce Papers, Yale Collection of American Literature, Beinecke Rare Book and Manuscript Library, Yale University (HHP)

Leo and Gertrude Stein Papers, Yale Collection of American Literature, Beinecke Rare Book and Manuscript Library, Yale University (LGSP)

Mabel Dodge Luhan Papers, Yale Collection of American Literature, Beinecke Rare Book and Manuscript Library, Yale University (MDLP)

Merle Armitage Papers, The Harry Ransom Research Center, The University of Texas at Austin (MAP)

Una and Robinson Jeffers Collection, Bancroft Library, Stanford University (JC)

Books and Articles

Abel, Elizabeth, Joyce Antler, and Sara Alpern, eds. *The Challenge of Feminist Biography: Writing the Lives of Modern American Women.* Urbana: University of Illinois Press, 1992.

Allen, Frederick Lewis. *The Big Change: America Transforms Itself, 1900–1950.* New York: Harper and Brothers, 1952.

Anderson, Wayne V. *Picasso's Brothel: Les Demoiselles d'Avignon.* New York: Other Press, 2002.

Bell, Millicent, ed. *The Cambridge Companion to Edith Wharton*. New York: Cambridge University Press, 1995.

Bernheimer, Charles, and Claire Kahane, eds. *In Dora's Case: Freud-Hysteria-Feminism*. New York: Columbia University Press, 1985.

Bland, Lucy. *Banishing the Beast: Feminism, Sex and Morality*. London: Tauris Parke Paperbacks, 2002.

Boone, Joseph Allen. *Libidinal Currents: Sexuality and the Shaping of Modernism*. Chicago: The University of Chicago Press, 1998.

Brandt, Allan M. *No Magic Bullet: A Social History of Venereal Disease in the United States Since 1880*. New York: Oxford University Press, 1987.

Brandt, Allan M., and Paul Rozin, eds. *Morality and Health*. New York: Routledge, 1997.

Brantly, Susan C., ed. *Understanding Isak Dinesen*. Columbia: University of South Carolina Press, 2002.

Brill, A. A. *Basic Principles of Psychoanalysis*. New York: Pocket Books, 1960 [1921].

Bruccoli, Matthew. *Dictionary of Literary Biography: F. Scott Fitzgerald's "Tender is the Night."* Vol. 273. Detroit, MI: Gale, 2003.

Buhle, Mari Jo. *Feminism and Its Discontents: A Century of Struggle with Psychoanalysis*. Cambridge, MA: Harvard University Press, 1998.

Burke, Flannery. *From Greenwich Village to Taos: Primitivism and Place at Mabel Dodge Luhan's*. Lawrence: University of Kansas Press, 2008.

Burnham, John C. "The Progressive Era Revolution in American Attitudes Toward Sex." *Journal of American History* 59, no. 4 (1973): 885–908.

———. *Jelliffe: American Psychoanalyst and Physician & His Correspondence with Sigmund Freud and C. G. Jung*. Chicago: University of Chicago Press, 1983.

———. *Paths into American Culture: Psychology, Medicine, and Morals*. Philadelphia, PA: Temple University Press, 1988.

Burns, Cherie. *Searching for Beauty: The Life of Millicent Rogers*. New York: St. Martin's Press, 2011.

Butler, Judith. *Gender Trouble: Feminism and the Subversion of Identity*. New York: Routledge, 1999.

Carpenter, Edward. *Love's Coming of Age: A Series of Papers on the Relations of the Sexes*. Manchester, UK: Labour Press, 1896.

Castle, Terry. "Mabel Dodge Luhan." In *The Literature of Lesbianism: A Historical Anthology from Ariosto to Stonewall*, edited by Terry Castle, 911–22. New York: Columbia University Press, 2003.

Chave, Anna C. "New Encounters with *Les Demoiselles d'Avignon*: Gender, Race, and the Origins of Cubism." *The Art Bulletin* 76, no. 4 (1994): 596–611.

Corbin, Alice. *Red Earth: Poems of New Mexico*. Edited by Lois Rudnick and Ellen Zieselman. Santa Fe: Museum of New Mexico Press, 2001 [1920].

Cowart, Jack, and Juan Hamilton, eds. *Georgia O'Keeffe: Art and Letters*. New York: New York Graphic Society, 1990.

Crosby, Alfred W. *The Columbian Exchange: Biological and Cultural Consequences of 1492*. Westport, CT: Greenwood Press, 1972.

Davidson, Roger, and Lesley A. Hall. *Sex, Sin, and Suffering: Venereal Disease and European Society since 1870*. New York: Routledge, 2001.

Davison, Carol Margaret, ed. *Bram Stoker's Dracula: Sucking Through the Century, 1897–1997*. Toronto: Dundurn Press, 1997.

Dawley, Alan. *Struggles for Justice: Social Responsibility and the Liberal State*. Cambridge, MA: Harvard University Press, 1991.

de Larrea, Irene Herner, ed. *Diego Rivera's Mural at the Rockefeller Center*. 2nd ed. Mexico City: Edicupes, 1990.

DeWitt, Miriam Hapgood. *A Taos Memoir*. Albuquerque: University of New Mexico Press, 1992.

Dinesen, Isak. *Out of Africa and Shadows on the Grass*. New York: Vintage Books, 1989 [*Out of Africa* originally published in 1937].

———. *Last Tales*. New York: Random House, 1957.

Dinwoodie, David H. "Indians, Hispanos, and Land Reform: A New Deal Struggle in New Mexico." *The Western Historical Quarterly* 17, no. 3 (July 1986): 291–323.

Duggan, Lisa. "The Trials of Alice Mitchell: Sensationalism, Sexology, and the Lesbian Subject in Turn-of-the-Century America." *Signs* 18, no. 4 (1993): 791–814.

Eakin, Paul John. *Fictions in Autobiography: Studies in the Art of Self-Invention*. Princeton, NJ: Princeton University Press, 1988.

Ellmann, Richard. *Oscar Wilde*. New York: Alfred Knopf, 1988.

Erlich, Gloria C. "The Female Conscience in Wharton's Shorter Fiction: Angel or Demon?" In *Cambridge Companion to Edith Wharton*, edited by Millicent Bell, 98–116. Cambridge: Cambridge University Press, 1995.

Everett, Patricia R. "Letters in Psychoanalysis and Posttermination Contact: Mabel Dodge's Correspondence with Smith Ely Jelliffe and A. A. Brill." *The Annual of Psychoanalysis* 26 (1999): 330–60.

Faderman, Lillian. *Surpassing the Love of Men: Romantic Friendship and Love Between Women from the Renaissance to the Present*. New York: William Morrow, 1981.

———. *Odd Girls and Twilight Lovers: A History of Lesbian Life in Twentieth-Century America*. New York: Columbia University Press, 1991.

Fass, Paula. "A. A. Brill—Pioneer and Prophet." Master's thesis, Columbia University, 1968.

Ferris, Kathleen. *James Joyce & the Burden of Disease*. Lexington: University Press of Kentucky, 1995.

Fitzgerald, F. Scott. *Tender is the Night*. New York: Charles Scribner's Sons, 1962 [1933].

Flora, Joseph M., Amber Vogel, and Brian A. Giemza, eds. *Southern Writers: A New Biographical Dictionary*. Baton Rouge: Louisiana State University Press, 2006.

Ford, Charles Henri, and Tyler Parker. *The Young and Evil*. New York: Arno Press, 1975 [1933].

Freud, Sigmund. *Dora: An Analysis of a Case of Hysteria*. New York: Simon & Schuster, 1997 [1905].

———. *Sexuality and the Psychology of Love*. New York: Collier Books, 1972.

Friedman, Susan Stanford. "Women's Autobiographical Selves: Theory and Practice." In *Women, Autobiography, Theory: A Reader*, edited by Sidonie Smith and Julia Watson, 72–82. Madison: University of Wisconsin Press, 1998.

———, ed. *Analyzing Freud: The Letters of H. D., Bryher, and Their Circle*. New York: New Directions Publishing, 2002.

Gammel, Irene. *Baroness Elsa: Gender, Dada, and Everyday Modernity: a Cultural Biography*. Boston, MA: MIT Press, 2003.

Gibson, Ian. *The Shameful Life of Salvador Dalí*. New York: W. W. Norton, 1998.

Gifford, Sanford. "The American Reception of Psychoanalysis." In *1915, The Cultural Moment: the New Politics, the New Woman, the New Psychology, the New Art, and the New Theatre in America*, edited by Adele Heller and Lois Rudnick, 128–45. New Brunswick, NJ: Rutgers University Press, 1991.

Gilman, Charlotte Perkins. *The Crux*. Durham, NC: Duke University Press, 2003 [1911].

Gilman, Sander L. *Disease and Representation: Images of Illness from Madness to AIDS*. Ithaca, NY: Cornell University Press, 1988.

———. *Sexuality: An Illustrated History*. New York: John Wiley & Sons, 1989.

———. *Making the Body Beautiful: A Cultural History of Aesthetic Surgery*. Princeton, NJ: Princeton University Press, 1999.

Gilmore, Leigh. *Autobiographics: A Feminist Theory of Women's Self-Representation*. Ithaca, NY: Cornell University Press, 1994.

Goldman, Schecter. "Syphilis in Modern Art." *Cutis* 17, no. 4 (April 1976): 770–72.

Gordon, Linda. *Woman's Body, Woman's Right: A Social History of Birth Control in America*. New York: Grossman Publishers, 1976.

Grosskurth, Phyllis. *Havelock Ellis: A Biography*. New York: Alfred Knopf, 1980.

Haag, Pamela. "In Search of 'The Real Thing': Ideologies of Love, Modern Romance, and Women's Sexual Subjectivity in the United States, 1920–40." *Journal of the History of Sexuality* 2, no. 4 (1992): 547–77.

Hahn, Emily. *Mabel*. Boston, MA: Houghton Mifflin, 1977.

Hale, Nathan. *Freud and the Americans: The Beginnings of Psychoanalysis in the United States, 1876–1917*. New York: Oxford University Press, 1971.

Hall, Lesley. "'The Great Scourge': Syphilis as a Medical Problem and Moral Metaphor, 1880–1916." Paper written for the Courtauld Institute Symposium, May 23, 1998. http://homepages.primex.co.uk/-lesleyah/grtscrge.htm.

Harding, M. Esther. "Obituary Notice." *Journal of Analytic Psychology*, vol. 13 (1968): 67–69.

Hayden, Deborah. *Pox: Genius, Madness, and the Mysteries of Syphilis*. New York: Basic Books, 2003.

Heller, Adele, and Lois Rudnick, eds. *1915, the Cultural Moment: The New Politics, the New Woman, the New Psychology, the New Art, and the New Theatre in America*. New Brunswick, NJ: Rutgers University Press, 1991.

Hirsh, Sharon L. *Symbolism and Modern Urban Society*. Cambridge: Cambridge University Press, 2004.

Horton, Susan. *Difficult Women, Artful Lives: Olive Schreiner and Isak Dinesen, In and Out of Africa.* Baltimore, MD: The Johns Hopkins University Press, 1995.

Hurst, Tricia. "Heiress Brings Lavish Lifestyle to Taos." *New Mexico Magazine,* November 1989, 28–33.

Ibsen, Henrik. *Ghosts, Last Plays of Henrik Ibsen.* New York: Bantam, 1962.

Jacobs, Margaret D. *Engendered Encounters: Feminism and Pueblo Cultures, 1879–1934.* Lincoln: University of Nebraska Press, 1999.

———. "The Eastmans and the Luhans: Interracial Marriage Between White Women and Native American Men, 1875–1935." *Frontiers* 23, no. 3 (2002): 29–54.

James, Charles, "The Brooklyn Museum Collection of Original Designs for Millicent Rogers, 1938–1948," Brooklyn Museum of Art, 1948.

Jamison, Kay Redfield. *Touched With Fire: Manic-Depressive Illness and the Artistic Temperament.* New York: The Free Press, 1993.

———. *An Unquiet Mind: A Memoir of Moods and Madness.* New York: Vintage Books, 1995.

Jelliffe, Smith Ely. "The Physician and Psychotherapy." *Medical Record* 90 (1916): 362–63.

Jung, Carl G. *Psychology of the Unconscious.* New York: Moffat, Yarl and Co., 1916.

Kellner, Bruce, ed. *The Splendid Drunken Twenties: Selections from the Daybooks, 1922–1930.* Urbana: University of Illinois, 2003.

Kelly, Lawrence C. *The Assault on Assimilation: John Collier and the Origins of Indian Policy Reform.* Albuquerque: University of New Mexico Press, 1983.

Lasch, Christopher. *The New Radicalism in America (1869–1963): The Intellectual as a Social Type.* New York: Vintage Books, 1967.

Lawrence, D. H. *Studies in Classic American Literature.* New York: Viking Press, 1964 [1923].

———. "Introduction to These Paintings." In *Phoenix: The Posthumous Papers of D. H. Lawrence,* edited by Edward D. McDonald 551–84. London: Heinemann, 1936.

Lears, T. J. Jackson. *Rebirth of a Nation: The Making of Modern America.* New York: HarperCollins Publishers, 2009.

Ledingham, John G. G., and David A. Warrell, eds. *Concise Oxford Textbook of Medicine.* New York: Oxford University Press, 2000.

Lewis, Simon. *White Women Writers and Their African Invention.* Gainesville: University Press of Florida, 2003.

Lowenthal, Michael. *Charity Girl.* New York: Houghton Mifflin-Harcourt, 2007.

Luhan, Mabel Dodge. *Lorenzo in Taos.* New York: Alfred A. Knopf, 1932.

———. *Intimate Memories: Background.* New York: Harcourt, Brace and Co., 1933.

———. *European Experiences: Volume Two of Intimate Memories.* New York: Harcourt, Brace and Co., 1935.

———. *Movers and Shakers: Volume Three of Intimate Memories.* New York: Harcourt, Brace and Co., 1936.

———. *Edge of Taos Desert: An Escape to Reality.* New York: Harcourt, Brace and Co., 1937.

Lunbeck, Elizabeth. *The Psychiatric Persuasion: Knowledge, Gender, and Power in Modern America*. Princeton, NJ: Princeton University Press, 1994.

Lunbeck, Elizabeth, and Bennett Simon, eds. *Family Romance, Family Secrets: Case Notes from an American Psychoanalysis, 1912*. New Haven, CT: Yale University Press, 2002.

MacDiarmid, Laurie J. *T. S. Eliot's Civilized Savage: Religious Eroticism and Poetics*. New York: Routledge, 2003.

Mack, Arien. *In Time of Plague: The History and Social Consequences of Lethal Epidemic Disease*. New York: New York University Press, 1992.

Magnuson, Harold J., et al. "Inoculation Syphilis in Human Volunteers." *Medicine* 35, no. 1 (1956): 32–82.

Marcus, Steven. "Freud and Dora." In *In Dora's Case: Freud-Hysteria-Feminism*, edited by Charles Bernheimer and Claire Kahane, 56–91. New York: Columbia University Press, 1985.

———. *Freud and the Culture of Psychoanalysis: Studies in the Transition from Victorian Humanity to Modernity*. New York: W. W. Norton, 1987.

Marnham, Patrick. *Dreaming with His Eyes Open: A Life of Diego Rivera*. New York: Alfred Knopf, 1998.

Martin, Ralph G. *Jennie: The Life of Lady Randolph Churchill*. Englewood, NJ: Prentice Hall, 1969.

Martinez-Herrera, Jose, et al. "Dalí (1904–1989): Psychoanalysis and Pictorial Surrealism." *The American Journal of Psychiatry* 160 (May 2003): 855–66.

May, Elaine Tyler. *Great Expectations: Marriage and Divorce in Post-Victorian America*. Chicago: University of Chicago Press, 1980.

May, Leila S. "'Foul Things of the Night': Dread in the Victorian Body." *The Modern Language Review* 93, no. 1 (1998): 16–22.

Meyer, Donald. *The Positive Thinkers: A Study of the American Quest for Health, Wealth, and Personal Power from Mary Baker Eddy to Norman Vincent Peale*. New York: Anchor Books, 1965.

Mohamed, Jan. "*Out of Africa*." In *Understanding Isak Dinesen*, edited by Susan C. Brantly, 72–100. Columbia: University of South Carolina Press, 2002.

Morrow, Prince. *Social Diseases and Marriage*. New York: Macmillan, 1904.

Morris, Roger. "Millicent Rogers' New Mexico Legacy." *Architectural Digest*, June 1993: 98–107, 188.

Mullin, Molly. *Culture in the Marketplace: Gender, Art, and Value in the American Southwest*. Durham, NC: Duke University Press, 2001.

Nin, Anais. *The House of Incest*. Chicago: Swallow Press, 1958.

Noll, Richard. "Styles of Psychiatric Practice, 1906–1925: Clinical Evaluation of the Same Patient by James Jackson Putnam, Adolph Meyer, August Hoch, Emil Kraepelin and Smith Ely Jelliffe." *History of Psychiatry* 10-2, no. 38 (June 1999): 145–89.

O'Connor, John S. "'Spirochete' and the War on Syphilis." *The Drama Review: TDR*, 21, no. 1 (1977): 91–98.

O'Keeffe, Georgia. *Georgia O'Keeffe*. New York: Viking Press, 1976.

Ostrowski, Carl. "The Minister's 'Grievous Affliction': Diagnosing Hawthorne's Parson Hooper." *Literature and Medicine* 17, no. 2 (1998): 197–211.

Owens, Mitchell. "Desert Flower." *New York Times Magazine*, August 19, 2001, 190–99.

Pankhurst, Christabel. *The Great Scourge and How to End It.* London: Lincoln's Inn House, 1913.

Parascandola, John. *Sex, Sin, and Science: A History of Syphilis in America.* New York: Praeger, 2008.

Peiss, Kathy, Christina Simmons, and Robert A. Padgug, eds. *Passion and Power: Sexuality in History.* Philadelphia, PA: Temple University Press, 1989.

Pelensky, Olga Anastasia, ed. *Isak Dinesen: Critical Views.* Athens: University of Ohio Press, 1993.

Poe, Edgar Allan. "The Masque of the Red Death." In *Selected Writings of Edgar Allan Poe*, edited by Edward Davidson, 174–80. Boston, MA: Houghton Mifflin, 1956.

Porter, Dean A., Teresa Hayes Ebie, and Suzan Campbell. *Taos Artists and Their Patrons, 1898–1950.* South Bend, IN: The Snite Museum of Art, Notre Dame University, 1999.

Porter, Roy, and Mitkulás Teich, eds. *Sexual Knowledge, Sexual Science: The History of Attitudes to Sexuality.* Cambridge: Cambridge University Press, 1994.

Quétel, Claude. *History of Syphilis.* Translated by Judith Braddock and Brian Pike. Baltimore, MD: The Johns Hopkins University Press, 1990.

Rado, Lisa. "Primitivism, Modernism, and Matriarchy." In *Modernism, Gender, and Culture: A Cultural Studies Approach*, edited by Lisa Rado, 283–300. New York: Routledge, 1997.

Randall, Teri Thomson. "Millicent Rogers: A Woman of Substance." *Santa Fe New Mexican*, June 28–July 4, 2002, 36–37.

Reed, Maureen. "Mixed Messages: Pablita Velarde, Kay Bennett, and the Changing Meaning of Anglo-Indian Intermarriage in Twentieth-Century New Mexico." *Frontiers* 26, no. 3 (2005): 101–34.

Rich, Adrienne. "Compulsory Heterosexuality and Lesbian Existence." In *The Lesbian and Gay Studies Reader*, edited by Henry Abelove, Michele Adina Barela, and David M. Halperin, 227–54. New York: Routledge, 1993.

Richard-Allerdyce, Diane. *Anais Nin and the Remaking of the Self: Gender, Modernism, and Narrative Identity.* DeKalb: Northern Illinois University Press, 1998.

Richardson, John, and Marilyn McCully. *A Life of Picasso: The Painter of Modern Life 1907–1917.* Vol. II. New York: Random House, 1996.

Robinson, Paul. *The Modernization of Sex: Havelock Ellis, Alfred Kinsey, William Masters and Virginia Johnson.* New York: Harper & Row, 1976.

Rodriguez, Sylvia. "Art, Tourism, and Race Relations in Taos: Toward a Sociology of the Art Colony." *Journal of Anthropological Research* 45, no. 1 (1989): 77–99.

———. *The Matachines Dance: Ritual Symbolism and Interethnic Relations in the Upper Rio Grande Valley.* Albuquerque: University of New Mexico Press, 1996.

Rosaldo, Renato. "Imperialist Nostalgia." *Representations* 26 (Spring 1989): 107–22.

Rosenberg, Charles. "The Bitter Fruit: Heredity, Disease, and Social Thought in Nineteenth-Century America." *Perspectives in American History* 8 (1974): 189–235.

Rosebury, Theodor. *Microbes and Morals: The Strange Story of Venereal Disease.* New York: Viking Press, 1971.

Rosenblum, Robert, Maryanne Stevens, and Ann Dumas. *1900: Art at the Crossroads.* New York: Harry N. Abrams, 2000.

Rudnick, Lois Palken. *Mabel Dodge Luhan: New Woman, New Worlds.* Albuquerque: University of New Mexico Press, 1984.

———. "The Male-Identified Woman and Other Anxieties of a Feminist Biographer." In *The Challenge of Feminist Biography: Writing the Lives of Modern American Women,* edited by Sara Alpern, et al., 116–38. Urbana: University of Illinois Press, 1992.

———. *Utopian Vistas: The Mabel Dodge Luhan House and the American Counterculture.* Albuquerque: University of New Mexico Press, 1996.

———, ed. *Intimate Memories: The Autobiography of Mabel Dodge Luhan.* Albuquerque: University of New Mexico Press, 1999.

Russett, Cynthia Eagle. *Sexual Science: The Victorian Construction of Womanhood.* Cambridge, MA: Harvard University Press, 1989.

Salman, Sherry. "The Creative Psyche: Jung's Major Contributions." In *The Cambridge Companion to Jung,* edited by Polly Young-Eisendrath and Terence Dawson 52–70. Cambridge: Cambridge University Press, 1997.

Samuels, Andrew. "Introduction." In *The Cambridge Companion to Jung,* edited by Polly Young-Eisendrath and Terence Dawson, 1–16. Cambridge: Cambridge University Press, 1997.

Sanger, Margaret H. *What Every Girl Should Know.* New York: Belvedere, 1980 [1916].

Satter, Beryl. *Each Mind a Kingdom: American Women, Sexual Purity, and the New Thought Movement, 1875–1920.* Berkeley: University of California Press, 1999.

Schwartz, Sanford. *The Matrix of Modernism: Pound, Eliot, and Early Twentieth-Century Thought.* Princeton, NJ: Princeton University Press, 1985.

Seitler, Dana. "Unnatural Selection: Mothers, Eugenic Feminism, and Charlotte Perkins Gilman's Regeneration Narratives." *American Quarterly* 55, no. 1 (2003): 61–88.

Showalter, Elaine. *The Female Malady: Women, Madness, and English Culture, 1830–1980.* London: Virago, 1985.

———. *Sexual Anarchy: Gender and Culture at the Fin de Siècle.* London: Penguin, 1990.

———. *Hystories: Hysterical Epidemics and Modern Culture.* New York: Columbia University Press, 1997.

Sicherman, Barbara. *The Quest for Mental Health in America, 1880–1917.* New York: Arno Press, 1980.

Smart, Carol. "Reconsidering the Recent History of Child Sexual Abuse, 1910–1960." *Journal of Social Policy* 29, no. 1 (2000): 55–71.

Smith, Sherry. *Reimagining Indians: Native Americans Through Anglo Eyes, 1880–1940.* New York: Oxford University Press, 2000.

Smith, Sidonie. "Performativity, Autobiographical Practice, Resistance." In *Women, Autobiography, Theory: A Reader,* edited by Sidonie Smith and Julia Watson, 109–15. Madison: University of Wisconsin Press, 1998.

Smith, Sidonie, and Julia Watson. *Reading Autobiography: A Guide for Interpreting Life Narratives*. Minneapolis: University of Minnesota Press, 2001.

Smith-Rosenberg, Carroll. *Disorderly Conduct: Visions of Gender in Victorian America*. New York: Oxford University Press, 1986.

Snitnow, Ann, Christine Stansell, and Sharon Thompson, eds. *Powers of Desire: The Politics of Sexuality*. London: Monthly Review Press, 1983.

Solomon, Andrew. *The Noonday Demon: An Atlas of Depression*. New York: Scribner, 2001.

Sontag, Susan. *Illness as Metaphor*. New York: Farrar, Straus and Giroux, 1978.

Spence, Donald. *Narrative Truth and Historical Truth: Meaning and Interpretation in Psychoanalysis*. New York: W. W. Norton and Co., 1984.

Spongberg, Mary. *Feminizing Venereal Disease: The Body of the Prostitute in Nineteenth-Century Medical Discourse*. New York: New York University Press, 1997.

Steinberg, Leo. "The Philosophical Brothel." *October* 44 (1988): 7–74.

Sterne, Maurice. *Shadow and Light: The Life, Friends, and Opinions of Maurice Sterne*. New York: Harcourt, Brace, & World, 1965.

Stone, Albert. "Modern American Autobiography: Texts and Transactions." In *American Autobiography: Retrospect and Prospect*, edited by Paul John Eakin, 95–122. Madison: University of Wisconsin Press, 1991.

Suleiman, Susan Rubin. *Subversive Intent: Gender, Politics, and the Avant-Garde*. Cambridge, MA: Harvard University Press, 1990.

Tapert, Annette, and Diana Edkins. *The Power of Style*. New York: Crown, 1994.

Thurman, Judith. *Isak Dinesen: The Life of a Storyteller*. New York: St. Martin's Press, 1982.

Tisdale, Shelby. *Fine Indian Jewelry of the Southwest: The Millicent Rogers Collection*. Santa Fe: Museum of New Mexico Press, 2007.

Torgovnick, Marianna. *Gone Primitive: Savage Intellects, Modern Lives*. Chicago: University of Chicago Press, 1990.

Tornabene, Lyn. *Long Live the King: A Biography of Clark Gable*. New York: G. P. Putnam's Sons, 1976.

Trimberger, Ellen Kay. "The New Woman and the New Sexuality." In *1915, the Cultural Moment: The New Politics, the New Woman, the New Psychology, the New Art, and the New Theatre in America*, edited by Adele Heller and Lois Rudnick, 98–116. New Brunswick, NJ: Rutgers University Press, 1991.

Tumber, Catherine. *American Feminism and the Birth of New Age Spirituality: Searching for the Higher Self, 1875–1915*. New York: Rowman & Littlefield Publishers, 2002.

Vance, Carole S., ed. *Pleasure and Danger: Exploring Female Sexuality*. New York: Routledge & Kegan Paul, 1984.

Venturini, Carol A. "The Fight for Indian Voting Rights in New Mexico." Master's thesis, University of New Mexico, 1993.

Vicinus, Martha. "Distance and Desire: English Boarding-School Friendships." *Signs* 9, no. 4 (1984): 600–622.

———. *Intimate Friends: Women Who Loved Women, 1778–1928*. Chicago: University of Chicago Press, 2004.

Walters, Ronald. *Primers for Prudery: Sexual Advice to Victorian America*. Englewood Cliffs, NJ: Prentice Hall, 1973.

Ward, Patricia Spain. "The American Reception of Salvarsan." *Journal of the History of Medicine and Allied Sciences* 36, no. 1 (January 1981): 44–62.

Waters, Frank. *Of Time and Change: A Memoir*. Denver: MacMurray & Beck, 1998.

Wilde, Oscar. *The Picture of Dorian Gray*. http://www.upword.com/wilde/.

Wilford, John Noble. "Genetic Study Bolsters Columbus Link to Syphilis." *New York Times*, January 15, 2008. D2http://www.nytimes.com/2008/01/15/science/15syph.html.

Williams, Roger Lawrence. *Horror of Life*. Chicago: University of Chicago Press, 1980.

Wilson, Philip K. "Bad Habits and Bad Genes: Early 20th-Century Eugenic Attempts to Eliminate Syphilis and Associated 'Defects' from the United States." *Canadian Bulletin of Medical History* 20, no. 1 (2003): 11–41.

Worboys, Michael. "Unsexing Gonorrhoea: Bacteriologists, Gynaecologists, and Suffragists in Britain, 1860–1920." *Social History of Medicine* 17, no. 1 (2004): 41–59.

Young-Eisendrath, Polly, and Terence Dawson, eds. *The Cambridge Companion to Jung*. Cambridge: Cambridge University Press, 1997.

Zaretsky, Eli. *Secrets of the Soul: A Social and Cultural History of Psychoanalysis*. New York: Alfred A. Knopf, 2004.

Index